M000305412

THE GARDEN *in* ANCIENT EGYPT

Alix Wilkinson

By the same author

Ancient Egyptian Jewellery (Methuen)

THE GARDEN
in
ANCIENT EGYPT

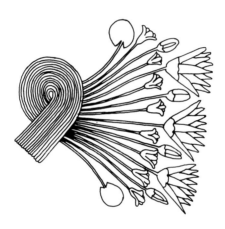

Alix Wilkinson

THE RUBICON PRESS

The Rubicon Press
57 Cornwall Gardens
London SW7 4BE

© Alix Wilkinson, 1998

British Library Cataloguing-in-Publication Data.

A catalogue record for this book is available from the British Library.

0-948695-48-X (hardback edition)
0-948695-49-8 (paperback edition)

All rights reserved. No part of this publication may be reproduced, stored in a retrieval system, or transmitted, in any form or by any means, electronic, mechanical, photocopying or otherwise, without the prior written permission of the copyright owner.

Printed and bound in Great Britain by
Biddles Limited of Guildford and King's Lynn

Contents

List of Illustrations

Fig. 30   Grove at Dahshur. Drawing by Juanita Homan from Rainer Stadelmann, 'Pyramiden und Nekropole des Snofru in Dahshur. Dritter Vorbericht über die Grabungen des Deutschen Archäologischen Instituts in Dahshur', *Mitteilungen des Deutschen Archäologischen Instituts Abteilung Kairo*, 49 (1993), Abb. 1b. Phillip von Zabern, Mainz-am-Rhein, by kind permission of Professor Stadelmann.

Fig. 31   Trees on the horizon. Drawing by Juanita Homan from François Daumas, 'Sur trois représentations de Nout à Dendara', *Annales du Service des Antiquités de l'Égypte 51* (1951), 373-400, pl. i.

Fig. 32   Mentuhotep. Photograph author. Reproduction by courtesy of the Trustees of the British Museum.

Fig. 33   Tree and soul-bird. Drawing by Juanita Homan from Sir John Gardner Wilkinson, ed. Samuel Birch, *Manners and Customs of the Ancient Egyptians*, iii, John Murray, London, 1878, no. 588, p. 349.

Fig. 34   Trees on the horizon. Drawing by Juanita Homan from Rosalie David, *Cult of the Sun*, Dent, London, 1980, fig. 23.

Fig. 35   View to Karnak from Deir el-Bahari. Drawing by Juanita Homan based on Alexander Badawy, *A History of Egyptian Architecture*, iii, University of California Press, Berkeley, 1968, fig. 112.

Fig. 36   Hatshepsut. The Egyptian Museum, Cairo. Photo Author.

Fig. 37   Hatshepsut's funerary temple. Drawing by Juanita Homan from Dieter Arnold, 'Deir el-Bahari', *Lexikon der Ägyptologie*, ed. Wolfgang Helck, Eberhard Otto, Harrassowitz, Wiesbaden, 1975, i, 1014, Abb. 1.

Fig. 38   Hathor in papyrus clump. E. A. W. Budge, *The Book of the Dead of the Papyrus of Ani*, Trustees of the British Museum, London, 1894, by courtesy of the Trustees.

Fig. 39   Hatshepsut. The Egyptian Museum, Cairo. Photo Author.

Fig. 40   Hatshepsut statues at Deir el-Bahari. Photo Author, by kind permission of the Polish-Egyptian Archaeological and Preservation Mission. Deir el-Bahari.

Fig. 41   Lettuce garden of Amun. Drawing by Juanita Homan from Edouard Naville, *The Temple of Deir el Bahari*, Egypt Exploration Fund, London, 1895-1908, v, pl. cxlii.

Fig. 42   Incense trees planted. Drawing by Juanita Homan from Edouard Naville, *The Temple of Deir el Bahari*, Egypt Exploration Fund, London, 1895-1908, iii, pl. lxxix.

Fig. 43   Incense trees in pots. Drawing by Juanita Homan from Edouard Naville, *The Temple of Deir el Bahari*, Egypt Exploration Fund, London, 1895-1908, iii, pl. lxxix.

Fig. 44   Temple of Amenophis III (?) Drawing by Juanita Homan from Norman de Garis Davies, *The Tomb of Two Officials of Tuthmosis IV*, (Nos. 75 and 90), Egypt Exploration Society, London, 1923, pl.xxxiii.

Fig. 45   The Ramesseum. Photo Author.

Fig. 46   Medinet Habu. Drawing by Juanita Homan from Uvo Hölscher, *Das Hohe Tor von Medinet Habu, Eine Baugeschichtliche Untersuchungen*, Leipzig, 1910, pl. iii.

Fig. 47   Temple avenue. Drawing by Juanita Homan from Siegfried Schott, *Wall scenes from the mortuary chapel of the Mayor Paser at Medinet Habu*, Oriental Institute of the

Colour Plates

To the memory of Jelisaveta 'Seka" Allen in gratitude
for her kindness toDumbarton Oaks Fellows over many years

Acknowledgements

Research for this book was begun at Dumbarton Oaks, in the Center for Studies in Landscape Architecture. I should like to thank Dumbarton Oaks, Trustees for Harvard University, for two Fellowships, (Summer and an academic year) which gave me time and space for study, and the use of their libraries. I am particularly grateful to Professor John Dixon Hunt and Professor Joachim Wolschke-Bulmahn who, as Directors of Studies in Landscape Architecture, gave me great help and encouragement. I should also like to thank Annie Thacher and Linda Lott in the Library and my colleagues at the time, Professors Craig Clunas, Edward Harwood and Terence Young. Many others have given me their time and help among whom I gratefully mention the late Dr. I.E.S. Edwards, the late Miss Nora Scott, Professor Alan Schulman, the Librarian and staff at the Herbarium Library in the Royal Botanic Gardens at Kew, and at the Natural History Museum and the British Library; Dr. Jaromir Malek and the Griffith Institute, Dr. Nigel Hepper, Dr. Mohammed Saleh, Professor Nabil Hadidi, Mrs. Reem Samir , Mrs. Thérèse Labib Youssef, Mr. Yasser Adel Hanafa Osman, Mr. Abd el Halim Abd el Mogali Mohamed, Mr. Badia Hassan Diwan, Mr. Magid Fransis, Mr. Harry James, Dr. Maurice Bierbrier, Mr. Eric Uphill, Mrs. Rosalind Janssen and the staff in the Petrie Museum at University College London, Dr. Peter Dorman and his predecessors as Directors of the American Research Center in Egypt, Dr. Ray Johnson, M. Larché of the French Institute in Cairo, Dr. Hassan Ragab, Dr. Rainer Stadelmann and the librarians at the German Archaeological Institute in Cairo, Professor Manfred Bietak and his staff at the Austrian Archaeological Institute in Cairo, Dr. Josef Dorner, Dr. Dieter Arnold and Dr. Dorothea Arnold and their staff at the Metropolitan Museum in New York, Mr. Jim Folsom of the Huntington Botanical Gardens, Mr. Henry Varney, Mr. Michael De Heart of the Getty Museum Santa Monica, Professor David Stronach, Dr. Fadwa el-Guindi, Dr. Suzanne Granger of Arcadia Botanic Gardens, Dr. Stuart Tyson Smith, and my travelling companions and hosts on many trips to Egypt.

Introduction

About This Book

Among the multitude of books about gardens there is none in English devoted solely to the gardens of pharaonic Egypt. The early chapters of general histories of gardens mention those of Egypt before passing on to more familiar and central matters. Gardens in general now receive more attention and are studied both for themselves, and the enjoyment and interest they provide, as well as for being a reflection of the tastes and aspirations of their creators. The gardens of the ancient Near East are of interest in themselves, as a reflection of their societies, and as the forerunners and models for Roman and Arab gardens.

This book is concerned with the way the ancient Egyptians designed the gardens around their buildings, with what motivated their choice of plants, and how they were arranged.

The Position of Ancient Egyptian Gardens in the History of Gardens

The Greeks and Romans expressed their admiration for the gardeners and gardens of Egypt. The Egyptians' 'hard landscape' contained elements which became standard in later gardens. They built terraces long before the Assyrians startled the world by imitating a mountain landscape with their 'Hanging Gardens of Babylon'. Egyptian gardens were cooled by channels of water before Persian gardeners adopted this device. The Egyptians even had atrium gardens long before the Romans made this style famous at Pompeii.

Re-creations of Ancient Gardens

We cannot visit an ancient garden, although there are attempts at re-creations of ancient paintings and the results of excavations laid out in the grounds of the Agricultural Museum in Cairo. At ancient sites, all we can see in the ground are the pits cut in the rock, or brick-built containers for trees, and the square plots with moulded mud rims for vegetables and flowers. From these remnants we can work out the overall design, and understand the way the plants were integrated into the complex of buildings, and the surrounding terrain.

The place where gardens were created was often itself holy and significant as the abode of a deity. Ancient gardens were not static. There is evidence for their being covered and built over at Karnak, destroyed and remade at Hermopolis, and totally abandoned and forgotten at Amarna.

Modern Studies of the Flora in Pharaonic Egypt

The flora of pharaonic Egypt has been admirably documented since the early Nineteenth Century by distinguished botanists, but the landscaping of the gardens has largely been discussed in the context of individual excavation reports, or descriptions of tomb-decoration. In this book an attempt is made, on the one hand, to examine the religious ideas which inspired the landscaping of the gardens and dictated which plants should be grown in them, and on the other, to consider the social and economic factors which had an impact on garden design.

Evidence for Ancient Gardens

Evidence for gardens consists of archaeological remains, areas of planting, documents written on stone and papyrus describing the layout, the size, the plants and the use made of gardens, and visualizations in paintings and models.

Garden research means studying the "geographical surroundings, historical events, and social and cultural contingencies that envelop a garden - as experienced by those who constructed it". A garden may be interpreted as "an *opposition* to certain aspects of its context, and as a *consequence* of others".[1]

Modern research can only reveal a few aspects of garden development, but it provides a way in for the reader, who can then develop a personal interpretation of the original scene.

Mythological Concepts on which Sacred Landscapes were based

The motivating forces for the design of pharaonic gardens around religious buildings were the beliefs the architects held about the primeval places which they tried to imitate in their designs.

The Egyptians created sacred landscapes by giving concrete reality to mythological places which were described in religious texts. According to the Egyptian mythology, Creation on earth started with an island which sprouted vegetation; and in heaven, the sun went on its journey by day and night through an imagined landscape. The Egyptians referred to gardens as being located 'at the proper places'.[2]

The Creators of Garden Design

The kings controlled most of the wealth of the community, and it was they who built for themselves, or sanctioned for their courtiers, tombs where many of the gardens which we know about were created. They also arranged for the building of temples and gardens for particular gods. These gardens gave actuality to the afterlife, and declared the power of the king to deliver to the gods what they required, even exotic plants which were hard to cultivate, like incense trees. The gardens, by their size, and the special plants which grew in them, symbolized the fertility of the land and the success of the king and the gods.

The Symbolism of Plants

Many of the plants had symbolic significance. Trees were sacred to certain deities: the date palm to Re and to Min, the doum-palm to Thoth, the sycamore fig to Hathor and the tamarisk to Osiris. Waterlily and papyrus were life-giving and dedicated to Horus and Hathor.

Activities in the Gardens and Groves

The activities which took place in these landscapes were rituals of burial and the maintenance of the cult of the dead, as well as the rituals concerned with the deities in the cult temples. The upkeep of the plants, watering them, picking fruit, and digging the ground was equally important and is recorded in paintings, as occurring at the same time as the rituals were taking place.

The accidents of preservation may distort the record, and, in an area with an expanding population, changes are quickly made, leaving no trace of what went before. The story was different for the cult temples. As long as they remained in use their avenues, orchards, places where the sacred animals were raised and enclosures for the sacred trees were all carefully tended.

Period of time covered by this book

The time span covered by this book is from Predynastic times until the Thirtieth Dynasty; in other words, the period during which Egyptian pharaohs ruled the Nile valley. The evidence is unevenly distributed, with the main landscaped buildings surviving from the Eleventh to Twentieth Dynasties (c. 2000-1000 B.C.). Over this period of a thousand years, although all the basic forms and ideas were established in the Old Kingdom (c. 2800-2000 B.C.), other art forms went through considerable changes. Gardens did not change greatly. Their purpose was to provide food, fruit, fuel, wood for building, perfumes and bouquets. Their forms varied according to the space available and precise purpose of their planting. But there is no obvious development from one style to another.

Artistic representations of Nature

Nature always fascinated Egyptian artists. Accurate representations were important because the plants and animals depicted had to live forever on walls and floors, perpetuating the prosperity of the estates of tomb and temple owners.

Adaptations of the Landscape to Human Ideas

Over the period of dynastic history the adaptation of landscape and vegetation to human ideas and needs went through several phases. For much of the period, the only evidence which has survived comes from royal monuments in desert areas. Kings and some of their officials planted trees around their tombs. Officials described their estates in words and pictures focussing on the quantities of produce, while celebrating the pleasure they would derive from contemplating their lakes and orchards.

More evidence remains from the New Kingdom with the plantations in both funerary and cult temples. Royal officials imitated their masters' burials, and some had plantations around their houses. Excavations in the eastern Delta have revealed the great extent of the orchards around the temples and palaces from the Thirteenth to Nineteenth Dynasties. At Amarna, traces of extensive gardens have survived because the city was abandoned and the terrain not disturbed until excavators arrived in the late Nineteenth Century. Pictures in temples and tombs give further ideas about the layout and plantings of gardens. Written documents record the extent of the estates belonging to temples and private individuals, and what they contained. But the evidence is tantalizingly incomplete.

All through pharaonic history, trees and flowers were incorporated into building schemes, and this practice continued into Ptolemaic and Arab times. Evidence for the ways in which this was done has survived unevenly, but the fact that the individual parts of a building continued to represent papyrus, waterlilies, palm trees and bouquets of plants, flowers and fruits, show how much the Egyptians were concerned to incorporate the natural world into their architectural environment.

The Theme of this Book

The theme of this book is the Egyptians' artistry in combining the natural terrain of mountains and river with buildings and plants, in order to create landscapes from their mythological imagination. The aim is to bring together the existing research and to focus on the landscaping of some of the religious buildings. The study of garden history is enjoying a renaissance at the moment, and this is an opportune time to draw attention to early examples of the combination of landscape, theology and horticulture.

The Sequence of the Contents of this Book

The early chapters in this book explain the design features of an Egyptian garden, the agricultural year, seasons, growing conditions, types of land in use, climate, and the plants grown in gardens. The next chapters explain the mythological basis for the landscaping of royal and private tombs and funerary monuments. The gardens painted in private tombs and described in literature reflect different views of the afterlife, all based upon water and vegetation. The later chapters describe the gardens in cult temples and cities as they can be discovered from excavation and from literary descriptions.

I   Features in Ancient Egyptian Garden Design and Ornamentation and the Conventions used in the Artistic Representations of Gardens

Ancient Egyptian gardens were constructed with many of the features known from the gardens of later eras. But the designers were often motivated by religious considerations which dictated the architecture and the plants which were used in them. The purpose of the gardens governed to a certain extent their layout. Surrounding tombs were 'sacred groves', which were planted with trees, which had a particular significance in the mythology and rituals of the dead. There were the utilitarian vegetable gardens and orchards on private estates. And there were similar utilitarian orchards around temples, but which had the additional attribute of being on sacred ground and serving a sacred purpose.

The Design of Gardens

The general layout of a garden and its buildings follows a time-honoured pattern, which can still be seen today in the humblest homestead, for example, in the oasis of Bahariya. The property is enclosed with a wall all round. Inside the gateway is an unroofed courtyard, filled with trees. Then, there is another wall and another door. The second courtyard is also unroofed, and contains more trees, providing shade and fruit, and here there is a vegetable patch and a vine shading a work area, or the entrance to the house. This arrangement is illustrated in ancient times at Amarna,[1] and in the tomb of Neferronpet (Theban Tomb 178) where the storerooms and workshops of the 'House of Gold of Amun' are laid out, with trees in both outer and inner courtyards outside the main workshop, with each area enclosed by walls and doors.[2]

The Egyptians were fond of symmetry in all their art, and landscaping was no exception. Twin groves, twin trees, and twin pools are frequently found in excavation and illustration, as are geometrical arrangements of rectangles within a garden. Gardens were laid out with strong structure, making use of different levels linked by terraces, and were often centred around pools of water. Areas with their own individuality were separated by walls or trees. The gardens were axially planned. A building, whether tomb or temple, was the focus and point of departure. The unity of the building and the gardens was usually evident. Straight lines predominated in the design on the ground and in the plantings.

Gardens, which might be described as 'formal', that is displaying symmetry, geometry and pattern in their design, are shown in the New Kingdom tomb-paintings. They are usually walled, protected from the wind by several rows of trees and have a central pool.

Nefersekheru drinking from a pool amid date palms. Theban Tomb 296. XIXth Dynasty. (Fig. 1)

The Use made of Gardens

The pharaohs provided space for festivities, religious processions and crowds, in some of the gardens they created. On the pathway beside the temple lake, processions passed on various festivals such as the Burial of Osiris at Karnak. The king was also rowed on a lake surrounded by gardens in a special barge in ceremonies for the opening the dykes; and after his death, his statue was rowed out on memorial days. Processions passed along the avenues between temples at particular festivals, such as the annual journey of the statues of Amun, Mut and Khonsu from the Karnak to the Luxor temple, or across the river to the funerary temples of the deceased pharaohs. The people who used the gardens were the priests, who collected offerings for the gods, and carried out rituals for the temple cult and for the dead. Estate owners enjoyed their gardens and included the gardeners who tended the plants in their illustrations of their gardens of eternity. Other inhabitants of gardens were lovers who tried to remain unnoticed, except by each other, and the friendly spirits in the trees. There were also the gardens where the produce necessary for the rituals and the upkeep of the personnel of the temple was grown.

The Egyptians had different words for different types of gardens. They classified gardens by their form, by what they grew, and by the buildings to which they were attached.[3] The forms could be a piece of cultivable ground divided into squares, a park, a park with a temple and a pool, an open terraced area, and a sunken or level peristyle or atrium within a building. The Persian and Moghul type of garden divided into four orchards, called a *chahar bagh*, was called in Egyptian a 'chamber of trees'. The 'chamber of trees' also had another characteristic feature of the *chahar bagh*: pavilions. Gardens could also be described by the plants growing in them: vineyards, vegetable gardens, olive groves, fruit orchards, groves of incense trees, groves of trees useful for their wood, and tree-growing country in general, usually abroad. Some of the same vocabulary was used again for describing the gardens attached to buildings. There were gardens belonging to palaces, and tombs, to funerary domains and estates, and to private estates of the living, and gardens of particular temples, such as those of Horus at Heliopolis, Re at Hermopolis, of Sekhmet, or Osiris at the Abaton on the island of Philae.

Names of Gardens

Gardens had names, just as buildings had names. The garden created by Akhenaten at Amarna for the globe of the sun, the Aten, was called 'The Seeing-Place of the Aten'. And the shrines on the route between the Karnak and Luxor temples which had gardens, had names like, 'Hatshepsut is united with the perfection of Amun'.

The 'Hard Landscaping' of Gardens

Within the arranged landscapes, arcades and colonnades provided a variety of textures and a background for plants. Steps and stairways emphasized changes in levels and viewpoint. A pond or garden house marked a focus of interest, and the garden kiosks were also vantage points from which to view the wider landscape or an indoor scene.

Terraces

Terraces provided view points: from the top the owner looked down on the surrounding countryside, and on anyone approaching from below; and from the bottom, the visitor was overwhelmed by the structure, which he then had to climb. Terraces emphasize who is in control. Hatshepsut's funerary temple at Deir el Bahari was the most steeply terraced of the funerary temples at Thebes, but all were terraced however slightly. Here trees were grown for certain on the lowest terrace, and possibly also on other terraces. The temple of Hathor at Deir el Medina is arranged on four terraces. Terracing may have been used in the garden of the 'King's House' at Amarna, and is indicated in an illustration of an estate at Karnak.[4]

Walls

High, plastered walls, sometimes with painted or tile decoration, hid the participants taking part in processions from the stares of the vulgar. Painted and tiled walls in gardens continued up to the 18th Century in Portugal. Sometimes, walls were serpentine (sinuous), as at Hermopolis, where they lined the avenue in front of the temple.

Gates

Gates are still an important feature of Middle Eastern gardens, and fine gates stood at the entrance to some of the ancient gardens. Their gateposts were particularly elaborately decorated. A vast orchard and vineyard in the Delta had door and doorposts of "gold mounted with copper, the inlay figures were "of every costly stone, like the double doors of heaven."[5] Those which gave entry to a garden surrounding a lake within the precinct of the temple of Amun, and called the 'Libation of Amun', were found at Karnak. Gate-houses were a feature of both illustrated and actual gardens: one of the most elaborate and extensive was at Amarna leading into the park-like temple called the *Maru*-Aten.

Buildings in Gardens

Temples, palaces and houses, all had their gardens. Pyramids were not fantastic "Follies", but tombs of the pharaoh, beside which a grove of trees was planted. Temples were the dwellings of gods, and could be magnificent stone structures covering several acres, or small, stucco-covered brick shrines, in the gardens of private houses. Smaller buildings in gardens were made out of papyrus, providing shade and somewhere to sit, or make love, or give birth.

Little booths in gardens are illustrated in tomb-paintings, where the owner sits to receive the produce of his estate. These kiosks were made of light materials: painted wood, papyrus and rushes. Sometimes they were quite elaborately decorated with papyrus- or lotus-topped columns supporting the curved roof. In shape they are like some of the shrines in which statues of the gods were placed. They provided shelter from the wind, and shade from the sun. They usually consisted of just one room, with space for a seat. An actual garden kiosk has been excavated at Tell Dabaa in the garden of a Thirteenth Dynasty palace.[6] Such garden-kiosks became a feature of Islamic gardens, and lasted into the Khedival gardens in Cairo in the 19th century.

Loggias

Loggias were a feature of both temple and palace architecture, and in both types of building they led out into garden areas. At Deir el-Bahari, the funerary temples of King Mentuhotep and Queen Hatshepsut both had extensive porticos opening onto the terraces where trees were planted. At Hatshepsut's temple, the inside walls of these loggias were decorated with painted relief carvings recording the deeds performed by the Queen for the god Amun. Her expedition to Punt to collect incense trees and bringing an obelisk for the temple at Karnak are perhaps the best known. The palaces at Tell Dabaa in the Delta,[7] and the royal bedroom of Amenophis III's palace at Malqata, on the west bank at Thebes, both opened into a grove of trees.

Gardens inside Buildings

Sunken atrium gardens inside buildings were found in excavations in four ceremonial areas at Amarna: in the central area or 'palace', in the southern and northern *Marus*, and the site to the south of the city, called Kom el-Nana.

Lakes and Canals

Water was brought in canals to feed the gardens. It was the central feature of many gardens. The temple lake was not only the water source for the temple, but was the place where rituals were performed. Some temple lakes were large: the one at Karnak measured 132m. by 80m. Private gardens sometimes contained lakes. Officials described the extensive lakes on their properties, and a lake large enough for a boat to travel on is illustrated beside Djhutynefer's house.[8] Smaller pools have been excavated in private gardens at Amarna. People valued pools as sources of refreshment and coolness. In them they bred fish and birds for food. There were also cisterns, which stored water for supplying the plants in the gardens. Wells were another source of water both in temples and in private gardens. Pools were stepped so that the water could be reached when the pool was nearly dry. The edges of some pools provided terraces for marsh plants.

The shapes of pools were rectangular and T-shaped. The T-shape was the form in which the channels in front of temples were arranged as landing areas. Both the T-shape and the rectangular reflect the form of a place where offerings were made.

Jetties and Quays

One of the features illustrated in the wall-paintings is a ceremonial landing platform surrounded by a low balustrade.[9] These platforms foreshadow the lakeside jetties still remaining in Moghul gardens. Bridges have not survived, but a long quay was found jutting out into the lake at Amarna in the *Maru*-Aten. A similar jetty remains in the Shalamar garden at Lahore.

Decoration - Sculpture and Statues

Statuary and sculpture were not just decorative features. They were bearers of religious and political messages. In tomb-gardens, a statue represented the owner himself, was the living presence of the deceased and had to receive the attention and respect due to him. He appeared in various guises and performed various actions, both in sculpture in the round, and in scenes in relief. In cult temples the garden statuary was of the gods of that temple and their worshippers.

Menageries

Menageries were included in gardens. Live animals in the royal gardens reflected the king's ambition to collect the living world around him, and to have animals of particular significance as his attendants. Lions, the royal animal *par excellence*, decorated his throne and chariot. Lions were kept in cages at the entrance to royal gardens at Karnak, and antelopes, oryx and ibex were kept at Karnak and Amarna. Birds illustrated at Amarna, and presumably living in the gardens, included rock pigeon, turtle dove, great spotted cuckoo, grey-lag goose, pied kingfishers, geese, and ducks.[10] Ducks and geese were ornaments as well as being edible, as were the fish. Animals were bred at various temples for food, and as offerings for the deity of the place.

The Plantings

Avenues

Avenues of trees lined the approaches to temples. Each tree was planted in its own container, or in a pit, so that it could be individually watered. There were also groves and orchards of trees, usually arranged in straight rows. A sacred tree, or grove of trees, was grown in its own enclosure in some temples. At temples up and down the river, trees were brought into the courtyards, enhancing the stone imitative plant elements with natural vegetation. Inside the court of the Roman temple of Khnum at Elephantine, real palm trees grew up in front of stone imitations of papyrus, lotus, and palms.[11] Pergolas for vines were the central feature of several gardens painted in tombs, and they also provided a long, cool tunnel through a garden. Vistas were controlled by the avenues of trees and their protecting walls, and concentrated the eye on a particular objective. From the funerary temples on the west bank at Thebes, the vistas converged on the Nile, and beyond it on the temples of Karnak or of Luxor. Pergolas for vines were the central feature of several gardens painted in tombs, and they also provided a long, cool tunnel through a garden.

Orchards

Fruit trees were planted in orchards in rows sometimes around a pool.

Vegetable gardens

Vegetables were grown in rectangular plots close to water.

Flower gardens

Flowers were grown beside and in water, and in fields.

Physical Conditions of Garden-Making

In order to create such magnificent gardens the Egyptian designers had to deal with two potentially overwhelming elements: the desert and the river. In the desert there was too little vegetation; and along the river bank there was too much, and the river itself overflowed every year. On the slopes of the western mountain at Thebes, the architects were trying to extend the river bank into the desert, and had to do it by artificially providing water. This mountain was the site of the royal funerary temples and courtiers' tombs. Here the dead rested 'Upon the Crag of the Lady who is the West of Thebes',[12] an area seen by the Egyptians as a hard, hilly desert in which they scattered the round-topped markers of many tombs. But somewhere at the foot of the mountain was a lush papyrus marsh where poppies also grew, and into which the sky goddess, as a cow, stepped to welcome the dead, when they came to their tombs in the tall, pink rock beside these markers. On the east bank of the river the landscape was verdant. The main temples of Karnak and Luxor had gardens inside and out.

The Architects who created the Gardens

Some of the architects who created these gardens are known by name: Ineni and Senenmut who advised Queen Hatshepsut, and Amenophis, son of Hapu, who designed the king Amenophis III's monuments, to mention just three of the most famous.

The Meaning of the Gardens

The meaning and message of the gardens was frequently in the sculpture, both in the round and in relief, which represented the owner in various guises and occupied in various activities. They frequently stressed the relationship of the owner to the gods. The status of the owner is demonstrated by the size of the garden and its enclosure, and by the size and splendour of the buildings and their decoration. The whole design of a building and its garden was used to imitate and represent the landscape of their religious mythology. Tombs and funerary temples were landscaped in imitation of the tomb of Osiris: that is, as a mound with trees around it. Symbolism could also be in the plants used, many of which had a particular religious significance. Man's dominance over nature is shown in bringing plants into the desert.

Summary

The sacred gardens of ancient Egypt included many of the garden features which survived through Roman and Islamic times and became fashionable in Eighteenth Century Europe. The Egyptians created buildings and gardens which were integrated with the surrounding natural scenery. The power and splendour of the ruler were demonstrated in extensive gardens in front of the funerary temples at Deir el Bahari, and in and around the temple of Amun at Karnak. At Amarna, the site sacred to the sun-god, the desert plain was made green by parks at either end; and temples, palaces and houses with their own gardens filled the built-up area. In between these parks, lay clusters of buildings with avenues leading up to them, and gardens, some of them with pools, around them, contrasting with the desert. In the *Maru*-Aten there was a large artificial lake, an ornamented quay, temples, garden walks, avenues, a gatehouse, and maybe even a banqueting house. The 'Northern *Maru*', included a sunken atrium garden and a menagerie, as well as a central pool and small shrines.

In the much more fertile Delta, a vast orchard and vineyard surrounded the palaces and temple at Avaris and Pi-Ramesses (Tell Dabaa).[13] Ramesses III ordered the planting of orchards here and at many religious centres. At Heliopolis he decreed that date and olive groves be established, and gardens and incense trees at Memphis.

Ancient Egyptian landscape gardeners created lavish plantations at temples and city sites. Great sweeps of desert covering over a mile at a time were kept full of trees. The Egyptians' problems were connected with the control and provision of water, which they managed to overcome by creating canals and pools inside, and in front of, their buildings, and by the constant use of the *shaduf* and bucket. Their success was sustained over many hundreds of years. The temples, with their gardens, lakes and canals, were in living and verdant contrast to the desert and rocky scarp of the mountains. They lasted - collectively, though not all at one time - for many hundreds of years.

The Conventions used in the Artistic Representations of Gardens

The Egyptians illustrated plants on the floors and walls of palaces, temples and tombs, as well as on jewellery, and vessels used in the temple rituals, and as architectural elements.

Many of the species are instantly recognizable, and thus qualify as botanical illustrations in the modern sense, being "concerned with accuracy allowing the identification of the plants to be shown."[14] Plants were also represented in the round, as pendants, containers and other artefacts. They are shown in relief sculpture, and as inlays for furniture, ritual vessels, jewellery and buildings.

"Botanical illustration is the portrayal of plants with enough accuracy and relevant detail for a particular kind to be recognized thereby and distinguished from other kinds".[15] The conventions adopted by botanical illustrators vary, even among the artists employed at Kew over the last twenty years. Some show the plants growing in natural conditions, together with other plants which belong in the same environment, including the type of ground, rocky or mossy, and the dead leaves which lie on it. Other artists show whole areas of forest, with the birds which visit the plants. While others show the different parts of the plant at different stages of development. The artist in antiquity "looked at plants with an enquiring interest essentially the same as that of his modern counterpart and portrayed them as faithfully in accordance with the needs and standards of a far distant past".[16] What were these 'needs and standards' in ancient Egypt? Here there is another level of interpretation: that of the

Recognition and understanding of the graphic languages and pictorial conventions employed. These are themselves influenced by the intended purpose of the image and by the materials and techniques used in the production . . . . . and by the innate culturally specific perceptions of the artist.[17]

The Purpose of Egyptian Illustrations, the Hieroglyphic Element

Modern writers suggest that botanical illustrations were for the benefit of physicians, so that they could recognize the plants needed in their remedies. The Egyptians apparently did not have this purpose in mind, since their medical treatises which remain have no illustrations of the plants prescribed in their pharmacopaea, and no illustrated herbal has survived.

Plant illustrations were used in paintings and relief sculptures in tombs and temples as background, and an adjunct for human activities. The plants provided the context for agricultural activities appropriate to the seasons of the year: marshlands, fields of flax and grain, vegetable gardens, vineyards and orchards and savannah. The illustrations were not regarded as representations of a plant, they were the plant itself, waiting to be brought to life by supernatural means.

In scenes of ritual in temples, the plants also indicate the location where rites were taking place; for example, in a papyrus marsh for rites of pulling up or shaking the papyrus for the goddess Hathor, and the birth of Horus. Plants were also used to decorate ritual objects and funeral garments, the spoons used for incense, jars, 'lotus' cups in which offerings were made to the gods, bowls, jewellery buried with the dead, where the choice of plant had a religious significance. The purpose of Egyptian paintings and relief sculptures of plants and gardens was:

1. to represent the activities going on there as continuing for eternity, in particular the cultivation of plants, and the performance of rituals;

2. to represent the place and the activities at their optimum condition: when the most significant part of the ritual was being performed and when the place was in its most perfect state, and with whatever part of the life-cycle of the plants, whether flowers or fruit, were important, being represented;

3. to have a record of the ritual being carried out;

4. to have a record of the best moments of the place, and of the life of the deceased.

The fact that many plants which are known from archaeological remains to have existed in pharaonic times were not illustrated, indicates that the mythological and symbolic connotation of the plants were among the main reasons for their being represented. Another is the importance of the plant as an agricultural product.

General Egyptian Artistic Conventions relevant to Botanical Representations

Egyptian artistic conventions are sometimes hard to interpret, although the Egyptians themselves had some fairly fixed conventions which can be explained. The ancient Egyptian artist represented both space and time in his compositions. Space could be shown as one place only, or as several views of the same place. Time could also be indicated by a sequence of events in cartoon style, or by the addition of an inscription, or as one significant moment.

The conventions which the Egyptians used to depict life are not the same as those which became current after the Greeks discovered perspective, although there are instances of drawings in which figures further from the viewer are smaller than those in the foreground. When the shape of the top of an article is significant that surface is drawn as if from on top. Waterlily flowers and papyrus heads are frequently represented from on top. This view is adopted in the decoration of ceilings where the painted flowers are 'looking down' on the viewer below. Plants can also be seen from below.

Enclosed spaces are sometimes shown in bird's eye view, and elements within the scene and the actors are drawn in profile. Individual items, such as cakes on a table could be shown in profile, or in bird's eye view. Certain objects, such as the food on offering tables, and legs of meat, were nearly always shown in a fixed manner so that there would be no doubt about their identification. Grapes, cucumbers and lettuces are always recognizable as such. Egyptian artists 'sought to strike a balance between the ideal and the actual when carving representations of plants, animals and objects'.[18]

There were fixed forms for most plants: the shape of the sycomore-fig was adopted as the determining sign for any kind of tree. This convention makes identification of a particular species difficult, unless there are other clues. The Egyptians established conventions for many scenes, emotions and objects. A few "signs" were enough to "evoke the image" of a familiar scene.[19] For example, a pool between date palms, in which the pool appears to be suspended between the trees, is derived from an Old Kingdom conventional rendering of a Holy Place in the Delta. These fixed forms had a religious significance, and could not be changed without losing their essential meaning. (Fig. 1)

Since the representations of agricultural scenes in the tombs were for religious purposes, namely to ensure the perpetuation of the seasonal cycle, little variation in their depiction was possible. The artists were producing a timeless reality, not a particular scene. The stress was on the permanent and immortal aspect of objects and activities, and not on one specific moment. 'Almost always (the artist) sought to portray a generalization of an action, not its transitory aspect on a particular day under certain conditions.'[20]

Plato commented on this apparently static aspect of Egyptian art:

> Painters and others who produce figures and such like were not at that period permitted to make innovations or to create forms other than the traditional one, nor is it permitted now, either in art or in any kind of music.[21]

Egyptologists vigorously contest this opinion. They maintain that the seeming immutability of Egyptian art comes from a modern outlook. Plato thought that the Egyptians were fulfilling his theory of 'ideas', but this interpretation depends much more on the Egyptians' understanding of their own culture, and their attempts to recreate Old Kingdom styles.

Egyptian art has been called 'a-spective', that is non-perspective. The artists drew what they believed constituted the essentials of an object or situation. They rendered objects "as known" rather than, in the manner of artists in the Greek or Hellenistic tradition, "as seen". They included details which would be hidden from the viewer in a perspective view, and changed their vantage point using frontal, side and bird's eye views simultaneously, for the same object or scene. The viewer has to re-orientate their point of view according to whether the object illustrated is being viewed by the artist from the top or the side: according to whether one view of an object is represented, or if several surfaces are being set side by side. The ancient Egyptians regarded an object as having six 'views': front, back and two sides, underneath and on top. These 'views' controlled how the artist represented objects, particularly human figures in sculpture, but this view of objects influenced his other productions. In addition to not wanting to depict "foreshortening and other optical departures from the 'normal aspect' they were also not concerned with rendering light and shade".[22] Symmetry was an important element, and gives a predictable balance to many compositions.

The system of 'registers', the lines of figures and scenes one on top of each other, indicated time and space. A vertical arrangement of scenes might indicate simultaneous events occurring in the same place, or it could be used to indicate movement from one place to another, or a sequence of events in time. Often the registers served to separate the scenes in time and space. Things further removed from the main scene were shown as smaller (but not in true perspective), thus enlarging the field of vision. e.g., the hippopotamus in a river scene, where he could be shown as very small indicating that he was deep under the water. The registers in a composition were arranged in proportion to the wall-space available. In some Old Kingdom tombs there was a system of one to twenty between the height of the register and the length of the room in which they were drawn.[23] But the important figures, such as the tomb-owner, would be drawn up to three times higher than the figures in the scenes in front of him. Sometimes the leading figure in a procession is shown with their back-view, as if moving away from the viewer.

Reliefs and paintings were usually coloured, although there were also line drawings in ink which were left uncoloured. Relief sculpture in the tombs was painted, or intended to be painted. Details of clothes, jewellery, hair and face were painted on statues. The colour indicates that an object belongs to a class of objects. "It does not show the color of a particular object, or of that object seen on a particular occasion". Green was the colour of growing plants, but that use did not prevent the Egyptians from adding fruit and flowers in their appropriate colours.

Egyptian artistic conventions were arrived at in the same period as the pyramids were built, in the 4th Dynasty, and maintained for hundreds of years, but with a flexibility that allowed for many stylistic and cultural changes. One such change came about in the reign of Akhenaten when "a conscious attempt" [was made] to make the visual "perception the actual appearance of nature".[25] Bak, Akhenaten's chief architect at Amarna, explained that he was the, 'Assistant whom His Majesty himself taught'.[26] Was he passing on the responsibility for altering the artistic conventions of the state? The new style in art has been attributed to Akhenaten's devotion to truth. Otherwise the artists are mainly anonymous, and seldom received recognition or signed their work.[27] But some are identified in the tombs by having their names over a representation of themselves at work.[27]

Accuracy of Drawings

Drawing in most instances is remarkably true to life in spite of being stylized to fit the norm current at a particular period. Some plants were also hieroglyphic signs, and as such their representation was standardized. Lotus (waterlily) flower, bud and stalk with leaf all mean what they represent, but a waterlily plant with a twisted stalk means 'offer'.[28] A single papyrus stem and head means 'papyrus' and 'green', and a clump of papyrus means the 'Delta' region. Grapes growing on props mean 'wine'. All these ideographs had a phonetic sound and could be combined with other signs to make other words.

At any given period plants are represented fairly uniformly, as if there were pattern books in circulation. This repetition is particularly evident in the fresco or secco painting at Amarna where the same groups of plants occur several times over. The reason why the artists were so accurate in their representations was that the plants were part of a scene which was intended to serve the eternal needs of the tomb-owner or deity, and so had to be as true a representation as possible. Another reason is that plants were shown in standardized ways so that they would be recognizable, first in the writing system, and this accuracy was carried over into purely figurative compositions. In many cases the distinctive shapes of trees were recorded and the characteristic fruits growing on them, rather than their less recognizable flowers. For example, the flowers of poppy are more generally illustrated than the pods, which could be confused with waterlily pods. The flowers of cornflowers were illustrated, presumably because the seeds just blow away. Mandrake is usually illustrated fruiting not flowering, (although on a casket in the tomb of Tutankhamun, the flowers with their purple petals are shown),[29] whereas waterlilies are shown flowering or in bud. Lettuces were shown in leaf before they had flowered and run to seed. The flowers of lily,[30] not the fruits, which have no perfume, are the part illustrated. The fruit, which is a determining part of the tree, is shown as present, even if, as in the case of date and doum palms growing side by side, they do not, in reality, bear fruit at the same time of year.

Summary

Egyptian art, was, in many instances, ideographic, that is to say, there were artistic conventions for certain objects and ideas, while other things were represented according to the individual artist's original thought. Egyptian art contains different levels of meaning which encompass indications of time, aspects of the social and economic life, and references to religion and mythology.

II   Cultivation

The Cultivated Areas

The conditions for gardening in ancient Egypt were unique. Although rain did fall, it was unpredictable, and the people depended on the inundation of the Nile. Because water came only once a year, it had to be collected and conserved, and this was done in lakes and pools, which were blocked by dykes to keep the water in, and then opened a little - usually by making a small tunnel through the lower part of the dyke - when required. Cultivation of orchards and vegetable gardens was around these pools, as far as can be seen from the illustrations in the tomb-reliefs and paintings.

A monkey going off to water a garden with another monkey on his shoulder, who is preparing to pick the fruit. A XIXth Dynasty sketch on a flake of limestone. (Fig. 2)

Excavation has provided evidence of cultivation plots, and most of these are near a water-source, such as a well or a pool. The richest citizens at Amarna had their own pools and wells in their gardens. The inhabitants of the oasis of Dakhleh also owned their wells, as they made clear to a royal official who came to inspect them.[1]

Plots

Square plots near lakes, or canals, full of papyrus and other water plants, are illustrated in the Fifth Dynasty Sun Temple of Niuserre at Abu Gurob, and also in private tombs of the Old Kingdom, such as those of Nyankhkhnum and Khnumhotep, Fetekta, Nyankhnesut, Mereruka, Neferherenptah, and Rashepses.

Old Kingdom example of squared beds near water in the tomb of Mereruka. VIth Dynasty. (Fig. 3)

A water source is shown near the rows of plots in a Middle Kingdom wall-painting at Beni Hasan. Here, rising ground leads up from a pool to the place where the gardeners are watering the plots from pots, and picking lettuces and onions. The edges of the squares are moulded in slightly raised relief, and there are depressions for runnels round the edges. They are coloured blue-green for the leaves of a vine on a trellis which is covering the crop. At el-Bersheh there is no pool visible beside the plots, but there is

Picking waterlilies: an illustration in the VIth Dynasty tomb of Zau at Deir el-Gebrawi. (Fig. 4)

a pool illustrated on the opposite wall (Fig. 5). Flower-growing is illustrated in tombs from the Old Kingdom onwards. Plants were used in bouquets, and flowers, such as waterlilies and lilies were squeezed in bags to make perfume. Bouquets of papyrus and other marsh plants are shown being gathered outside the palace at Amarna. Mandrakes, poppies and other flowers were used to decorate the large bouquets which were carried on formal occasions, such as funerals and festivals.

Crops were planted in rectangular beds, surrounded by low dykes, so that water could be retained around them. Such beds have been found in the Eastern Delta site of Tell Dabaa (Fig. 7), ancient Avaris,[2] in Middle Egypt at Amarna,[3] and in the Sudan at Mirgissa,[4] Soleb,[5] Kerma[6] and Amarah West,[7] where the Gufti workmen recognized what they had found,

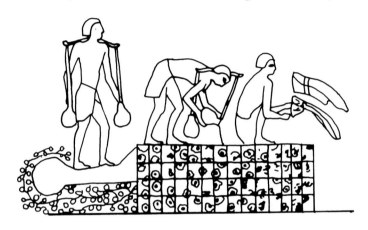

Vegetables in rectangular beds which are shaded by a vine. The man on the left is bringing water in pots on a yoke from a pool, or well, beside the plots. The man on the right has pulled up some onions and lettuces. A painting in the Middle Kingdom tomb of Khnemhotp III at Beni Hasan. (Fig. 5)

and unhesitatingly declared them to be seed-beds. The plots in the Workmen's village at Amarna measured from 45-52cms. square. The dykes round the square beds were probably used as paths. At Mirgissa, Iken, the fortress which "no Nubian may pass", the plots covered an area of 13 x 13m., and were in the enclosure outside the fort, and not connected with any building. Each plot was 45cm. square and had small irrigation channels.[8] There was also a basin of larger size to store water. Flower-beds were also arranged in rectangles, as can be seen in reliefs from Memphis of the late Eighteenth and Nineteenth Dynasties. The hieroglyphic sign *sepat*, which was the determinative for district, nome, estate and garden represents either the criss-crossing of dykes in a field, or the squares of plots under cultivation. A system of runnels in fields at the time of Napoleon's expedition is clearly visible in a sketch made by his draughtsmen.

The water supply was very close to some of the plots excavated, for example, to the houses at Amarna, which have wells and pools, but for others, water had to be carried for some distance. The well which supplied the workmen's village at Amarna was outside the wall about 1400m. away in the direction of the town.[9] But there was a stand of pots about 20m. from the wall. The stables of the so-called 'Military Police Headquarters' at Amarna had a large pond and a well.

At all times, poor people cultivated vegetable gardens for their own use. The widow of a gardener said she had made enough money to buy slaves, by selling the produce from her garden. State taxes were levied on produce. Henenu, a local lord in Middle Egypt during the Eleventh Dynasty, boasts of collecting taxes for the king, and inspiring fear throughout the land. Extortion became such a problem, that Horemheb forbad his officials to 'plunder the poor by taking the best of their vegetables', or to keep produce for themselves.[10]

Vineyards

Gardening in Egypt began with the cultivation of grapes, and the vineyards remained very important throughout the historical period. Vine-growing is illustrated in twenty-four Old Kingdom tombs. In the succeeding period, up to the end of the Middle Kingdom, nine tombs show vine-growing, four have orchards, and six have vegetable-patches. Two methods of supporting the vines are shown. In earlier times forked props were used, and occasionally pergolas, which became more general in the New Kingdom.

Vines supported on forked props illustrated in the Middle Kingdom tomb of Khnemhotp III at Beni Hasan. (Fig. 6)

A pergola from a wooden model in a tomb was found at Saqqara.[11] It has 'little arches of wood supported on wooden pillars', and is painted blue. The holes in which the uprights for a pergola were fixed have been found at Tell Dabaa, Avaris, in the period of the Hyksos.[12] Separate pits were dug for the vines 1.2m. in diameter and 3m. apart.

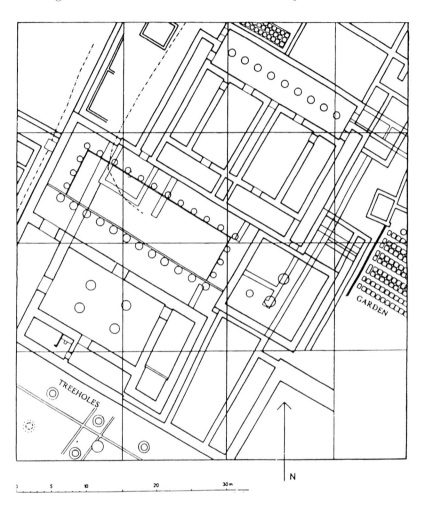

Palace gardens at Tell Dabaa in the eastern Delta. XIIIth Dynasty. (Fig. 7)

The brick pillars in a large hall beside the ceremonial buildings at Amarna may have been for a pergola. Some of the vines illustrated in the tombs do not appear to have any support, but they may had a frame hidden underneath which was only exposed when all the grapes had been picked. Vines were sometimes trained across pools to protect the workers drawing water and to shade the fish and birds living in the pools.

Picking grapes is illustrated in several tombs. These scenes are not just concerned with the material harvesting; there was a ritual of the grape harvest. In the New Kingdom the vine was equated with the papyrus thicket as the place where the sun sheltered just before its birth.[13] Whole burial chambers were covered with a painted vine across the ceiling, as a symbol of the rebirth of the owner.

Orchards

Illustrated beside the square plots and the vineyards were the orchards; orchards are depicted in thirteen tombs (Fig. 48). They also needed artificial irrigation. This could be provided by a well sunk to reach ground water, or a pool left behind after the inundation, which might eventually dry up. Such a pool can be seen in the tomb of Menna (Theban Tomb 69), with men ploughing beside it. But the inundation might reach too high, and damage or destroy the trees. There was a saying that: "If a gardener becomes a fisherman his trees perish",[14] which may refer to an extraordinarily high Nile, rather than to the gardener choosing another occupation. Methen, who lived during the Third Dynasty, described how he dug a 'very large lake' and planted figs and vines.

The earliest orchards illustrated contained a great variety of trees: sycomore figs, common figs, and even incense trees. Other trees which were illustrated were date and doum-palms, Christ's thorn and olive. Samentuser who lived at Thebes in the Eleventh Dynasty and whose stela is in the Florence Museum (no. 6365), and Harkhuf, Governor of Upper Egypt, both spoke of their ponds and sycomore-fig trees.

Trees were planted in rows, and were either watered from a channel running alongside them, or individually, usually in a pit, with a wall around them. This technique is demonstrated at Hermopolis,[15] and at Abydos, where six trees were planted round the 'Osireion',[16] and at the temple of Taharqa at Kawa in Nubia.[17] Mud and brick containers are illustrated in wall-paintings at el-Bersheh, and in New Kingdom tombs at Amarna and Thebes. (Fig. 8) The excavators at Amarna described how the pits were made:

> As there is little nourishment in the desert soil, a hole was dug and filled with imported earth; this earth was mounded up and round it was built or plastered a mud wall, circular and rising like a flower pot to a height of anything up to 60cms. according to the size of the tree and rounded off at the top with a neat coping: these mud tubs are still regularly used in Egypt, but nowadays more to prevent goats eating the plants, and, represented in section, they appear in ancient Egyptian drawings of trees.[18]

And not only trees, but a clump of cornflowers is illustrated in one of these mud containers.

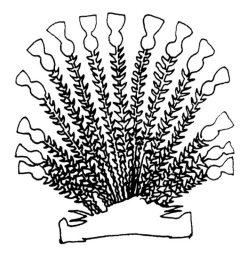

A clump of cornflowers in a mud container, painted on the floor surrounding the T-shaped pools in Building I in the Maru-aten at Amarna. XVIIIth Dynasty. (Fig. 8)

Another way to ensure that the plants had enough water was to plant them inside large pots . Such pots have been found at Tell Dabaa, and Amarna.[19] At Tanis, the pots, with their bases broken off, were arranged in three rows.[20] A pottery pipe was also found at Tanis made of jars fitted together, and another was found at Armant dating from Roman times.[21] At Elephantine there was a system of jars fitted together vertically to bring water to the roots.[22]

Some plant holders instead of being solid were made out of bricks with air spaces between them. These too are shown surrounding trees at Amarna. Their position may be significant. The ones illustrated in the tomb of Meryre are in a passageway between two buildings, and so could be exposed to the ravages of goats. The quay in front of the palace is another exposed place where bricks were used to protect trees. In modern times such tubs are used to prevent young trees being attacked by goats. A circular fence of sticks or basketwork was also a way of protecting trees from being chewed by animals.

Trees were grown for their fruit, which was usually picked by men and boys, who climbed the trees. The fruit was collected in baskets, pots, and in nets. In one illustration (Tomb 29 at Beni Hasan) a man is using a tool for holding bulls' horns, to pull down branches of a tree. It consists of a long pole with a hook at the end, but he may just be scaring away birds with anything that came to hand. A ladder is only illustrated once, in the Satirical Papyrus of Turin. Occasionally other details of cultivation are shown in the tomb paintings, such as a bag placed over part of a date tree in the tomb of Neferhotep (Fig. 66), either to protect it from birds, or to promote the fertilization of the female flowers.

According to the Old and Middle Kingdom paintings and reliefs, gardens do not appear to have been fenced. But in the New Kingdom, the illustrations show walls round orchards, and walls round separate areas within a garden. And wooden models found in the tomb of Meket-re of gardens and dating from the XIth Dynasty are walled. In the centre is a pool, surrounded by sycamore fig trees, in front of a portico. Painted on the back wall of this building are doors and windows. The building has been interpreted both as a tomb and as a dwelling. There is also a stone model in the British Museum (EA 36903) of a walled orchard which has holes for the miniature trees cut in the floor (the trees have disappeared). The pools are also cut fairly deeply into the floor, one has steps leading down into it; and there are lines arranged in a grid to represent the irrigation channels, or individual plots. The top of the wall is crenellated, like the wall illustrated in the tomb of Ineni (Fig. 48); it has two doors carved on the outside. There is a portico on one side and a stairway.

A stone model of courtyard containing an orchard. The dots represent depressions in the floor where miniature trees would have been arranged. In the centre are rectangular and circular 'pools'. The wall is crenellated and has doors. There are steps to an upper floor. Possibly XVIIIth Dynasty. (Fig. 9)

Pottery versions of courtyards with trees, pools and vegetable patches have been found dating from the end of the Old Kingdom into the early New Kingdom. Usually a building is part of the model; it has also been interpreted both as a dwelling house and as the façade of a tomb. One model has palm trees growing in front of the building.[23] Others have a pool, or several pools, in front of the building. These so-called 'Soul houses' were pottery substitutes for offering tables, and, like them, receptacles for libations of water. Some of the pools have holes round them for trees, or a canopy or pergola. The reason for having walls was to keep out marauders, both human and animal. The threat from wild animals was real enough at Thebes in the Late Period, since an owner had to promise her gardener that she would carry a spear and sword when visiting the garden because of wolves and hyenas, and also that she would wear something on her head.[24]

Area of Plantations

Very little information is available about the dimensions of cultivated plots, vineyards and orchards. And even when measurements survive, there is no agreement about what their modern equivalents are. Methen had a walled vineyard, and also a field of 200 araura. Ineni, who was Overseer of the Granary of Amun, and responsible for providing the offerings to the temple of Amun during the early part of the New Kingdom, lists about 451 trees in one orchard. A few high officials at Amarna had private gardens measuring over sixty metres by thirty.[25] The vineyard outside the late Eighteenth Dynasty temple at Tell Dabaa was about thirty metres wide.

The Gardeners

The Labourers

The small figures of workmen (shabtis) found in great quantities in tombs are often inscribed with an instruction that they must: "Cultivate the fields, flood the banks (of the fields, i.e. water them) and carry away sand to the east and to the west".[26] These figures were evidently supposed to continue in the hereafter the regular agricultural work, which consisted in transporting soil to the required position, and building up the dams with sand mixed with mud. They would also have had to remove sand blown in from the desert, which would be an unwelcome invader of the cultivation. Manuring was also part of their work. Bricks from disused buildings were probably collected for this purpose. Natural marl may have been spread on the fields, and sand brought from the desert to lighten the mud.

Labourers evidently had a hard life:

> The gardener carries a yoke
> His shoulders are bent as with age;
> There's a swelling on his neck
> And it festers.
> In the morning he waters vegetables,
> The evening he spends with the herbs,
> While at noon he has toiled in the orchard.
> He works himself to death
> More than all other professions.[27]

But these were not his only duties; there was all the digging, earth-moving and watering. According to his contract preserved on a pot, a gardener had to water the vineyard, and in the evening he had to make baskets.[28] Not all gardeners were male. Women, and also children, are listed and illustrated as workers.

A gardener working a shaduf raising water from a canal to water the plants in front of Ipuy's shrine. Theban Tomb 217. XIXth Dynasty. (Fig. 10)

Instructions from a landlord to his workers confirm the impression of their hard life: "Take great care, hoe all my land, sieve with the sieve; hack with your noses in the work".[29] But they could go on strike. Gardeners, who normally brought supplies of vegetables for the people building the royal tombs of the 19th and 20th Dynasties, struck with the other workers over lack of pay. Their status was similar to fishermen and watercarriers. Occasionally their names are recorded. Three gardeners are named in the tomb of Khnumhotep at Beni Hasan. A gardener, called Amenhotpe, was among the workers building Senenmut's second tomb; it is not clear whether the tomb had a garden, or whether this man was simply an assistant in the work. Neternakht is named as a gardener in a scene of grape picking. The gardener, Harmose, was listed among the people given by Sheshonk, to the temple at Abydos, together with the garden 'which is in the high district of Abydos'.[30] Tomb owners arranged for gardeners to maintain the gardens at their funerary chapels. Ker, a suspect in a royal tomb robbery, was such a man. The cemetery workmen may also have included gardeners, since people like Hapzefa, Nomarch of Siut, had gardens outside their tomb-chapels. Gardeners are named as some of the people setting up booths at a funeral ceremony. Foreign gardeners were brought to the temple of Osiris at Abydos during the 26th Dynasty, where Peftuaneith said he made an orchard:

Planted with all fruit trees
Its gardeners being foreigners
Brought in as prisoners.[31]

Asiatic prisoners were employed in the vineyards, even as far away as
Kawa in Nubia, where Taharqa provided gardeners for the vines at the
temple. They were described as "Good gardeners of the Mentiu of Asia".[32]
The staff needed to maintain a vineyard on the Delta estate of the funerary
temple of Sethos II at Thebes, is listed as seven men, four young men, four
old men and six boys. In general, these workers were bound to the soil, to
their village or region, and could not move freely. However a class of
landowning peasantry, who had been given land in return for performing
a mortuary cult for the king, or for a rich landowner, were freeholders. And
retired soldiers and officials who had been granted land, owned it outright
and could trade it. The gardeners had many enemies. Goats and monkeys,
locusts, mice, cattle, hippopotami, and snakes; a gardener is mentioned in
the Coffin Texts as someone who will remove a snake from the path of the
deceased. Monkeys and baboons probably stole fruit. They are often
depicted climbing fruit-trees, and it is not clear whether they have been
trained to collect the fruit, or whether they are predators. In one

Monkeys stealing fruit. Painting in the Middle Kingdom tomb of Khnemhotp at Beni Hasan. (Fig. 11)

illustration, (Berlin 14149) however, the fruit pickers are chasing away a baboon. Goats are so often shown chewing the lower branches of trees that

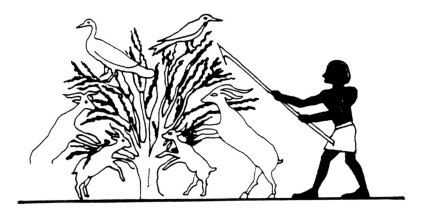

A man scaring birds, and goats grazing on the lower branches of a tree. A painting in the Middle Kingdom tomb of Bakt I at Beni Hasan. (Fig. 12)

perhaps they were allowed to do so by their keepers, since they were productive animals. Birds also helped themselves to fruit. Hippopotami, being such large, heavy vegetarians, could do an enormous amount of damage to plants. Geese, which are illustrated in so many agricultural scenes, could destroy dates in summer, emmer in winter, and eat the seed the sowers threw on the ground. The extremes of the climate were always dangerous. In the early part of this century a professional gardener's main problems were still dangers from flooding, drought, and birds, which could destroy trees by nesting in them.

Tools

Tools were limited to ploughs and Egyptian hoes for digging. The hoe is a spade-like tool which is worked towards the body. Baskets were used for carrying produce and soil, and pots for carrying water, either singly or on yokes.

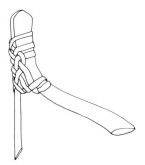

An ancient hoe. The copper blade is tied onto the wooden handle with leather thongs. (Fig. 13)

31

Water-skins, were used for holding drinking water, as the painting in the tomb of Nakht (Theban Tomb 52) shows, where a man is drinking from a skin. In the tomb of Khety at Beni Hasan, a skin is shown hanging on a tree ready to be used.

In the New Kingdom, the *shaduf* was introduced, although it was known much earlier in Mesopotamia. By this invention it was possible to lift a bucket of water up to two metres vertically using a ball of clay as a counterweight to the bucket. The pole holding the clay was fixed to an upright post and worked in see-saw fashion as the bucket was dipped and raised. (Figs. 10 & 66) More accurate directing of the water could be obtained by an extension to the *shaduf* consisting of a cylindrical runnel leading to the plant-container. A man in the tomb of Neferhotep (Theban Tomb 49) pours water from a leather bucket into such a device. This is the earliest illustration of a *shaduf* and dates from the XVIIIth Dynasty. The arm and pot visible in the tomb of Meryre at Amarna, probably belong to a yoke not a *shaduf*. A rather surprising and laborious way of watering a plot was with a scoop, like the tool used for winnowing. However the man who is shown using it may be moving mud rather than water. The water-

A man using scoops to move water or mud. Part of a scene in the Book of the Dead of Nebhepet in Turin. (Fig. 14)

wheel, or *saqqieh*, may have come into use in the New Kingdom. Petrie thought he had found a pit where a *saqqieh* had been installed in the garden of the central palace at Amarna. But it is more generally thought to have been introduced in Ptolemaic times. Water could be delivered mechanically to plants by means of pottery water-pipes. Such pipes were found in the temple palace of Seti I at Thebes, but dating from the Late Period, and belonging to another installation, also at Tanis, and in the temple at Elephantine, and at Kawa. Donkeys were used to transport water in big earthenware pots which were illustrated in the tomb of Mahu at Amarna, and for supplying the workmen constructing the royal tombs.

A donkey transporting water pots. A relief in the tomb of Mahu at Amarna. XVIIIth Dynasty. (Fig. 15)

The Officials

There was a wide social gulf between the labourers who did the work, and the state officials in charge of the temple gardens. In the New Kingdom, priests with the title "Gardener of Amun" occupied an elevated social position, passed their offices on to their sons, and had tombs on the West Bank at Thebes. One such official was Nakht, Son of Guraru, "Gardener of the Divine offerings of Amun" (Theban Tomb 161); another was Sennufer (Theban Tomb 96), who was Mayor of the Southern City, Prince and Count, and held other important titles. Senenmut, who was Queen Hatshepsut's adviser, was "Overseer of the Gardens of Amun", according to the inscription on his statue. Semirem was "Overseer of the Garden" at Amarna. Other titles closely associated with that of "Gardener of Amun", were, "Bearer of the Floral Offerings of Amun", which was another office exercised by Nakht (Theban Tomb 161) and by his sons, and "Gardener of the Divine Offerings of Amun", the title held by his father, and his son, Huynufer. Scenes in his tomb show him inspecting fields of grain and flax, and a large plantation of lettuces. The food may have been grown for the funeral meal for many guests which is shown in the next register, or for the supply of the temple of Amun. In the Sixth Dynasty, the high official, Mereruka, had the title "Overseer of the Plantation". Even at Buhen, in far off Nubia in the Thirteenth Dynasty, a gardener was prosperous enough to have a stela put up for himself. Gardeners are mentioned together with "Carriers of Floral Bouquets" in a list of temple personnel in the time of Ramesses II.[33] The only time an upper class Egyptian worked in a garden was after his death, when he tilled the ground, and reaped a harvest in the fields of the afterlife.

Lower down the social scale would have been the 'Heads of Gardens' whom prophets of Amun in the temple at Karnak instructed to provide extra offerings for the temple of Mentuhotep at the behest of Sesostris III.[34] The duties of these officials were to oversee the cultivation of the products needed for the offerings in the temple, and the preparation of the elaborate bouquets which were carried in processions and required for all ritual occasions. Pharaoh's Butler was instructed to bring back blue flowers and "Katha" from Nubia, according to a letter addressed to the Viceroy of Kush in the time of Ramesses XI.[35] But the gods were the ultimate gardeners:

> [Flowers of sweet] odor [given] by Ptah and planted by Geb....Ptah has made this with his hands to entertain his heart. The canals are filled with water anew and the earth is flooded with his love.

Mereruka, in front of an easel, painting symbolic representations of the three seasons as seated figures with their names over their heads. In the ovals are the hieroglyphic signs for 'moon', indicating the four 'moons' in each season. VIth Dynasty. (Fig. 16)

The 'Hymn to the Aten' emphasizes the power of the sun god, Aten, in promoting plant growth:

> Thy rays nourish every garden (or field), when thou risest they grow by thee (or for you).[37]

The Seasonal Cycle

Egypt had three seasons which controlled life: inundation, winter and summer. Just after the inundation, Egypt was a 'black cloth' of mud, according to the Arab poet Masudi. From January to March it was a 'green cloth', and from April to June, a ripening 'nugget of gold'. At the time of inundation people took advantage of the increase in water for fishing, fowling and visits by water. The grapes were ready for harvesting. As the water went down they prepared the ground, and sowed the seed. The pools left by the receding water kept the arable land moist.

The activities of each season: fishing and fowling during the inundation in the tomb of Paheri at el-Kab. XVIIIth Dynasty. (Fig. 17)

Winter was the time for tending the crops, at the end of which, the grain and flax were harvested. The period until the inundation came was a hot, dead and difficult time, with only the olive harvest and some fruit-picking to look forward to.

The activities of each season: fruit-picking during summer in the tomb of Paheri at el-Kab. XVIIIth Dynasty. (Fig. 18)

The number of times a piece of land could bear crops within a year has been debated. The lands too high to be reached by the inundation, and which were watered artificially, could possibly grow up to three crops in a year, whereas the inundated land may only have borne one crop, as it did in the Nineteenth Century.

In the tomb-reliefs, the whole cycle of the year is represented. Tomb-owners say they are: 'Beholding the seasons of summer, [inundation] and winter."[38] The importance of keeping the life-cycle going, in both the vegetable and animal kingdoms, is expressed in Seti I's decree establishing an estate to provide offerings for a temple of Osiris at Abydos:

> The bulls mount, the herd receives increase, the herbs multiply in leafage, the stalks come in due season, they multiply millions, and their numbers increase anew.[39]

Inundation

The climate of Egypt has not altered greatly since the Middle Kingdom, but the area covered by deserts has increased. Rain was evidently not totally absent, since the Egyptians had words for rain, and they built gutters and spouts on temples. A satisfactory level of inundation was vital for all types of agriculture. People wanted a flood without disaster, which was not so high that it would flood areas of habitation, and not so low that insufficient new soil and moisture would be deposited. Nile levels recorded on an offering table of the Old Kingdom in the Cairo Museum, specify twenty-five cubits at the inundation, twenty-three cubits in the winter, and twenty-two in the summer. The height of the flood seems to have varied at different periods, with particularly high levels in the Middle Kingdom, followed by lower levels in the succeeding years. The bed of the river was lower in antiquity than it is now, probably by about 3.5m., having been filled over the centuries with the deposit from the mountains, and the water-table was also lower.

The heights of the Nile were recorded at various points along the river as the flood progressed. At Thebes, one of the places at which an observer noted this event, was just below the highest peak, the Qurn, from which the whole plain could be seen. He had to write the month, day, and year of the current king, when "the water returned". What the observer actually saw was probably the sun glistening on the spreading water, as the canals and pools filled, and the peasants ran to remove the earth and stone dams to let it in. The inundation usually came between July and August. On the day when the inundation reached their part of the valley, landowners went out to see the 'Opening of the Dykes'. Amenophis III's excursion in his boat on Queen Tiyi's lake at Djarukha, described on several commemorative scarabs, was in celebration of the 'Opening of the Dykes', when 'His Majesty celebrated the "Festival of Opening the

Pools".[40] The actual breaking of the dyke may be illustrated on the mace head found at Hierakonpolis and now in the Ashmolean Museum, of king Scorpion, who ruled before the First Dynasty.

The king 'Scorpion' cutting the dyke to allow water to flood the fields. Early Dynastic Period. (Fig. 19)

A festival of Opening the Dykes was still celebrated in the Sixteenth Century when Prospero Alpini visited Egypt. He was amazed to see the people throwing flowers, gifts and themselves into the water.

Summary

Gardens were economic units producing fruit, vegetables and flowers. They were part of a larger estate which consisted of several areas, such as: a lake, containing papyrus, reeds, waterlilies and birds, a "hall of natron for pouring out fresh water", a bird-farm in the marshes, cattle stalls, herbs, that is, wild plants on the land, goose-ponds, marshes, wild plants in the water, fields along the banks of the river or canals where the cattle could graze, low-ground islands and high-ground islands for growing crops. The cultivated land consisted of different qualities, according to how far the plot was from the river. There was highland, away from the river, lowland and islands, and the newly appearing land. Crops which should not be flooded, such as vines, were grown on higher ground, whereas annual crops such as vegetables, which need rich, fresh soil were grown near water.

Gardens were part of the system which produced supplies for a landowner, his family and dependents, and for his memorial cult after his death, and in the same way, for the upkeep of the staff of temples and of the pharaoh. In tomb-scenes long lines of estate-workers are shown converging on the owner, bringing him the produce of his estate.

Agricultural methods hardly changed at all from ancient Egyptian times until the Nineteenth Century. The climate of Egypt was similar to modern conditions, but there was more natural vegetation, and a much lower population. The ancient texts seem to indicate a local responsibility for the control of water supply, rather than central control of the irrigation system.[41] Water conservation was a main concern of the Egyptians, who built elaborate networks of dykes and canals in order to preserve the available flood water, but the system of conservation changed in the Nineteenth Century, and there is apparently no continuity of systems from ancient times to the Twentieth Century.

III   The Trees in the Gardens

The range of plants known to have existed in pharaonic Egypt was extensive. Some were native to Egypt, but many others arrived at different times from the surrounding regions: from the south, including the Sudan, the Horn of Africa and the Zambesi regions, from the north, the Irano-Turkish regions, from round the Mediterranean, and from the east, as far as Arabia. During the pharaonic period the flora was fairly stable, and fairly limited. In Hellenistic and Roman times there was a great increase in the number and variety of plants. During pharaonic times timber and nuts were imported from the surrounding countries.

Sources of Information about Plants

Excavation

The most specific information about the plants in Egyptian gardens and orchards comes from excavation, from the analysis of roots, seeds, pollen and carbonized and decayed remains, and from the wreaths and garlands, as well as manufactured items, such as furniture and weaponry, which were placed in the tombs at the time of burial, and reburial. Museums all over the world have plant remains which were buried with mummified bodies, or laid on coffins and other furnishings in the tombs. A few of these collections have been examined and published.

The amount of exact information about the species of plants largely depends on the interest and technical expertise of the excavator. In pools excavated at Amarna in the 1920's, for example, only the debris of "lotus and papyrus" was identified, although other plants must have been present.

Studies of predynastic, early dynastic and pharaonic sites show that there were four endemic species, nineteen African species, fifty-six Middle Eastern species and nineteen paleo-tropical species. From the middens and animal-pens of the workmen's village at Amarna come fruits and seeds of crops cultivated for food or other purposes: pomegranate, date and doum palm, sycamore-fig, olive, almond, and varieties of *Mimusops* and *Grewia*. The bouquets and wreaths left in tombs by mourners, show that many different flowers were growing near the tombs, possibly in special herb-gardens. These plants included hollyhock (*Alcea ficifolia*), mayweed, (*Anthemis pseudocotula*), blue cornflower (*Centaurea depressa*), golden mayweed (*Chrysanthemum coronarium* L.), convolvulus, cordia (*Cordia gharaf* and *myxa*), *Cressa cretica*, *Delphinium orientale*, jasmin, lettuce, madonna lily, *Melilotus indica*, mint, *Mimusops laurifolia*, waterlily, olive, poppy, pomegranate and wild celery. The bouquets were constructed on a strong central core of date-palm leaves and ribs, cloth and bundles of papyrus with colourful, sweet-smelling posies attached to this core. There were ring-stands and pots for bouquets. Botanical research in excavations has been carried out over the last few years at Hierakonpolis,[1] Amarna,[2] Tell Dabaa,[3] Kom el-Hisn,[4] and Saqqara.[5]

The packing used to fill the cavities in mummified bodies has yielded a range of vegetation, both from the plants themselves and the pollens of other plants adhering to them and to the bandages.[6]

Illustrations of Plants in Paintings

The trees which are most frequently shown growing in gardens are, date and doum palm trees, sycomore-fig, pomegranate, olive, vine and willow. Trees were arranged in straight rows, usually of particular species. In the tomb of Amenemhab Mahu (Theban Tomb 85), the innermost row was of sycomore-figs, the middle row was of alternating date and doum-palms, and trees with spreading branches stood in the outermost row.

Fruit, which tomb-owners wanted to be sure they had on their tables in the afterlife, is illustrated piled up in heaps. It included grapes, yellow, heart-shaped *Mimusops laurifolia*, carob pods, dates and figs. Fruits which were passed round at banquets by the guests, were either mandrakes or *Mimusops laurifolia*. The vegetables prepared for banquets were lettuce, onion, melons and cucumbers. In the illustrations of vegetable gardens of the Old Kingdom there were onions and lettuce, and the trees were date and doum palm, pomegranate, juniper, common fig, sycomore-figs, and vines.

Incense trees are mentioned, and occasionally illustrated in the tombs and temples of the Old and New Kingdoms. The flowers which appear both in the Old and in the New Kingdom tomb-paintings most frequently are poppy, cornflower and hollyhock, and members of the daisy family. In marsh scenes many reeds and rushes are shown growing in, and near, water.

Imitations of fruit and flowers as containers, spoons for incense and models left in tombs, confirm what is known about the plants used by the Egyptians.

Documents - Words for Plants

The names for particular plants can be identified when they are written beside the illustration. But the Egyptians referred to plants which do not survive in illustrations, for example, in medical texts, poems, or descriptive passages, and these identifications are not always certain.

Many remedies for ailments included parts of plants, but it is not always clear which species is meant, and the meaning of words in the medical texts has to be gained from documents outside them.

Trees growing in Ancient Egypt

In an Egyptian landscape the most important plants were the trees. They formed avenues in front of temples and surrounded the gardens within them with a protective wind-break. Date and doum palms, and sycomore-figs are the most frequently illustrated, but excavation shows that tamarisk, cedars and *Mimusops* also grew on sacred sites.

The earliest representation of a tree is on a sealing from the reign of the first kings of the First Dynasty, Ka and Narmer; a circular plot of ground, or town-sign, is shown next to a tree, which species it is, is not certain.

Trees beside the signs for 'town' on a sealing of the First Dynasty. (Fig. 20)

All trees had economic worth, either as food: such as, carob, dates, pomegranates, apples, olives, figs and grapes, or as building material for temples, houses, boats, furniture and weapons, for which, date palm, willow, sycomore-fig, and the imports, ash, conifers and elm were used. Trees and vines provided shade and food. Dates, figs, and doum-palm were used for sweetening at a time when sugar cane was not known.

Fruit-producing Trees in the Orchard[7]

Orchards were a regular part of an estate. Ramesses III gave two 'sycomore gardens' (orchards of sycomore-fig trees), to the temple at Heliopolis.[8] There are several illustrations of orchards and even a written description accompanied by an illustration in the tomb of Ineni (Theban Tomb 81), which mentions many more trees than are shown in the illustration. The trees in this orchard are arranged in rows and some are easily recognizable.

In the orchards, the most distinctive trees were the date and doum palms and the sycomore-fig. Date palms (*Phoenix dactylifera* L.) grow to a height of about 20m. They have been cultivated since prehistoric times. Date wine and date syrup were made from the fruit. The 'Land of the Date Palm', called by the Egyptians 'the sweet land', lay between Xois and Sebennytos in the Delta. But palms grew all over Egypt. Dates were much used in medicine.

The stem of the doum-palm, *Hyphaene thebaica* (L). Mart.*Cucifera*, is divided low down, so that the tree appears to have two trunks, which are light brown with dark stripes and usually about 30cm. thick. On each stem are about forty oval fruits, 7-8cms. long, which have a very sweet outer skin and an inner nut about 4.0cms. long which contains sweet juice. Doum trees grow currently both in Lower Egypt, and in the oases of Upper Egypt. Illustrations of the tree are found from early dynastic times. The fruits were left in tombs for the dead to enjoy, and were illustrated on the tables of food placed before them. The dried fruit was used as an astringent. The words for doum-palm tree was *mama* and for the fruit, *kuku*.

Argun-palm, *Medemia argun*, is a smaller version of the doum-palm. It reaches 10m. high. and has a tasteless fruit with purple skin and yellow flesh. It is a native of Nubia. Fruits have been found in Fifth Dynasty tombs. Ineni, the royal gardener in the early part of the Eighteenth Dynasty, who listed and illustrated some of the trees he had planted, included argun palms among them. The Egyptian name was *mama-en-khannet*.

Sycomore-fig (*Ficus Sycomorus*), is a large, spreading, evergreen tree which grows fairly rapidly to a height of about 15m. Its leaves are rough and leathery. The sycomore-fig produces fruit all the year round. The figs, which grow on short, slender stalks, need cutting with a knife in order to get them to swell and ripen. The ancient Egyptians enjoyed their sweet taste. They were used as a laxative and a cure for worms. The juice was a treatment for cuts. The sycomore-fig belongs to the same family as the common fig. It was planted in gardens in order to provide shade as well as fruit. The tree was called *nehet*.

Olive-trees, (*Olea europaea* L.), grow to over 10m. tall. They need good drainage and can withstand salt and drought. Olive trees have been cultivated since about 3000 B.C. The seeds have been found in tombs of various periods, and the leaves in garlands in tombs of the Seventeenth Dynasty at Thebes, and in Tutankhamun's burial. Olive trees may be illustrated on an early Dynastic ceremonial slate palette now in the Cairo Museum. The king Akhenaten is shown offering an olive-branch in a scene on a carved and painted block from Amarna, and olive trees are illustrated in wall-paintings and reliefs also at Amarna. Olives were planted in the Delta. Classical writers wrongly thought the Egyptians could only grow olive trees in a few places, such as in the gardens of Alexandria and the nome of Arsinoe, and some modern writers have followed this opinion. The word *dedtu*, used since the Nineteenth Dynasty, became in Arabic *Set setun*.

There were several evergreen trees which also produced fruit and which are now rare, if not extinct, in Egypt. One of the most intriguing is *Mimusops laurifolia* (Forssk), (the previously named *Mimusops schimperi*), roots of which were found at the entrance to Hatshepsut's funerary temple at Deir el-Bahari. Garlands made of *Mimusops* leaves and fruits, were found at Medinet Habu,[10] at Deir el-Medineh,[11] and in Tutankhamun's tomb, and remains were found in the workmen's village at Amarna.[12] Although it was not native to Egypt, some specimens were re-introduced at the end of the last century, and are still growing in the front courtyard of the Egyptian Museum beside Mariette's tomb, and at the back of the building.[13] The tree has oval leaves, and yellow or green,[14] strongly flavoured fruit, about 4cm. long with two to three shiny seed kernels, and sweet green pulp. The stems contain a milky juice. The trees grow to a height of 15-30m. The trunk is dark brown, with a rough, grooved bark. There is a problem distinguishing the representations of the fruit of *Mimusops* from that of mandrake. The botanical difference is that the mandrake has a calyx covering the lower part of the fruit, and the *Mimusops* has reflexed sepals.[15] Both are green in colour ripening to yellow. Hollow blue faience fruits, identified as *Mimusops*, were found at Deir el-Bahari,[16] and two of glass inscribed with the name of Tuthmosis III, were found in the tomb of Tutankhamun. *Mimusops* has been identified with the Greek word persea, which has been identified with two Egyptian words: *shwab* and *ished*.[18] The balance of opinion now favours *shwab* as the Egyptian word. And so Ineni, Tuthmosis I's architect, who planted thirty-one *shwab* trees in his garden would have had *Mimusops* growing there. In Greek times it was said that when the persea fruit ripened the Nile would rise: 'May the persea fruit not fall the night when the waters of the Nile rise and may the wind not blow them off'.

The carob tree, *Ceratonia siliqua L.*, is an evergreen reaching a height of over 4m. Pods and seeds, which are sweet, were found in Eighteenth Dynasty burials at Deir el-Medineh. Illustrations of long pods which are described as 'acacia' in some instances are probably carob, especially those which are being eaten.

Another evergreen, Christ's Thorn, *Ziziphus spina Christi L.* is a shrub or small tree, with small flowers and yellow, sweet, juicy fruit. It is native to North Africa. The fruit becomes sweeter with age.[20] Fruits were left in tombs, including those of Hemaka at Saqqara,[21] and Tutankhamun. The leaves could also be eaten. In Egyptian the tree was called *nebes*.

Seeds from the cones of Stone Pine, *Pinus pinea L.*, a delicacy tasting like almonds, have been found in Egyptian tombs, for example, at Gebelein.[22] The tree is tall with a single trunk and umbrella-shaped head.

Vines, *Vitis vinifera L.*, were illustrated even more frequently than the date palms, and probably from earlier times. A vine growing over a pergola was often placed in the centre of an orchard; vines in this position can still be seen in the oasis of Dakhlah. Two types of grape were cultivated, *Monopyrena Chasselas*, and *cornithiaca*. The grapes, 2cm. long and dark red, thick skinned, and sometimes with a blue 'bloom', were similar to those still grown in the Fayum. The leaves are hairy on the underside. Vines were grown all over Egypt, with special centres of cultivation in the Delta and the oases. Jar-sealings of the early dynastic period have the imprint of the word for grapes: a grape-vine growing on a forked support. Grapes were found in Zoser's tomb complex, and among the fruits provided for Tutankhamun, as well as a quantity of wine. The earliest representation of the cultivation of grapes is found in the Old Kingdom. In later times there are illustrations of vines shading the winepress, or around a pool, and as canopies for people in the gardens, such as the tomb owner, and musicians. Vines are shown growing in temple and palace gardens as well as in agricultural scenes.

Seeds of castor oil, *Ricinis communis L.*, were found in a prehistoric burial. Castor oil grows as a bush. The oil, which acts as a laxative, comes from the seeds which are enclosed in a prickly pod. The seeds and leaves are toxic to humans and animals. The bush may be illustrated on a relief at Amarna, in the tomb of Meryre, in the orchard with a pool in the centre, but equally this illustration may be of a vine.

Pomegranates, *Punica granatum L.*, grow where there is rich soil. Imitation pomegranate fruits have been found in tombs of the Middle,[23] and New Kingdoms,[24] and real ones in other tombs. Pomegranates are frequently illustrated among the fruits brought to the tombs as offerings. The bark of the tree is used for tanning leather, and the roots as a vermifuge.[25] It has been suggested that the wine from pomegranate was called *shedeh*, but this word may refer to a type of wine made from grapes. The ancient name for the plant was *inhemen*.

Common figs, *Ficus carica* L., produce fruit twice a year: an early crop on the existing growth, and a late crop on the new year's growth. A dish in the form of fig leaf was found at Abydos dating from the First Dynasty.[26] Fig-trees are illustrated in tombs of the Old, and Middle Kingdoms as well as in those of later periods. Models of figs were found in tombs. The reason for this provision is explained by a Pyramid Text which indicates that figs are necessary for the deceased: "Those whom the god loves ... who live on figs, who drink wine, who are anointed with unguent."[27] Baboons are elevated to the state of immortals - or representatives of the baboon god Thoth - and are often shown eating figs.

Baskets containing two kinds of juniper berries were found in Tutankhamun's tomb: *Juniperus oxycedrus* and *J. excelsa*. The trees of *Juniperus excelsa* grow to a height of about 6 m. and live for hundreds of years. *Juniperus oxycedrus* (prickly juniper) is a shrub which grows up to 8m. high on mountain slopes. The red berries have a strong flavour. Juniper berries, coloured light blue, are illustrated in the Fifth Dynasty tomb of Neferherenptah. Wood of *Juniperus phoenicea* has also been found in Egypt.[28]

Apples, grew in an orchard in the Delta Residence of Ramesses II.[29] Ramesses III ordered baskets of apples to be given to Hapy, the inundation,[30] but where they were grown is not known.

Fruits, and pieces of wood from Egyptian plum, *Balanites aegyptiaca* L., have been found in excavations. It is a spiny tree with thorns, which grows in very dry places to a height of about 3m. Balanos oil is obtained from the kernels of its small, pear-shaped,[31] brown fruits, which have also been described as green, turning to yellow.[32] It has small greenish yellow flowers which have a spicy scent. It is also known as Soapberry Tree, or Desert Date. *Balanites aegyptiaca* has been identified with the magical *ished*, which was a kind of 'Tree of Life', or 'Family Tree' on whose leaves the gods recorded the names of the kings. But, the *ished* was more likely to have been modelled on the *Cordia myxa* than the *Balanites*, since the latter is thorny, and no thorns are shown on the *ished*; but that tree may be completely imaginary. The idea of names being written on the leaves of a tree is found in the Koran; there the tree is the Christ's Thorn (*Ziziphus spina-christi* L.).

Another tree which can withstand very dry conditions is *Moringa peregrina* (Forssk), the so-called 'horseradish tree', because of the flavour of its root. It was one of the trees listed by the architect and gardener, Ineni, as growing in his orchard, if the identification with the ancient name *bak* is correct. Seeds are listed in the Berlin collection, but their provenance is not certain. Moringa pods have been identified in an illustration of an offering table in a tomb at Beni Hasan.[33] The tree is slender, with arching branches and long needle-like leaves, with small, flat leaflets. It has small, sweet-scented, pink or yellow flowers and pods longitudinally ribbed, containing a three-sided, bitter-sweet fruit. The flowers are also described as being yellow. The seeds of *M. oleifera* were a source of *behen* oil,[34] and they could have been used as a water purifier. The pods and seeds are edible, and the tree yields gum as the result of an insect's activities. Although once native to Egypt, it now grows only in the Orman Botanical gardens in Cairo, in the desert east of Thebes, near the Red Sea and in Sinai.[35]

Trees less likely to have been grown regularly in Egyptian orchards were almonds (*Prunus dulcis* (Mill,) D.A. Webb = *P. amygdalus* = *Amygdalus communis*) the nuts of which were found at Amarna in the workmen's village, and in the tomb of Tutankhamun.

Remains of pistachios, *Pistacia vera* L., were found at Mostagedda, and at Memphis.[36] The pistachio tree grows to a height of about 10m. It has dark green leaves which grow together in groups of three to five. The fruit, which is about the size of an olive, also grows in bunches. It has a mesocarp around the greeny-purplish nut. The tree is indigenous to Persia and Syria, but is cultivated in the Mediterranean regions.

The orangy-red fruits, which taste like maize and grow in clusters, of *Grewia tenax* (Forssk.), were found in the tomb of Tutankhamun. It is a shrub which grows to about 3m. in hot areas around Aswan[37] and the Red Sea, as well as in Arabia. It has smooth, dark green leaves and large white flowers.

Cordia myxa L. (and *Sinensis*) with slender, hanging branches and large, ovate leaves, has reddish fruit held in a cup-shaped calyx, rather like that of an acorn. Seeds of *Cordia sinensis* have been found in Old and New Kingdom burials. Remains have also been found in Middle Kingdom tombs at Thebes. The fruits are used for making a bird lime.

Inside the gardens and along the banks of the canals and rivers grew willow-trees, *Salix subserrata* Willd. Its wood was used for boxes, and the branches for garlands in the tomb of Tutankhamun; medications were concocted from some parts of the willow. A pollarded willow tree is illustrated in the Nineteenth Dynasty tomb of Ipuy at Deir el-Medina. A willow shades a plot of ground where one large symbolic lettuce is growing behind, or beside, a statue of Min on a stela in the Museum at Lyon. A prophetess of Mut, Heruben, is shown, in her funerary papyrus in the Cairo Museum, kneeling beside water in the shade of a willow tree.

Date palm (*Phoenix dactylifera*) growing in the Kharga Oasis, Egypt. (Pl. I)

Doum palm (*Hyphaene thebaica*) growing in the Kharga Oasis, Egypt. (Pl. II)

Castor oil bush (*Ricinis communis*) growing at the Royal Botanic Gardens, Kew. (Pl. III)

Tamarisk bushes (*Tamarix*) growing in the Kharga Oasis, Egypt. (Pl. IV)

Carob tree (*Ceratonia siliqua*) growing in Spain. (Pl. V)

Christ's thorn (*Ziziphus spina Christi*) growing at Chicago House, Luxor, Egypt. (Pl. VI)

Lentisk bush (*Pistacia lenticus*). (Pl. VII)

Nile acacia (*Acacia nilotica*) growing in the Kharga Oasis, Egypt. (Pl. VIII)

The giant reed (*Arundo donax*). (Pl. IX)

Henna (*Lawsonia inermis*). (Pl. X)

Poppies (*Papaver rhoeas*) growing at the Royal Botanic Gardens, Kew. (Pl. XI)

Pomegranate fruit (*Punica granatum*) growing at Dumbarton Oaks, Washington, D.C. (Pl. XII)

Resin-producing Trees

The Egyptians burnt incense in their temples and in funerary rituals. Resin of frankincense, *Boswellia* species, was found in the tomb of Tutankhamun.

Frankincense trees, *Boswellia species*, grow in the Horn of Africa, and in southern Arabia, but the *Boswellia sacra* Flueck., which produces the best gum, grows in Dhofar, in the arid zone behind the mountains, beyond the reach of the monsoon rain, and can still be found in the eastern Hadramaut.[39] Frankincense is a resin which is released from the trunk by cutting the bark, and letting the sap drain out into bowls tied to the trunk, or held by the harvester. *Boswellia sacra* grow to a height of about 2 to 10m. The bark is ash-coloured, and papery, and the gum is white. The flowers are white, or wax coloured, and the fruit is a three-valved capsule. The trees flower in late September, and the resin used to be harvested May and December. Nowadays the best frankincense is harvested at the hottest time of the year in the autumn season. It is white, and could be moulded into shapes such as animals and obelisks.[40] Heaps of white ointment in special metal vases are illustrated in tomb paintings such as those of Nebamun (British Museum EA 37985). Frankincense trees grow in Somalia (*Boswellia carteri*, *B. frereana*, *B. bhau-djiana*) and in Ethiopia, the Sudan and as far west as the Central African Republic (*B. papyrifera*). *Boswellia carteri* grows to a height of 8m. and maintains itself on rocks by means of the bulbous base of its trunk.[41]

The Egyptians made great efforts to cultivate incense trees. The most spectacular attempt, of which illustrations have survived, was when Hatshepsut's envoys brought back living trees in baskets from Punt, and planted them at Thebes.[42] The trees brought by Hatshepsut may have been frankincense *(Boswellia Spec.)*,[43] or myrrh[44] (*Commiphora Spec.*).

Myrrh is derived from various species of *Balsamodendron* and *Commiphora*. The difference between frankincense and myrrh trees is that, myrrh is a shrub and frankincense a tree. Myrrh has a thorny trunk and branches, and the gum is reddish. The bark of the *Commiphora myrrha* (Nees) Engl. is peeling and papery like that of the *Boswellia*. It has trifoliate leaves and oval, mango-shaped fruits, about 1 cm. long and reddish tubular flowers.[45] It grows in Arabia and in Africa.

In the ancient inscriptions the words for myrrh and frankincense, are not clearly distinguished. A number of words are used for both incense resin and the trees, of which *anty* and *sentjer* were the most common in dynastic times.[46] There is confusion in the translations over *anty* and *sentjer*, both being translated as myrrh and as frankincense. An attempt was made to separate the two words, saying that *anty* is myrrh and *sentjer* frankincense,[47] but it is doubtful if the Egyptians made this distinction.

The word *anty* is used in Hatshepsut's inscriptions for the trees brought back from Punt, and for the heaps of red aromatic substance illustrated in the Deir el-Bahari reliefs. The god Min, who was believed to have come from Punt, received "perfume of *ant* in the temples during each day".[48] At banquets, guests were "perfumed with *anty*",[49] as ointment to be rubbed on the body.

But, the word *sentjer* was also used for trees and resin.[50] It can be interpreted as meaning 'to make divine'. *Sentjer* is the name of a tree on an Old Kingdom relief sculpture in Berlin, and in the lists of Ramesses III's gifts to temples. At other times it is used to describe the resin. The Egyptians imported *sentjer* since the Fifth Dynasty, according to records on the Palermo Stone, dating from the time of Sahure.

Because incense-bearing treees were not native to Egypt, rulers after Hatshepsut and Tuthmosis III continued to bring trees from Punt, which are recorded in a temple at Athribis, even as late as Ptolemaic times. Incense of a kind could be made from *Commiphora opobalsamum*, some of which was found in a Theban tomb of unknown date. It still grows in Egypt on Gebel Elba.

Gum from acacia, was found in Tutankhamun's tomb. The Nile acacia, *Acacia nilotica* or *Arabica L.* has yellow flowers and grows in places which need be only slightly damp. The pods are "strongly constricted between the seeds giving them a necklace-like appearance".[51] The white acacia, *Acacia albida* Del. grows in even dryer places and has white flowers and yellow, fleshy pods. *Acacia tortilis* (Forssk.) has small leaves, yellow flowers and a curled pod. Acacia trees grow abundantly in Egypt. The yellow flowers of the acacia were illustrated in the Old to Middle Kingdom tombs at Beni Hasan, where the immense size of the acacia is indicated by the many stems of the trunk clustered together. An acacia growing by water shades fishermen netting their catch in an illustration in a New Kingdom tomb of Ipuy (Theban Tomb 217). The gum was used for fixing pigments and in medicine. The ancient word for acacia was *shendjet*. There was an official called "Overseer of Acacia-trees", which indicates the importance of the products of the acacia.

Tamarisk produces a resin like frankincense gum. The habit of the different species varies. Some grow in dry soil along coasts, others in the desert, and others near water. The species found in ancient Egypt are *Tamarix nilotica*, and *Tamarix articulata* = *aphylla*. *Tamarix aphylla* (L.) Karst. is a large tree which grows in very dry conditions, and stores water in its roots which can hold the tree firm in sandy soil. Its leaves are minute, and the sprays of small flowers are pink. The salt crust from its leaves can be used as a salt substitute. The remains of tamarisk bushes were found in pits around the Osireion at Abydos, and at the funerary temple of Mentuhotep at Deir el-Bahari in pits 10 m. deep. The bushes can grow to about 12 m. high. They have pinkish white flowers arranged spirally along a spike. The green stems give the appearance of leaves. Dye was obtained from small nodules formed by insects, and the plant was used medicinally.

The tall, slender, evergreen cypress, *Cupressus sempervirens* L. with its pointed top and rounded base, now typical of Italy, but originally native to Iran, and the eastern Mediterranean, can grow up to about 30m. high, though more usually, only to 15 or 20m.; it can live for 500 years. Oil comes from the leafy shoots. It was thought that the king Taharqa said he gave seeds of this tree to the temple at Kawa in the Sudan, but the word used means almond,[52] rather than cypress.

Maerua crassifolia fruits were found in an Eleventh Dynasty burial at Gebelein, and may be the *ima*-plant listed as growing in Ineni's garden. It is a bush, or even a tree, found in oases and in the Sudan. Here it grows as a small tree, usually six metres wide, with a flat rounded crown and twisted branches. There are several illustrations of trees which are labelled as *ima*. An oil is produced from its buds. Another member of the same family is *Capparis aegyptiaca* which was illustrated on tiles at Amarna.

Myrtle, *Myrtus communis* L., has oil in its leaves. It is an evergreen bush which grows both near water, and on dry soil.

Imports of resins were derived from the tree *Pistacia atlantica* Desf., the shrubs, *Pistacia lentiscus*., and *Pistacia terebinthus* L., which grow around the Mediterranean, and in the Horn of Africa.

Summary

Our impressions about ancient orchards are formed by the illustrations which show palms, vines and sycamore-figs predominating, and the documents, particularly the list of trees in the orchard under Ineni's care, which shows a much greater variety of species. Excavation demonstrates that the reality was nearer to Ineni's list than the paintings. Outside the cultivated areas, in the desert, and along the waterways, grew a wide variety of trees which the Egyptians made use of for food, carpentry, perfumes and medicine.

IV   The Flower Garden

Introduction

> I belong to you like this plot of ground
> That I planted with flowers
> And sweet-smelling herbs.
> Sweet is its stream
> Dug by your hand,
> Refreshing in the northwind.
> A lovely place to wander in,
> Your hand in my hand.[1]

So a young girl sings to her lover. The ancient Egyptian flower garden would have looked, to the modern eye, which is accustomed to especially bred blooms, like a herb garden, or even a collection of wild flowers. Recent reconstructions of historical gardens give us some idea of the limited range of plants known at a particular place and time. The Egyptians were similarly constrained in the variety of plants at their disposal. The purposes for which they grew their plants were for offerings in temples and tombs, for garlands to wear on special occasions such as banquets, and for use in embalming and medicines. Many of the flowers illustrated in wall-paintings, and placed in tombs, could have been growing wild on the edge of the cultivation, or under the trees in the orchards.

'Gardens of Rebirth'

The combinations of planting most frequently illustrated in reliefs and paintings of the New Kingdom are mandrake, poppy and cornflower growing at the edge of a pool, which contains waterlilies and papyrus. (Fig. 56) On a casket found in the tomb of Tutankhamun are scenes of the king engaged in various ceremonies to do with rebirth in the afterlife. On the lid a girl, sitting in a patch of poppies, is picking mandrake fruits. Opposite her is a girl in an arbour, or plantation, of mandrakes or poppies. Tutankhamun fishes amid mandrake fruits surrounded by flowers.

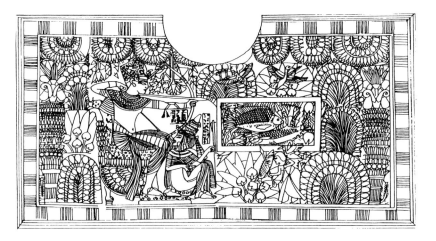

A panel from a wooden box. Tutankhamun fishing with a bow and arrow amid mandrake fruits and flowers. (Fig. 21)

The scenes depicted in many paintings are funerary, and so we can assume that the plants are to do with the rebirth of the deceased in the afterlife. Even the decorations in palaces probably have religious meaning, and so purely 'secular' illustrations have not survived.

The range of plants known from illustrations is greatly increased by finds made in the tombs: the wreaths and bouquets laid on the bodies, and packing used in embalming. Further information about flower cultivation comes from the lists of floral offerings presented in the temples, but the species required in the rituals are limited to papyrus, waterlilies and *isi*-flowers.

Flower Arranging

It is clear from the elaborately constructed bouquets which have been found in the tombs, and which were illustrated on the walls of the tombs, that the art of flower arranging was very important in Egypt. The bouquets were based on a foundation of palm leaves and fibres and each item was tucked or sewn on to this framework. The idea of a bouquet was used by the jewellers who made Princess Khnumet's diadem which was found at Dahshur. A miniature bouquet or 'tree' was fixed into a holder at the back of the diadem. This bouquet is composed of a central stalk to which are attached lapis lazuli and carnelian flowers, representing waterlilies and pomegranate flowers, together with long, thin gold leaves which may be intended for willow leaves. Spoons in the form of bouquets were another variation on this theme.

Making garlands of flowers is illustrated in the tomb of Nezemger, the chief gardener at the Ramesseum.[2] The gardeners would have been responsible for providing the flowers for the bouquets, and may indeed have had the task of constructing them.

The Planted Garden[3]

Many gardens had a pool and plants round and in it. Formal arrangements of plants were illustrated at Amarna on the pavements in the *Maru*-Aten, which was a park containing temples and offering places, and in the central building. (Figs. 80 and 86. See Chapter 8)

In the scenes of the funeral rituals on a lake the plants around the water's edge are papyrus, cornflower, mandrake and poppy. All of these plants would have grown wild, as well as being cultivated. Some of the plants are illustrated in their flowering state and some only in their fruiting state.

Poppies and mandrakes growing beside water in the afterlife. Tomb of Sennedjem. Theban Tomb 1. XIXth Dynasty. (Fig. 22)

The fruit and flowers of mandrake, *Mandragora officinalum* L. are both illustrated. The fruit, which appears in summer and autumn close to the ground, resembles that of *Mimusops laurifolia*. The difference is that the mandrake has a calyx, whereas the *Mimusops* has smaller reflexed sepals.[4] Mandrake is illustrated, but actual examples have not been found in tombs. The plant is Mediterranean, but was said to have come from Elephantine. It grows on the edge of cultivation. The fruit smells sweet, induces sleep, and is supposed to have aphrodisiac properties. The ancient word for mandrake was *reremet*.

The oriental cornflower, *Centaurea depressa* Bieb. grows to a height of about 40cms. Although its blue flowers have disappeared from Egypt, it is frequently illustrated in the tomb gardens, and was used for garlands, and embalming.[5] Faience pendants were made in imitation of its flowers. Its Egyptian name is not known. The cornflower and the poppy were probably both cultivated in ancient times.[6] The cornflower was believed by Parkinson in the Seventeenth Century to be a remedy for scorpion stings and effective in healing wounds. The juice of its petals could be used to dye linen.

Bouquet of papyrus flower between two poppies, lotus petals, poppies, cornflowers, and man-drakes. From incised alabaster casket from Tutankhamun's tomb. XVIIIth Dynasty. (Fig. 23)

The dark red corn poppy, *Papaver rhoeas* L. is frequently illustrated in garden scenes. It was certainly part of the ancient flora and was probably cultivated. Flowers were found in a wreath of the Twenty-First Dynasty. The seeds can be used in cakes, and an oil is made from them which is a substitute for olive oil.[7] The leaves can be eaten as a vegetable, and the petals as an ingredient in soup. It is not opium-bearing.[8] Opium comes from the white or red-violet poppy, *Papaver somniferum* L. which has a poisonous white, milky juice.

Papyrus sedge is the best known and most frequently illustrated of all the Egyptian sedges and reeds. *Cyperus papyrus* L. grows about 3m. high. Wild papyrus was until recently believed to be extinct in Egypt. It now grows in Egypt thanks to the efforts of horticulturalists who have restored it to the Nile valley.[9] In ancient times it was used for many purposes, from making boats to a writing material,[10] and as a food plant. The name for a papyrus-marsh was *idhu*.

Floating on the pools were the waterlilies, the plant referred to in many Egyptological books as 'lotus'.[11] It was presented as an offering to the dead and in temples. In the prayer in his tomb Nebamun asks for:

> An offering of good and pure things, lotus flowers and buds and all kinds of herbs of fragrant smell (O Amen Re) that thou mayest give health to the Ruler ... on the part of the Ensign Bearer, Nebamun.[12]

Two species of waterlily grew in ancient Egypt: the blue and the white.[13] The blue, *Nymphaea caerulea* Savigny, which is found in the Delta, has a perfume, and opens from the early morning to about midday. The ancient Egyptian word for the flower was *seshen*, with *sapet* for the bud, *kha* for the leaf, and *red* possibly for the root.

The white , *Nymphaea Lotus* L., opens in the afternoon and stays open all night until almost midday. Waterlilies close after pollination and submerge, and then the pod surfaces and disperses the seed. Waterlilies need plenty of sun, and a minimum temperature of 75 F. Neither waterlily was much used as a medicine.

Flowers of the Field

Growing among the emmer and barley, and on the edges of the fields, were plants which were used by the ancient Egyptians for bouquets and burial with the dead. Some of these 'invaders' are illustrated in the fields, for example, in the tomb of Menna (Theban Tomb 69).

Mayweed, (camomile), *Anthemis pseudocotula* Boiss., is an annual herb which grows in cultivated ground. It has white daisy-like florets around yellow disc florets. It has been found at the predynastic site of Nagada.[14] Tutankhamun's sandals were decorated with inlays representing these flowers, as were tiles from Amarna. True camomile *Matricaria recutita* L., was used as a filling for the corpse of Ramesses II.[15]

A similar flower, except that all its florets are yellow, is *Chrysanthemum coronarium* L. Crown Daisy. It grows to a height of 80cm. in cultivated ground on the margins of fields. The leaves and flowers are aromatic. In Egyptian it was called, 'beautiful face' and 'golden flower'.

Narcissus flowers have a fragrant smell. *Narcissus tazetta* L. was found on the neck of the mummy of Ramesses II, and on the eyes, mouth and mummification cut. It grows spontaneously in the Mediterranean region in barley fields and irrigated land,[16] but requires cool rooting conditions.

The small brightly coloured members of the pea family such as *Lathyrus aphaca* L., and *Vicia sativa* L., which grew in the fields then, as they do now, were used for animal fodder. *Lathyrus aphaca* grows to a height of about 30-60cms. and has pointed upstanding leaves and light yellow flowers. It was found under Zoser's pyramid complex and also on a Twelfth Dynasty site.

A trailing plant with pointed leaves, in scenes showing women suckling their infants in leafy bowers, may be bindweed, *Convolvulus arvensis* L., which grows on the edge of the cultivation, in dry places, and flowers in spring. Musicians sometimes draped similar plants across their shoulders and over their arms. The deified Ahmes-Nefertary was often shown with this trailing plant around her. The leaves are not always the same in appearance, and so different plants with similar characteristics are intended. It is also shown twined round bouquets in various tombs, but no firm identification has been made. Other suggestions are, ivy, *Ecballium elaterium* (L.) A. Rich, or possibly *Cocculus hirsutus*, (J. R. & J. Forst.) Diels, fruits of which may have found their way into Tutankhamun's tomb.

Nightshade-like fruits were found in the garlands in the tomb of Tutankhamun, and were first identified as woody nightshade, *Solanum dulcamara* L., and then with withania nightshade, *Withania somnifera* (L) Dun., and now, possibly, with *Solanum villosum* Darracq. This perennial plant grows in waste places to a height of about 30cm. It has small white scentless flowers with reflexed petals, hairy on the outside. Its small yellowish berries are enclosed in a green inflated calyx.

Sandy Soil

On the edges of the fields, in sandy places, grew the asphodel, *Asphodelus fistulosus* L. to a height of about 20-50cms. It belongs to the ancient flora of Egypt.

Alkanet, *Alkanna tinctoria* Tausch., a herb with grey leaves and blue flowers grows in sandy places along the coasts and in the desert. Its ancient name was possibly *nestyu*, which was mentioned in medical texts.

The daisy-like flowers of ox-tongue with its yellow head, *Picris hieracioides*, *Picris radicata* (Forssk.) = *P.coronopifolia* = *Picris asplenioides*, was found in wreaths in Tutankhamun's tomb, and in the left-overs from his embalming, as well as among the flowers given for the reburial of the kings at Deir el-Bahari, during the 21st Dynasty, and in the burial of Nesi-Khonsu also 21st-22nd Dynasty, at Deir el-Bahari.

Gourds, *Citrullus colocynthis* (L) Schrad. with very bitter, poisonous fruits grew on the edges of the desert. The pollen was found in the mummy-wrappings of Ramesses II.

Cressa cretica L. was found in bouquets in tombs. It grows in salty areas. Tufts appear on the surface of the soil and are attached to long 'runners' just under the surface.

Moist Soil

Sesbania sesban (L.) Merrill or *aegyptiaca* was found in garlands on the mummies of Ahmose and Amenophis I. This member of the leguminosae family has yellow flowers, flecked with purple, and long, slender pods. It is widespread today in slightly moist spots. Keimer believed that it was cultivated in ancient times.[17]

Bulbs found in the burial of Nesikhonsu may be of *Crinum zeylanicum*. A *Crinum* was found in the tomb of Ramesses II.[18] The plant needs partial shade and frequent watering.

There is only rather ambiguous evidence for oleander, *Nerium oleander* L., having grown in ancient Egypt. It is an evergreen bush which grows up to 3m. tall and has pink or white flowers.

The Herb Garden

Herbs found in tombs include wild thyme, *Thymbra spicata* L., a sprig of which was found in a box in the tomb of Tutankhamun. Mint, *Mentha piperita* L., peppermint, was part of a wreath dating from the Twentieth to Twenty-Sixth Dynasties. It grows on a purple stem up to 60cms. high in well manured moist soil.

Safflower, *Carthamus tinctorius* L., was a cultivated plant, which grew in sandy places. Its seeds were found in Tutankhamun's tomb, and flowers in wreaths in other Eighteenth and Nineteenth Dynasty tombs, and on the mummy of Amenophis I. Red and yellow dyes were made from the yellow flowers of this thistle-like plant. Its ancient name was *ket*.

Seeds for giving flavour were provided by numerous herbs. A basket of seeds of chervil, *Anthriscus cerefolium* L. Hoffm. was found in the tomb of Tutankhamun.

Wild celery, *Apium graveolens* L., which is a biennial herb, grows in moist places to about 60cms. high and has small white flowers. The leaves have a strong flavour and smell, and were probably cultivated for their fragrance. Celery was found in the foundation deposit of Hatshepsut's temple at Deir el Bahari. Its ancient name was *matet*. Wild celery was used in making garlands for burial with the dead.

Several coriander seeds, *Coriandrum sativum* L., were found in Tutankhamun's tomb, and in burials at Deir el Medineh.

Trigonella foenum-graecum L., fenugreek, has been found in predynastic excavations, and in the tomb of Tutankhamun.

Pepper, *Piper nigrum*, was found in the cavity of the mummy of Ramesses II.

Other herbs used by the Egyptians included charlock, dill *Anethum graveolens L.,* mustard, *Sinapis allionii,* cumin, *Cuminum cyminum* L., wormwood, *Artemesia absinthum* L., and camel grass, *Cymbopogon schoenanthus* Spreng.

Medicinal Plants mentioned in Texts[19]

Many plants had medicinal uses. Papyri survive from dynastic times prescribing the use of herbal remedies for wounds, the treatment of eyes and teeth, bladder and intestines, the chest and coughs, pregnancy and the purging of worms. Those of which the identification of word and plant is certain are: Nile acacia, tamarisk, common fig, sycomore fig, date palm, willow, Christ's thorn, horseradish tree, vine, castor oil, onion, leek, flax, dill, cumin, *vigna (sinensis)* L. Walp., *unguiculata,* nut grass, emmer, barley, and *Commiphora* species identified with the word *anty,* and *Boswellia* species identified with the word *sentjer.* But these identifications may not be sure.

Some plants were only rarely used in medicine including, papyrus, blue and white waterlilies, carob, pomegranate, and *Mimusops laurifolia,* the Egyptian word for which is probably *shwab,* and identified with the Greek word persea. In the cases of juniper, a kind of ebony, *Dahlbergia melanoxylon* Guill. & Perr. alkanet, and wild celery, the identification of plant and ancient word are slightly doubtful. There are many other words used for plants and parts of plants of which the identifications are uncertain.

Some flowers have been identified from texts rather than from illustrations or debris found in tombs. The scented wormwood, *Artemesia absinthum,* which grows at the edge of fields, may be the *saam*-flower mentioned in a love poem.

Perfume from Flowers

In such a hot, dry climate perfume was greatly prized. The husband is urged in the 'Instructions' of the vizier, Ptahhotep, to provide ointment for his wife which 'soothes her body'.[20] On festive occasions, perfumed oils were worn by both men and women. The perfume could be liquid or solid.[21] The liquid was poured, or smoothed, on by servants. In tomb-paintings a white cone is shown on the heads of people taking part in funerary rituals. These cones are often said to be of unguent, which in the heat would gently melt in a sweet, sticky mass into hair and clothing. But it is possible that the cones are a sign of resurrection.[22]

Anointing guests with perfume; a painting in the tomb of Paheri at el-Kab. XVIIIth Dynasty. (Fig. 24)

There are several scenes of making perfume at different periods.[23] The most characteristic activity is squeezing a sack to get the juice out of the flowers. Other activities included pounding something in a mortar, stirring a pot on a fire, and filtering a liquid through a sieve.[24]

Flowers provided the perfume. One of the most strongly scented flowers were the white Madonna lily, *Lilium candidum* L., which grow to a height of about a metre from perennial bulbs. Scenes of collecting and pressing these flowers remain from the Late Period.[25] It is thus clear that they were cultivated. Remains of a lily are in the Louvre.[26]

Henna, *Lawsonia inermis* L., is a shrub which grows to a height of a metre. It has small, creamy-white, delicately perfumed flowers. Henna has been identified as an ingredient of perfume.[27] Since the dried leaves mixed with sarson oil,[28] are used as an orange-coloured dye for hair and hands in modern times, they may have been similarly used in ancient times, but the staining on the hands of mummies, which is sometimes attributed to henna, may simply be the effect of the embalming oils.. The seeds yield oil. The ancient name *ankh-imi* has been suggested.

Other plants which produced perfumes include myrtle, *Myrtus communis*, which has oil in its leaves. Rosemary was found in tombs, and was mentioned at the time of Ramesses III.[29]

Other odoriferous plants were myrrh, terebinth, (*Pistacia lentiscus, P. atlantica, P. palaestina*) date palm, jasmin - only *Jasminum sambac* or *grandiflorum* have been identified, not altogether certainly, before Roman times, and conifers, including cypress. Styrax produces perfume, but may not have grown in Egypt in dynastic times.

The Vegetable Garden

The vegetable garden is shown in paintings and reliefs in tombs as being close to water. The vegetables which are illustrated and mentioned most frequently were onions and lettuce. Other vegetables are known from burials and isolated illustrations.

Onions, *Allium cepa* L., need rich soil, have dark mauve flowers and hollow leaves. They are shown growing close to water in Old Kingdom reliefs in the tombs of Neferherenptah, Nyankhkhnum and Khnumhotep, and in Middle Kingdom tombs at Lisht,[30] and Beni Hasan. They were found wrapped with mummies,[31] and are illustrated on offering tables. The word for onion was *hedu*.

Lettuce, *Lactuca sativa* L.is an erect sparsely branching leafy herb, about a metre tall with reddish brown flowers 8m. wide; the narrow leaves have small spines along the mid-rib on the underside.[32] They belong to the original flora of Egypt, and were cultivated in the Old Kingdom, as is shown by illustrations in tombs such as those of Neferherenptah, Khnumhotep, and Mereruka and at Beni Hasan. A wild form of this lettuce still grows in Egypt.[33] The ancient name was *ab* and *abu*.

Garlic, *Allium sativum* L., was buried with the dead even in prehistoric times. Leaves of wild garlic were found in Tutankhamun's tomb entwined in a garland, and on other mummies. It grows to about 80cm. high. Its flowers are whitish and the leaves flat. Garlic bulbs were often placed in the armpits and groin of mummies. There were several Egyptian words for garlic.

Cucumbers and melons have much the same appearance in the Egyptian paintings, but the people recognized different kinds by giving them different names. The snake cucumber, or musk melon, *Cucumis melo*, L., which is curved, and has numerous longitudinal grooves, is illustrated in paintings in the tombs of Nakht, Userhet and Ipuy as well as on a piece of linen. *Cucumis sativus* L. is also a cucumber. Seeds of the small cucumber (Chate) have been found in excavations.

Water melon, *Citrullus lanatus* (Thunb.) Mansf. (= *C. vulgaris*) trails along the ground, and has yellow flowers, and large dark green fruit. The seeds have been eaten since prehistoric times, and baskets of seeds were found in the tomb of Tutankhamun.

Pulses were an important addition to the diet. Chick pea, *Cicer arietinum* L., grows about 20cms. high and has white flowers. The pods contain seeds shaped like the head of a chicken or hawk, which explains the ancient name, falcon's head. A few seeds were found in the model granary in Tutankhamun's tomb.

Lentils, *Lens culinaris* Medik. = *esculenta*, were used for food, and were found in Tutankhamun's tomb. The plant is like a vetch with minute blue flowers, and pods containing flat green lentils.

Broad bean, *Vicia faba*, and bean, *Vigna sinensis*, are mentioned in texts under the name *per*. There was some argument as to whether peas, *Pisum sativum* L., were known before the Second or Third centuries B.C., but evidence has been found of *Pisum sativum* being present on the Old Kingdom site at Kom el-Hisn in the Delta.[34]

Mallow, *Althaea ficifolia* L., was found in garlands on the mummies of Amosis and Amenophis I. Mallows have large mauve or pink flowers, and the leaves are used as a soup thickener.

Marsh and Water Plants

With so much marshy ground around the river and lakes, many water plants were part of the economy of an estate. The papyrus and blue and white waterlily grew wild as well as being cultivated.

The true lotus, *Nelumbium speciosa* Willd., stands tall in a pool, about 30cms. above the level of the water with its large, rounded leaves. Its flowers are white tinged with a delicate pink. The fruit is like a large shower head, composed of separate carpels, in each of which is a single black seed, looking like an olive. It has been identified with Pythagoras's 'Egyptian Bean', and Herodotus reported that the roots and seeds were eaten by the Egyptians.

Growing in shallow water was reed-mace, *Typha domingensis* Pers.= *australis*, which is a perennial, is distinguished by its long, erect brown inflorescence. Baskets were made from the leaves.

Cyperus alopecuroides is a reed grass which grows by water. It was illustrated at Amarna on the palace floor and elsewhere. *Cyperus esculentus* L. nuts were found at Saqqara dating from the Late Period.[35]

Common Reed, *Phragmites australis* (Cav.) Trin. ex Steud = *P. communis*, grows to over 2m. high, from rhizomes which spread under water in marshy and salty areas. It is depicted growing beside water in Old Kingdom tombs. Ramesses III hunted among these reeds according to the reliefs on the walls of Medinet Habu. The stems were used for pens and arrows, including those in Tutankhamun's tomb.

Also able to live in salty places in the desert, and coastal salt marshes,[36] the rush, *Juncus arabicus* (Asch & Buch.) Adamson = *J. rigidus* = *J. maritimus*, is a perennial, which grows to a height of about a metre. The stems contain a white pith. Pens found in Tutankhamun's tomb were made from these rushes.

The mop-headed Giant, or Persian, reed, *Arundo donax* L., which grows abundantly in stagnant water in Egypt today, is illustrated in scenes of bird-hunting in the marshes.

The robust long-stemmed pond weed,[37] *Potamogeton lucens* L. and *natans*, was frequently illustrated under boats in pools and canals.[38] Flowering in April and May, it grows in fresh to brackish water and is regarded as a severe nuisance even in modern times because it blocks canals and can cover the whole surface of the water.

It is not certain if the perennial Sweet Flag, *Acorus calamus* L., grew in Egypt, but there may be an illustration of it in the tomb of Rekhmire.

Field Crops

Emmer wheat, *Triticum dicoccum* Schrank, was the normal source for flour in ancient Egypt. It has been found in tombs in bread and in a model granary in the tomb of Tutankhamun.

Barley, *Hordeum vulgare* L., grows on fairly dry soil. It has been found on excavated sites,[39] and in tombs, particularly as the symbolic growing vegetation planted in Osiris 'gardens' which were placed in tombs, including that of Tutankhamun, and grown for the ceremonies in the festival of Osiris. Barley is the raw material for making bread and beer. It was grown from very early times and remains have been found near Abu Simbel and Aswan which date from 8000-7000 B.C.

Another grass, Halfa grass, is a name given to several grasses including *Imperata cylindrica* (L), and *Desmostachya bipinnata* (L.) Stapf. A bundle of *Desmostachya bipinnata* was found in Tutankhamun's tomb. Baskets, sandals and roofing were made of reeds and rushes. Hemp, *Cannabis sativa* L.,[40] is a tall annual shrub which has been used for ropes since the second millennium B.C. if the word for it was *semsemet* which is found in the Pyramid Texts in the context of rope-making.

Flax, *Linum usitatissimum* L., with its pale blue flowers, supplied the linen needed for all the clothes, bedding and mummy bandages used by the Egyptians. It must have been grown in quantity. When grown for fibre it is planted close together and reaches about a metre high. It needs water and a fairly light soil. The part which is used for making thread is the fibre inside the stalk, the average length of which is about 60cms.[41] This fibre is a long, smooth, cylindrical tube, 2-3cms. long. It is creamy white in colour. The plants should be harvested before the seed capsules and leaves have become yellow.[42] The seeds are removed from the stalks by threshing with a hammer or comb. The fibre is obtained by soaking the stalks to the point of putrefaction (retting) in order to remove the gum from the fibre and decompose the outer stalk. In modern times, flax was soaked upright in pools. The fibres are then cleaned and straightened by means of combs.

Next, they are drawn out and doubled to make a strong yarn. Illustrations show the harvesting of flax and its manufacture into linen. When grown for linseed oil the plants were more widely spaced.

Clover - Arabic 'berseem', *Trifolium alexandrium* L., was grown for the cattle to eat. Evidence comes from the remains of dung used as fuel at the Old Kingdom site at Kom el-Hisn. The cut forage was called *semu*, which is the same word as for plants in meadows.

Summary

A 'flora' of ancient Egypt can be compiled from archaeological remains, paintings in tombs, temples and on papyrus, and from deduction based on words used for plants in the medical, religious and secular literature. Some of the plants which grew in ancient Egypt are still to be found in the country, others only survive in Saudi Arabia or the Horn of Africa. Some have been re-introduced recently like *Cyperus papyrus*. Many of the plants are raised in botanical gardens around the world. The Mediterranean species are fairly common, but the African and Arabian species usually need hothouse care.

V Groves around Royal Tombs and Terraced Funerary Temples

Introduction

The great landscaping enterprises in ancient Egypt were undertaken under the direction of the kings, for their benefit and use, and to please the gods; as the Sage, Ipuwer, observed: "It is good....when ponds are dug and orchards made for the gods".[1] It was also to demonstrate the king's power and influence to his people and to foreigners.

Monumental tombs placed in magnificent settings have been built by powerful rulers down the ages. The Mausoleum of Augustus in Rome and the Taj Mahal are among the most famous of these shrines, which, even at a great distance in time, echo features of some of the ancient Egyptian monuments which preceded them, particularly in the use of water and trees.

The Religious Beliefs connected with Tombs and Tomb Gardens

Royal burial places were modelled on beliefs about the appearance of the tomb of the god Osiris. It was sometimes illustrated as a tomb-chamber covered by a mound, with trees growing out of the top. Other

The tomb-chamber of the god Osiris at Abydos, covered by a mound from which trees are growing. On the coffin of Petosiris now in Marseilles. XXXth Dynasty. (Fig. 25)

representations show the tomb of Osiris with a tree beside,[2] rather than on top of it, which is the design described by Plutarch, who says that the tomb of Osiris was shaded by a tamarisk tree (*de Iside et Osiride, 21*). One of the

63

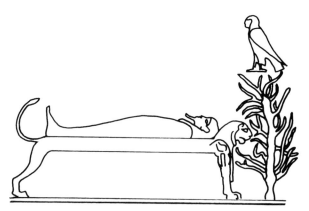

Burial and revival beside a tamarisk tree, on which the soul-bird of Osiris is resting. A relief-carving in the East Osiris chapel on the roof of the temple of Hathor at Dendera. Ptolemaic-Roman Period. (Fig. 26)

explanations of how the world came into being, was that a Mound, or an island, appeared out of the water. A stepped mound surrounded by water is shown in the mythological scene on a coffin in Cairo, and in the Book of the Dead of Hunefer (in the British Museum) as the place where Osiris is seated, or lies, covered by the canopy of heaven. This stepped mound came to be regarded as the place where Osiris was buried.

A particularly detailed realization of the Mound of Creation as the tomb of Osiris, is the so-called 'Osireion' at Abydos, which was built by Seti I, for his memorial tomb as Osiris. The whole building was completely

The deceased as Osiris lying under a stepped mound on which the god Osiris is enthroned. A painting on the wooden coffin of Istemkheb. Cairo Museum. XXIst Dynasty. (Fig. 27)

covered by a mound of earth, around which were planted six trees in large pits more than 15m. deep. The walls around the tree pits were roughly semicircular, and made of bricks and small lumps of limestone. Remains of tamarisk and conifer were found in them.

A view into the Osireion at Abydos. The channel around the central platform is now filled with vegetation. Reign of Seti I. XIXth Dynasty. (Fig. 28)

Tamarisks reflected the belief expressed in the Coffin Texts that the sky goddess Nut gave birth to the deceased king in the Field of Tamarisk.

Tamarisks growing on mounds, illustrating the idea of the tomb of Osiris. (Fig. 29)

Wepwawet, a jackal-like deity, who led the way for the dead, 'emerged from a tamarisk bush', according to Pyramid Texts 126. The conifer appears to reflect the story recounted by Plutarch of how Osiris's coffin, washed up at Byblos, became enveloped by a tree, which would have been of a kind which grew in Lebanon, probably some kind of conifer. The Osireion was designed like a royal tomb with a long entrance passage making a right-angled turn into a cross room, which then led to an island surrounded by a water-channel. Steps led down from the island into the channel. A ledge on the bank in front of the alcoves could have served for towing the boat of Osiris. The channel round the island was intended to be fed by a canal which went under the temple of Seti I from the Nile. There would thus have been ample water for the trees. The burial chamber is off the island, at the opposite side from the entrance, and shaped like a coffin with a sloping, pyramidal roof.

The idea of an island in the midst of water was current at Abydos, for, there was an island in the middle of a lake on which the statue of the king was rowed. The lake was beside a temple which has now disappeared.

> The lake in front of [the Residence] is like the Great Green (sea) whose circuit is not known, when one gazes upon it bright like the colour of lapis-lazuli, its middle part of papyrus and reeds, and lilies abounding daily, and lo, a swan enters to move about; surrounded by trees reaching to the sky, that are set like the pine on its native land. The great *neshemt* barge enters its lake to convey the [king] Father-of-his-Monuments when he is rowed thereon. Behold he is in exultation and his crew rejoice; the Followers of Horus they too cry: "Give unto him an eternity of Sed-festivals (jubilees), to double his years of life upon earth, accomplishing the reign of Atum".[3]

Royal Funerary Monuments from the Earliest times to the Eleventh Dynasty

Since each king regarded himself as becoming Osiris when he died - together with other beliefs about perpetuating his existence in the other world - a grove, if not a garden, was a necessary adjunct to each individual tomb. Trees were planted in avenues leading up to the royal tombs and funerary temples and in groves around or beside them. Water, in a canal or pool, often lay in front of the structures, which were stepped, at least since the Old Kingdom.

The practice of making a grove beside a royal tomb goes back to the First Dynasty. The Horus king Aha,[4] who is equated with Menes, the first king of the First Dynasty, and the conqueror, who united Egypt, was buried at Saqqara in a tomb with a crenellated façade. In the front of each of the large niches of this façade, holes, some of which contained stumps of wood, were found. The wood may have been part of holders for bouquets, palm branches, or standards. A somewhat similar arrangement was found at Tomb 2185, also at Saqqara.[5] A coffin from Gebelein, a place occupied since early times, twenty-eight miles south of Luxor, is decorated with palms and bouquets which gives an idea of how the early tombs may have looked.[6]

The pyramids at Giza may have had gardens around their temples in the valley down by the river. The Valley Temple of Chephren, with its 'T'-shaped hall, abutted on a canal. Cheops' Valley temple was even lower in the flood plain, and so may have had vegetation growing around it. Basins connected with the valley temples of Mycerinus, Shepseskaf and the tombs of Queen Khentkaus and Neferirka have been found. They are all about 6m. long and 5m. wide. Their use is unclear, and it is not known whether they held any water. Their purpose may have been symbolic rather than practical. The area between the cultivation and the desert served as gardens and fields for the inhabitants of the pyramid town in the Fourth to Sixth Dynasties. There was a plantation in the funerary estate in the pyramid complex named the 'Soul of Sahure appears in splendour', according to the autobiography of a vizier.[7] The barren appearance of the terrain now does not reflect how it was in the Old Kingdom, for the cultivation was closer to the pyramids in ancient times. Somewhere in the area of Memphis was a palace, with a garden where there was a shrine of Sekhmet, for there is a record of: "The master craftsman of the barque of Amun in the inundation district and of the barque of Sekhmet in the lake (or garden) of Pharaoh."[8] The first king of the Fourth Dynasty, Seneferu,

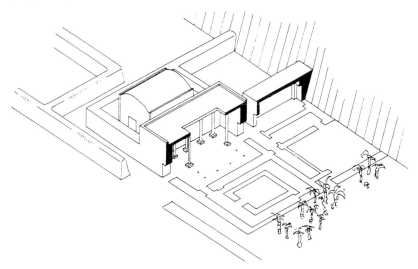

A grove on one side of the pyramid-temple of Seneferu at Dahshur. A reconstruction of the temple beside his IVth Dynasty pyramid. (Fig. 30)

of the Fourth Dynasty, Seneferu, had a grove on the north side of his pyramid temple at Dahshur.[9] Unfortunately no vegetation remained in the tree-holes which were filled with sand and Nile mud.

Gardens and groves may have surrounded lakes and pools, several of which were dug during the Old Kingdom according to entries on the Palermo Stone, which is a record of important events during the early part of the Old Kingdom. And in the Sixth Dynasty, King Isesi, commanded his chief architect, Senezemib, to make a lake, but there are no descriptions of any surroundings. Offering tables in the shape of pools were made for the

presentation of offerings to the dead, at the jubilee festival and in sun worship. These stepped offering basins represent the pool in a garden. Sometimes they have the word for sycomore-fig written on them, and sometimes a picture of a tree.

11th Dynasty Mentuhotep Nebhepetre (2061-2010 B.C.)

Memphis lost its supremacy and Thebes became the new capital. Mentuhotep decided to place his tomb,[10] with its cult temple, right against the mountain sacred to the Goddess of the West, Hathor, even on the site of a shrine dedicated to her. She, in her role as sky-goddess, it was believed, swallowed the dead king, just as she swallowed the sun, and carried them inside her body to the eastern horizon, to be born from her the next day.

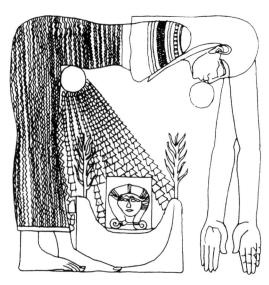

The sky goddess swallowing and giving birth to the sun. The goddess is bending over a representation of the horizon, with trees on either side, between which is the symbol for the temple, a head of the goddess Hathor, on which the newly born sun rays are streaming down. Roman Period. (Fig. 31)

Earlier rulers of the Theban region had built their tombs further north in the area called el-Taraf. They were substantial buildings, but nothing has remained as spectacular as Mentuhotep's monument.

Mentuhotep ruled for fifty-one years. He was a warrior, who reunited Egypt after a period of dissolution of central power during the First Intermediate Period between the Old and Middle Kingdoms. He undertook a large building programme all over the country, in addition to his tomb and funerary temple. At Deir el-Bahari, Mentuhotep created a magnificent vista by using as a background for his burial place, the great sweep of the cliff itself, the Western Mountain; below it stood the mound of the tomb, stepping down in terraces to a grove of trees.

Sycomore-fig trees formed an avenue beside the ramp up to the temple. On either side of them were rows of tamarisk trees. Between the sycomores were two rectangular flower beds, measuring about 2 x 7m., with roots still remaining in them when they were excavated. Unfortunately the plants could not be identified. The area covered by the plantation was about 50m. square, (which is the length of an Olympic standard swimming pool). The rest of the irregularly shaped enclosure, not covered by the grove, measured a further 150m., i.e., three times the length of the grove, and at its widest, at its eastern limit, about 230m.

Mentuhotep's pyramid and courtyard were a replica of the grave of Osiris with the trees in front. The terraces represented the steps up to the mound of Osiris, and the mound itself was the primeval hill which came into existence at the first moment of creation. The king's actual burial was in the cliff behind the temple, although originally it was to have been directly under the mound. The sycomore-figs had been planted as cuttings close together, covered with about 15cm. of soil, in pits 10m. deep, which were filled with black soil and river sand. The excavators described the remains as follows:

> There were found in the earth of the holes several round poles of sycomore fig branches, each about six feet in length and five to six inches in diameter. They were laid horizontally placed quite close together and were buried five or six inches below the surface. Out of the knots of their branches shoots and roots were sprouting everywhere so that the gardeners had quick results and a thick clump of green.[11]

As long as they had been watered they grew, but when care stopped they withered. Beside this central row were fifty-five pits, nine to 10m. deep and 5-6 m. across the top, narrowing as they became deeper, in which stumps of *Tamarix aphylla* were found. The plant is very tolerant of salt, wind and drought as long as it has become established and it is also very fast growing.[12] The plan was for an avenue of sycomore figs, the traditional sentinel in front of temples, between which the processions would pass,[13] and a waving feathery forest of tamarisk, stretching away on either side. The tamarisks grew to quite a size, their trunks reaching a diameter of about 10 cm.

> All of them showed well-rooted trees and those against the colonnade had spread even into the *gebel*. It is possible that the ground was shaded there and that it stayed moist.[14]

Some of the roots had reached a depth of 70cm. How long they remained before they withered might be established by counting the rings. Both tamarisk and sycomore were cut down after they had died from lack of water.

There were various stages in the development of the temple-grove; pits for trees were dug, and later were filled with rocks and levelled. Only the pits in front of the temple were filled with earth and had trees planted in them, although two rows of fourteen trees either side had been planned.

The Statuary

Statues of the king would have lined the avenue of sycomore fig trees. Some torsos were found in their original position, at the inner edge of the

A head from a statue of King Mentuhotep from his funerary temple at Deir el Bahari. XIth Dynasty. (Fig. 32)

tree holes facing the processional way. They were in front of eight trees on the southern side, and under five on the northern. But the heads were found separately. The statues were over life-size, two and a quarter metres high, and mounted on pedestals which would have been buried in the ground. The figures were of painted sandstone, showing Mentuhotep standing, with his hands crossed over his chest and wearing a white cloak which reached to his knees. This cloak was his jubilee robe. The later style of this garment is illustrated in Hatshepsut's temple, where a statue, whose cloak has a pointed collar, is brought in a boat to Deir el-Bahari.

Some of the heads of Mentuhotep have Red Crowns, and others, White Crowns, representing Lower and Upper Egypt. Two seated statues, wearing the same dress as the standing statues, were found at the end of the rows of trees, on the east-west axis of the large tree holes near the shaft entrance to the original tomb, called locally, 'Bab el Hosn'. They were also just over life-size. Under a sycomore-fig tree beside the approach to the temple was an altar. It may have indicated a particularly sacred tree. The excavators described the spot as:

> Outlined by two concentric circles of brick......The whole garden had a diameter of about 13.50m. The bricks of the outer circle were laid end to end and their outside was plastered. The interior of the circle consists of a coherent mass of mud much cracked from watering. It is likely that a tree larger than any other stood in the centre. Although a stump no longer remains, deep and very large roots are still preserved.......Leaves found here seemed to prove that it was a sycomore fig.
>   The altar beside the tree was made of mud brick.
>   The south side of the circle is broken by a roughly rectangular patch of brickwork measuring 1.65 m. from north to south and 5.20 m. from east to west. This may have been a large mud altar. Evidently it was divided into two compartments.[15]

The temple was surrounded by a series of white plastered walls, entered through a gateway 4m. wide, with towers on either side. There were four smaller gates with inscribed stone jambs in the enclosure wall.

The sacred grove was similar in position to the one at the Middle Kingdom temple of Osiris at Medamud, where there was a sacred grove (or a sacred tree) enclosed within a wall.

Mentuhotep's temple is landscaped, in the sense of the terrain having been physically altered in order to achieve an effect. The platform of the temple was cut out of the living rock. The courtyard in front of the temple was a 100m. wide and double that in length. Mentuhotep cut away the hillside in order to make a route from the river to his funerary temple. This route, 33m. wide, was paved with mud-bricks, and screened by a wall on either side, 3.5m. high. The causeway was more than a kilometre long.

Mentuhotep's tomb and temple followed in a tradition based on the idea of the tomb of Osiris with its trees beside it, which had been realized in some Old Kingdom tombs, and may have been more evident at the Saqqara and Giza pyramids than it is possible now to know. The symbolism of sycomore-fig and tamarisk trees connects them with a resting place for the soul, in the case of both trees, and with the belief that the sycomore-fig was sacred to Hathor, provider of nourishment for the deceased, and a sentinel on the eastern horizon.

A tomb at Hu (Diospolis Parva). Beside it is a tree, on which the bennu-bird of Osiris is resting. A drawing from a painting in the sarcophagus chamber of Marsiesi, called Dionysius. Ptolemaic Period. (Fig. 33)

The tamarisks reflected the belief that the sky goddess, Nut, gave birth to the deceased king among tamarisks: 'His mother Nut bore him in the Field of Tamarisk which protected the god in the nest'.[16] Cults which were observed at Mentuhotep's temple were that of the king himself, Amen-Re, and Hathor. The place was also sacred to the god Mont-Re, and rituals for the Hebsed or Jubilee of the king were performed, and also funerary rites connected with Osiris.

A plan of part of the temple was found on a piece of limestone. It may be the design for the planting of trees in front of the temple, or more likely, for the colonnade around the pyramid. A 'T'-shape covers two rectangles drawn on the plan, and may indicate a pool, or a statue base.

Two sycomore-fig trees on the horizon. The newly risen sun is seated on a calf riding out into the sky. A painting in the tomb of Sennedjem. Theban Tomb 1. XIXth Dynasty. (Fig. 34)

There was another Eleventh Dynasty temple on the west bank at Thebes, at the site of Medinet Habu, which was obliterated by the 'small temple' which was begun by Hatshepsut, and added to at various times until the Ptolemaic period.

Middle Kingdom

Sesostris II

One of the pyramids, high on the desert plateau at the entrance to the Fayum, was surrounded by a grove of trees. This was the pyramid of Sesostris II (1875-1836 B.C.) at el-Lahun, where there were trees planted in pits, cut in the bedrock.[17] The remains of the roots which were found could not be identified. Petrie described what he found:

> Around the great brick wall on the east, south and part of the west sides there were pits sunk in the rock, on the chip platform, in which trees had been planted in Nile mud and soil.

There were forty-two holes on the south side, forty-one on the east, and twelve on the west. Petrie connected the numbers with the numbers of nomes of Egypt, suggesting that there was one for each nome. He noted that the trees were planted 10 cubits apart (1 cubit = 52cm.), in pits nearly a metre across.

New Kingdom

Queen Hatshepsut's Landscaping of Deir el-Bahari

The next great landscape architect at Deir el-Bahari was Queen Hatshepsut (c. 1475-1458 B.C.), widow of Tuthmosis II. The site she chose was directly beside Mentuhotep's temple, also enveloped within the

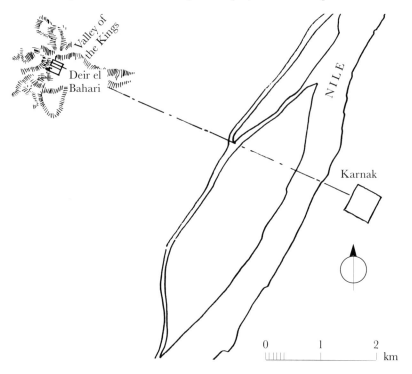

Plan of the sight-line between the temples at Karnak and Deir el-Bahari. (Fig. 35)

mountain sacred to Hathor. The place had become more holy through the burials of the kings of the Seventeenth Dynasty on the northern slope. She, however, made her tomb the other side of the sacred mountain, where her father, Tuthmosis I, had his tomb, deep in the mountain crevaces, in the place which became known as the Valley of the Kings. She sited her tomb directly west of her funerary temple, and in line with the temple of Amun across the river at Karnak.

The Nile between them was part of the symbolic landscaping, in which the sun rose in the east, on the temple of Karnak, and, set at the summer solstice, behind Hatshepsut's temple in the mountain, and her tomb. Tomb and temple were not physically connected, as were Mentuhotep's tomb and temple, but the symbolism of a unit was there.

The face from a statue of Queen Hatshepsut, which stood in her funerary temple at Deir el-Bahari. Early XVIIIth Dynasty. (Fig. 36)

Hatshepsut's temple was not only landscaped in geographical relation to the mountain and the river; there was a religious imperative to place the temple where Hatshepsut would be honoured, in the very mountain where the goddess, Hathor, resided, and among the tombs of her royal ancestors. Its harmony with its setting, which might be regarded as due to purely aesthetic considerations, is in reality the result of theological considerations.

Hatshepsut is famous for attempting to change the rules of inheritance from the males to the females of the royal family, thus demonstrating that, if there was no direct male descendant, then the female should rule. Her architect, Ineni, expressed the situation on the death of her husband, Tuthmosis II, clearly and with tact, in view of the fact that the male successor was not Hatshepsut's son, and she was not Queen Mother:

(Tuthmosis II) rose to the sky and united with the gods. His son rose in his stead as King of the Two Lands. He reigned on the throne of his father. His sister, the Wife of the God, Hatshepsut, directed the affairs of the country according to her will.[18]

She was crowned as king either two, or seven years later, while the male representative of the family, her young nephew Tuthmosis III, was associated with her, but not recognized as equal in kingship. She may have been ambitious and greedy for power as some have described her, but she was not a usurper, since her blood claim to royalty was better than that of Tuthmosis III, and she did not exclude him from royal honours. The destruction of Hatshepsut's monuments was carried out late in Tuthmosis III's reign as part of his building scheme at Deir el-Bahari.

Hatshepsut followed Mentuhotep in making use of the idea of the grave of Osiris and the mound of creation in her funerary temple, which combined the elements of grove, stairway and pool. The temple had been begun by Tuthmosis II. It rises in terraces, clinging to the mountainside. In front was an avenue of sphinxes, but no trees, as Naville had thought, leading from the Valley Temple near the river, which was probably surrounded by trees. At the gateway of Hatshepsut's temple were pits for trees cut into the limestone of the desert floor, which contained the roots of *Mimusops schimperi*.[19] Nowadays the spot is marked by notices saying that the stumps protected by a metal cage are the trunks of Hatshepsut's trees. They are, in fact, successors, which have also not survived.

On the first terrace inside the enclosure, in front of the colonnade, the early excavator, Naville, noted that:

> On both sides, the open space was used as a kind of garden. There were many small round pits about ten feet deep, filled with Nile mud in which trees had been planted. The stumps of two palm trees are still in situ, but there were other trees.[20]

Winlock, who dug the site twenty or so years after Naville, notes that the palms belonged to a later development on the site. He was sceptical about any grove of trees in the temple area, and said that he,

> Had been on the lookout for a grove of trees such as that in front of the Mentuhotep temple. We can say positively now that no such grove existed. Except for one in the northeast corner of the forecourt, and one on either side of the temple ramp, there were no trees in Hatshepsut's day in front of the temple. The stumps of some palms are still to be seen there, but they clearly belong to the much later grave pits.[21]

Naville wondered how the plants were watered, but his explanation is not very clear. He seems to imply that *sakkiehs* were used:

> The natives call them sagiehs, and they say that there are a great number of them along the avenue where the sphinxes stood. The two

perseas (*mimusops*) which stood on each side of the door in the enclosure wall, were planted in similar pits, and were watered in the same way.

Since *sakkiehs* were not introduced until Ptolemaic times, Naville may have been misled by his informants. He himself did not find any water channels.

The great feature of the landscape design, as one approached the temple, passing between the mimusops trees, and entering an open area - whether filled with trees or not - were two great pools in which waving papyrus had been planted. The pools were on both sides of the steps leading up to the first terrace, and were shaped like a 'T', with the head of the 'T' against the steps (which later became a ramp). They had sloping sides, and were 10m. wide (north to south) and 6m. across the top of the

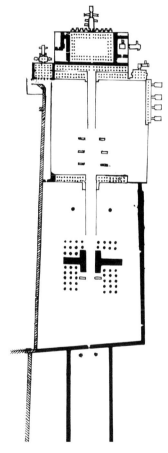

Plan of the funerary temple of Queen Hatshepsut at Deir el-Bahari showing the 'T'-shaped pools and the surrounding planting holes as well as the position of the Mimusops Laurifolia trees at the entrance. (Fig. 37)

'T'. When they were investigated, papyrus was still visible in them, and pieces of cut papyrus were found. Around the papyrus pools were about 66 pits cut in the rock. Judging from their depth of 3m. and their arrangement, they were for trees or bushes rather than for flowers, as indicated by Winlock.[22] The roots which were found in them were of apricots which were not introduced until Ptolemaic-Roman times. But some other tree, such as tamarisk, or acacia, could have been planted there in Hatshepsut's time. The pools provided a setting for several rituals. One was connected with the dedication of the temple, in which papyrus was cut down. The other rituals were funerary:

> May you pluck papyrus plants, rushes, lotuses and lotus buds. There shall come to you waterfowl in thousands, lying on your path; you cast your throwstick at them, and it means that a thousand are fallen at the sound of its wind...[23]

The goddess Hathor, in the form of a cow, coming out of the mountain into a papyrus clump. A vignette in the papyrus of Ani in the British Museum. XIXth Dynasty. (Fig. 38)

A scene of the deceased hunting birds in the marshes is illustrated in many New Kingdom tombs. A boomerang found in the 'T'-shaped pools suggests that the ritual of hunting in the papyrus marsh was performed here. Fishing was sometimes part of the hunting ritual, and a 'T'-shaped pool is sometimes the place where it was staged. 'T'-shaped pools were also used for receiving offerings. The 'T'-shaped pool may also be derived from the 'T'-shaped waterway in front of the tent of purification illustrated in Old Kingdom tombs. At Deir el-Bahari it would have been a place to make offerings to the dead queen.

It gave actuality to a place illustrated in the Book of the Dead (ch. 186), and on funerary stelae, which showed Hathor as a cow coming out of the mountain into a papyrus thicket, which represented the primeval world. A ritual of welcoming her would have been enacted beside the pools. While urging her with songs and incense to come out, two priests would take hold of papyrus stems and make an arch for the goddess, in the form of a cow, to step through. As the home of the cow goddess, Hathor, papyrus was the frontier between life and death. At the New Year festival celebrating the new creation, papyrus was offered to the gods for the produce of the marsh: birds, fish and vegetation. The discovery of papyrus in the 'T'-shaped pools at the foot of the ramp up to Hatshepsut's temple at Deir el-Bahari may be connected with this ritual.

Queen Hatshepsut as a sphinx. These brightly painted statues lined the approach to her funerary temple at Deir el-Bahari. XVIIIth Dynasty. (Fig. 39)

Garden Statuary

Statues of the queen, as a sphinx, made a continuous avenue from the river to the foot of the second stairway within the temple. These statues were massive in size - three metres long and a metre wide, carved in sandstone, and painted. They stood at intervals of about ten metres. All 120 statues had been removed and broken up, but the traces of their original positions were still visible in the early Nineteenth Century when Napoleon's savants made their maps and plans. The way across the second court, to the foot of the second ramp, was also lined with seven pairs of granite sphinxes representing the queen. The sphinx represented the power of the ruler of Egypt over foreigners, and as if to emphasize this point, the bases of these sphinxes were carved with bound captives. The sphinxes were thus guardians of the way into the temple.

Statues of Queen Hatshepsut as Osiris on the uppermost terrace of her funerary temple at Deir el-Bahari. (Fig. 40)

On the second and third terraces in front of the colonnades were statues of the queen standing, wearing the tight robe associated with Osiris. This dress may also be to do with the jubilee ceremony, and a perpetual representation of the queen at that ceremony, much as Mentuhotep was also presented in his statues, in a jubilee costume. Or, indeed, the costume may be a kind of mummy wrapping - like Osiris - but signifying the revival of the dead queen with her full powers. The way into the sanctuary on the uppermost terrace was flanked by figures of the queen kneeling, holding out jars of offerings to Amun.

If we compare the position of trees and statues at Hatshepsut's and Mentuhotep's temples can we assume that, since the statues in Mentuhotep's grove of trees were wearing jubilee costume, the statues on the second terrace of Hatshepsut's temple wearing a type of jubilee costume were also placed among or beside trees? Only one tree-pit has been found on this level. But, before the temple was built, there had been a garden round an earlier shrine, dedicated to Amenophis I, called Amenophis of the Garden, which Senenmut removed.

The terraces were linked by steps with a balustrade in the form of a great serpent, curling its way up the mountain side. Its head was that of a falcon, and carved on the ends of the balustrade were seated lions. The wall delimiting the temple precinct, the 'garden wall' was crenellated and each section was crowned with the relief-carving of a falcon wearing a crown, representing the queen.

Hatshepsut dedicated this temple to Amun-Re, and called it the 'House of Maat-ka-Re (Hatshepsut) (with the name) "Amun is the Holy of Holies"'. She also declared that Amun dwelt there in the Holy of Holies. The goddess of the mountain, Hathor, was honoured in a special chapel.

On the topmost terrace of the temple, in the 'Holy of Holies', the innermost shrine, there were two carvings representing gardens devoted to growing the lettuces for Amun-Min, beside a pool full of waterlilies and fish.[24]

This sanctuary was where the boat of Amun would have rested when it visited the temple at the annual commemorative festival, called the Festival of the Valley; it was a place where offerings were made. The niches along the wall were inscribed with lists of offerings. Representations of the barque of Amun, resting in the shrine, decorated both walls. The gardens carved on the walls consisted of three rows of rectangular plots with raised borders. The lettuces growing in them are shown beside the plots. Behind, or beside the lettuces, and drawn to a smaller scale, are sycamore-fig trees (alternatively they are small plants between the lettuces), or simply the sign for 'tree'. On the north side of the shrine, the rows of cultivation plots are bordered by a tall *was* sign, which stands for both the city and temple of Thebes, as well as for 'milk'. At the end of the pool, on the south side of the shrine, are four small oblong offering tanks for milk. Clumps of papyrus and lotus flowers grow in the pool. Birds and fish swim there, and ducks fly above, or rest on the papyrus umbels. The garden on the northern wall is mostly destroyed.

After the procession had climbed up the steps and entered the dark vault, servants handed the priests burning torches. After they had laid down the boat, and made sure everything was in order, they plunged their torches into four small basins containing milk. Libations of milk and water

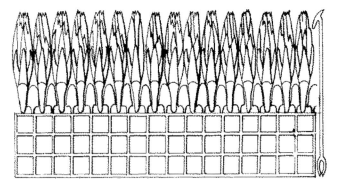

a. Lettuces sacred to the god, Amun-Min, growing beside cultivation plots.

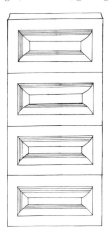

b. Small offering tanks for milk which are carved beside the garden.

c. Birds and fish amongst waterlilies in the pool in the centre of the garden.

d. Birds flying amongst the papyrus beside the pool.

Schematic representations of elements from the gardens carved on the walls in the inner sanctuary of the funerary temple of Queen Hatshepsut at Deir el-Bahari. XVIIIth Dynasty. (Fig. 41)

were offered for purification, and, in the cult of the dead. These basins were exactly like the four carved beside the pool on the walls.

Outside the shrine, in the Hall of Offerings, Amun's garden of lettuces is illustrated again. Although he has the appearance of the god Min, the inscription above his head calls him "Amen-Re, Foremost in Djeseru". The lettuces growing in the nine rectangular beds beside him are of enormous size, as tall as the plumes on his crown. Small trees are shown between the lettuces. These plants have the spikey appearance of incense trees. They may also represent the doum-palms sacred to Min.

Lettuces were sacred to Min: the milky sap of the plant being regarded as the semen of this fertility god. The garden of Min is usually illustrated beside or behind him, growing out of a square of ground divided into nine beds separated by low dykes. The lettuces also grow out of, or beside a shrine. In some representations of Min and his garden, the lettuces are in the shape of trees. The lettuces were indeed like miniature trees, since they could grow to the height of one metre, and in late representations an actual tree is shown. Lettuces were regarded as being aphrodisiac.

Work on Hatshepsut's temple at Deir el-Bahari was begun in her sixth, or seventh year, went on until Year 20, and was never finished. It was directed by Senenmut, who was also 'Overseer of the Gardens', and responsible for much else in the queen's administration. He was helped by other officials including the vizir, the treasurers and the Second Prophet of Amun. In the same year, the expedition which the queen had sent to collect incense trees, resin, tusks, skins and other products from Punt, returned. Hatshepsut gathered her court together and told them of this remarkable achievement.[25]

I speak a great thing which is set amongst you... a decree of my Majesty commanding to send to the incense terraces...

Trees were taken up in God's Land, and set in the ground in Egypt...for the king of the gods. They were brought bearing incense therein for (giving of themselves) ointment for the divine limbs, which I owed to the Lord of the Gods...he commanded me to establish for him a Punt in his house, to plant the trees of God's Land beside his temple, in his garden.

I made for him a Punt in his garden, just as he commanded me for Thebes. It is large for him. He walks abroad under them.

Some years later, Hatshepsut's successor, Tuthmosis III, commissioned two of his officials, Puyemre and Rekhmire to bring more incense trees from Punt, and this achievement they proudly recorded in their tombs (Theban Tombs 39 and 100). Another official reported the successful completion of his mission in these words: "Travelling to Thebes ... carrying thousands (?) of various products of Punt: myrrh .... incense trees..."[26]

There are three problems to do with the trees from Punt: the location of Punt, the identification of the trees brought from Punt, and where the trees were indeed planted.

There has been much debate about the location of Punt, whether it was a trading centre on the Somali coast, where produce from many areas was exchanged, or a wider area including part of the Sudan. Punt is now generally thought to be the former. The expression 'God's Land' probably means a far-off place, which has particularly attractive vegetable or mineral resources. The expression 'God's Land' has been discussed widely, the god being identified with the god of Egypt, Amun. An interesting interpretation is provided by the modern day Masai in Kenya who call the territory over which they roam grazing their animals, 'God's Land', meaning that it is available to all users for their individual purposes, but that it belongs to no one person or community and cannot be divided. Arabia is probably the place of origin of some of the aromatics.

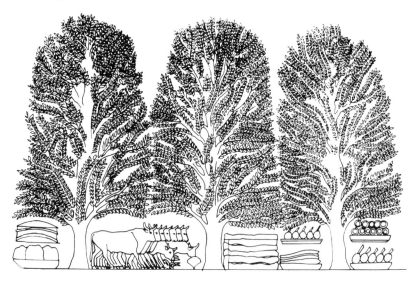

Incense trees from Punt planted in Egypt, with cattle grazing beneath them. Other produce of Punt is arranged under the trees. A painted relief in the funerary temple of Queen Hatshepsut at Deir el-Bahari. (Fig. 42)

Hatshepsut said she brought *anty* trees from Punt. *Anty* has been identified both with myrrh, and with frankincense. The Egyptians themselves knew two kinds of incense: *anty* and *sentjer*. Ramesses III's lists of donations to temples in Memphis mentions both *anty* and *sentjer* together, and so it is clear the Egyptians recognized a difference. The trees and the piles of gum or resin illustrated at Deir el-Bahari are called *anty*.

The trees from Punt illustrated in the Deir el-Bahari reliefs appear to be of two kinds: those with individually delineated leaves, 'leafy', and those with the trunk and branches clearly indicated, but the leaves painted as a continuous area of green, apparently, 'bare'.[27] Hepper identified the leafy trees with frankincense,[28] *Boswellia frereana*, which grow in Africa.[29] These trees can reach a height of one to ten metres,[30] "with a central stem about two feet in circumference and branches springing out rather scantily from the top."[31] The appearance of frankincense trees varies considerably, according to their environment and species. The other possibility is that Hatshepsut's trees were myrrh. Myrrh is derived from various species of *Balsamodendron* and *Commiphora*. Myrrh trees have been described as like a low spreading cedar, and also as a bush. They are very thorny "With gnarled and ash-grey coloured branches.....The leaves grow in small tufts and the flowers are white to light green."[32] The resin is yellowish red, and the piles of resin illustrated in Hatshepsut's temple are indeed coloured red, which could indicate that the trees were myrrh, but the resin and the trees need not be the same. Both frankincense and myrrh trees can be grown from seeds and cuttings, but not without difficulty. Myrrh is more widespread than frankincense, and grows both in Arabia and in Africa.

Hatshepsut said she was giving Amun ointment, which is another indication that the incense trees were probably myrrh, since myrrh resin, particularly that derived from *Commiphora erythraea*, var. *glabrescens*,[33] is the source of what is called in modern times, opoponax, which can be mixed with oil to create an ointment, whereas frankincense resin can only be burnt. *Commiphora erythraea* also grows in Saudi Arabia on Dumsuk island. It is a substantial tree 'four metres tall and ten metres wide with a creamy, peeling bark, large hard trifoliate leaves, and branches sweeping the ground'.[34]

Incense trees were believed to provide a resting place for the soul of a dead person. In his funerary inscription a priest of Amun and Hathor says: "My soul ... will assume the form of a swallow of God's Land in order to .. [signs not recognizable] on the incense (*antyw*) trees".[35]

It is not clear from her inscription whether Hatshepsut planted the incense trees at Amun's temple at Deir el-Bahari, her funerary temple, or at Amun's temple at Karnak. Her mention of creating a 'Punt' does not indicate what characteristic of Punt she had in mind: whether the terraces or the type of trees, or a combination of both.

> He commanded me to establish for him a Punt in his house, to plant the trees of God's Land beside his temple, in his garden.

The only pits for trees which have been excavated at Deir el-Bahari were round the 'T'-shaped pools, and one or two on the two terraces. These pits did not contain any remains of myrrh or frankincense trees. But some scholars have assumed that the trees which came from Punt were planted at Deir el-Bahari.

Some trees are shown in the wall reliefs growing in pots. Therefore pots could have been placed on the terraces to contain the trees from Punt, and indeed other trees. There was plenty of room for them. The middle terrace measures 85m. E.-W. and 80m. N.-S. The lower terrace was 130m. E-W. and 80m. N.-S.

Incense trees from Punt planted in pots in Egypt. A painted relief in the funerary temple of Queen Hatshepsut at Deir el-Bahari. (Fig. 43)

After the queen was buried, there was an annual pilgrimage to her funerary temple at Deir el-Bahari, not to her tomb, which was sealed. The Festival of the Valley was the occasion of the annual visit by the gods from Karnak, the living gods, to the dead gods on the western bank of the Nile at Thebes. The scene is illustrated in her temple together with the main festival of Amun, the Opet when the gods of Karnak went to the Luxor temple.

The focal point of Hatshepsut's garden at Deir el-Bahari was the twin pools, surrounded by trees or shrubs. One would expect to find sycomore figs, as the home of the goddess Hathor, or tamarisk such as those planted in Mentuhotep's garden. Steps led to a terrace where there is evidence only for one tree, but the site is very eroded, and there is space (50m. x 70m.) for quite a display. The trees from Punt came in baskets; the trees could well have been arranged on the terrace in pots. Indeed, some of them are shown as being in pots in the reliefs. There were certainly enough people to water them.

The approach to the temple was up an avenue of trees culminating in the two *Mimusops laurifolia* trees on either side of the entrance: like the two sycomores depicted on the horizon of heaven. When the visitor passed these trees, he was entering heaven. The protective sphinxes, the pools marking the territory of the goddess Hathor, and the stairway of the mound of creation, led to the ultimate garden, the garden of Amun-Min carved in the Holy of Holies, in the innermost sanctuary.

Other Gardens at Deir el-Bahari

Tuthmosis III built a shrine between Mentuhotep's and Hatshepsut's temples with an avenue of trees leading up to it; pits for trees have been found at 6m. intervals along part of the approach way,[36] which runs parallel with the approaches of Mentuhotep and Hatshepsut. The walls were 3.50m. high.[37] The pits for trees were about ten metres deep (about the height of the highest diving board from the water's surface) and filled with black earth. Round their edges was a low brick wall.[38] Fragments of roots and tree stumps were found in them.

Other Funerary Temples with Gardens

Hatshepsut's father, Tuthmosis I, built a funerary temple, which has since disappeared. It was mentioned on the shrine she built at Karnak, and may be illustrated in the tomb of Userhat (TT 51) who was Chief Priest of Tuthmosis I, in his funerary temple. In this tomb there is a scene of a statue of the king being conveyed in a barque along a tree-lined canal to a temple.

Tuthmosis III

Mentuhotep and Hatshepsut built their funerary temples high on the mountain, where they had to dig pits into the rock to provide places for trees to grow. Later pharaohs built lower down, nearer the edge of the cultivation, where water was more accessible. Pools are the feature which the later pharaohs mention as the embellishment of which they are most proud. Thus the water element of the tomb of Osiris is emphasized rather than the trees, although where evidence has remained, the trees were very much part of the design.

Tuthmosis III's own funerary temple was on the outer edge of the cultivation. It has all but disappeared. Palm trees may have been growing in the vicinity, since there was a Chief of the Guardians of the Date Trees at this temple.[39] It had a quay,[40] which means there was a water channel and presumably a garden. This temple may be illustrated in the tomb of Khons (Theban Tomb 31), but no garden is shown there. Trees are shown in a lower register, but they are part of another scene. (Alternatively, this illustration may be of the VIth pylon at Karnak). The valley temple of Tuthmosis III's funerary temple may be represented in an illustration on a board purchased in Thebes and now in the Metropolitan Museum in New York.

An Avenue and Lake at Amenophis III's Funerary Temple

The next funerary temple to have a garden in front of it, of which any evidence remains, is that of Amenophis III.[41] (c. 1390-1353 B.C.) The entrance to the temple is marked by the two lonely looking seated statues of the king known as the 'Colossi of Memnon'. Amenophis described on the stela which he put up at this temple, how he made a pool for Amun, filled with great Nile, Lord of fish and fowl'.[42] But he does not mention trees or a garden, although there may have been water-channels along the approach, which suggests that there was an avenue in front of the temple. This pool was on the east side of the temple and the 'filling with great Nile' happened annually. The lake may be illustrated in the tomb of the priest of the funerary temple of Amenophis III, Ameneminet (Theban Tomb 277), where a boat carrying a shrine, which may have contained the statues of the king and Queen Tiye, is taken across a lake towards a landing platform. Amenophis III's temple, may also be illustrated in the tomb of one of his officials, Nebamun (Theban Tomb 90). Two trees, which could indicate an avenue, are shown in front of it.

Two trees in front of a shrine or temple, which may be the funerary temple of Amenophis III, painted in the tomb of Nebamun. Theban Tomb 90. XVIIIth Dynasty. (Fig. 44)

A Garden at the Ramesseum

Ramesses II's (1279-1213 B.C.) garden at his funerary temple, the Ramesseum, is illustrated in the tomb of its chief gardener, Nezemger (Theban Tomb 138), whose title was "Overseer of the Garden in the Ramesseum in the Estate of Amun".[43] In the centre of the garden is a 'T'-shaped canal. The garden contained olive trees in mud pots, date, doum and argun palm trees. Beyond the pylon there is a lake surrounded by palm and sycomore trees. Part of the enclosure wall of the temple is also shown next to the pylon, and the 'T' of the canal abuts it. On the bank, six gardeners are working *shadufs* in order to keep the trees in their mud pots supplied with water. On the right is the tomb owner and two kneeling figures. One of the men is laying some plants on a table and the other holds up a baton. The texts give the name and titles of the owner. The pylon is on the left, which may mean that this part of the garden around the canal was outside the temple, and was, in fact, on the canal leading up to it. Alternatively, if the movement is from left to right, the pylon forms the entrance to the garden; in this interpretation, the pool or canal is inside the temple complex, and the owner is standing on a platform at the entrance to the temple, which is like a terrace overlooking the canal. However, the canal illustrated in Nezemger's tomb may simply be an imaginative representation, and not have been located in front of the Ramesseum, or in any other part of this temple. The orchard represented may have been to the north-east of the enclosure wall where there is still plentiful water and palm trees.

The Ramesseum. The area between the pylon and the temple where the garden tended by Nezemger may have been. XIXth Dynasty. (Fig. 45)

Nowadays acacia trees with their yellow flowers and long pods, and ancient tamarisk trees are growing between the pylon and the restored exterior of the temple, which shows that this ground is fertile and well watered in an area where the canal in the picture may have been. Gardens are known to have been inside as well as outside temples, and this may have been so at the Ramesseum.

The only other indication of a garden at the temple is an illustration of an *ished* tree in the so-called 'Astronomical Room'. The *ished* tree was a magical tree on which it was thought that the gods wrote the names of the kings at coronations and jubilee festivals, to assure them that their names, and thus their lives, would be perpetuated. In the scene in the Ramesseum, the Goddess of Writing, Lady of the Library, Sefkhet-'abu and the god Thoth do the writing in front of Atum, who is seated on a throne, with the seven gods of sky and earth depicted on the base of his throne. The goddess says to Ramesses II:

> I make your years on earth last in unending number. I make your life span more secure than the life span of heaven remaining in your own temple.[44]

And Atum says:

> I write your name on the holy *ished* tree with my own hand. I have proclaimed you king on my throne.

There is a similar scene also in the Ramessum on the first pylon, but it is partly destroyed. Ramesses had this scene carved on many of his temples. The scene developed out of the idea of finding the king's name on the sacred tree, and then recording it in the Annals, on a palm rib. The *ished* tree illustrated in the interior of the Ramesseum has fruits, on which Thoth writes the king's name. They are egg-shaped, and grow with the pointed end downwards. The *ished* tree represented in the Small Temple at Medinet Habu, built by Hatshepsut and Tuthmosis III, has only leaves and no fruits.

A living representative of this sacred tree may also have been grown in the temple, or it may be a purely symbolic part of the scene of recording the king's name at his accession. The original *ished* tree was believed to have been in Heliopolis, in the temple of Re.

Ramesses II was a powerful ruler who had to fight in Palestine and Syria to maintain Egypt's position. He boasted of his victory at Kadesh on the Orontes, but in fact it was a narrow escape. He was an energetic builder leaving his mark on many temples all over Egypt.

The Funerary Temple of Merneptah

Merneptah's (1213-1202 B.C.) funerary temple, was arranged on a slope in a system of terraces which would indicate that there might have been a garden in front of it. But no garden remains have been found so far.

The Gardens of the Funerary Temple of Ramesses III at Medinet Habu

One of the purposes of this temple of "Millions of Years" was to provide a place for the king to bring the statues of Amun at the Festival of the Valley.

> The king appears like Re in the palace of his august broad hall to cause his father Amon to appear at his Feast of the Valley.[45]

The spiritual relationship with the temple of Amun was stressed by Ramesses saying that his temple was opposite Karnak. Ramesses III (1187-1156 B.C.) described this vast funerary temple, as having 'towers of stone reaching to heaven', a wall round it and 'ramps and towers of sandstone'.[46] He says it was:

> Surrounded with gardens and arbor areas (literally, palaces of chambers of trees) filled with fruit and flowers for the Two Serpent Goddesses.
>
> I built their chateaux with windows, and dug a lake before them supplied with lotus flowers.[47]
>
> I dug a lake before the Temple of Millions of Years, supplied with lotus flowers, flooded with Nun, planted with trees and vegetation like the Delta.[48]

Excavations have revealed several places in and around the temple where there are remains of tree-pits and pools. In his reconstruction of Medinet Habu, Hölscher shows the first courtyard inside the High Gate as filled with trees. On the south side of the approach to the first pylon there is an oblong pool, lying east-west. It is surrounded by trees and cultivation plots. On the north side, there is the Eighteenth Dynasty temple, also surrounded by trees. He does not indicate any planting round the pool and canal beside the quay. The main garden areas inside the temple were:

1. Between the High Gate and the first pylon on the south side, where there was an enclosure containing a row of trees along the west wall, east of a pool, which was roughly in the centre of the enclosure. The pool reached ground water.

2. A grove of thirteen trees laid out between the Small Temple and the first pylon.[49] The pits were in three rows spaced at 3.50m. apart. Each pit was surrounded by a small wall.

3. Inside the main temple, west of the 'palace', there was a 'T'-shaped pool.[50] This may have been the main lake of the temple at one time. In this

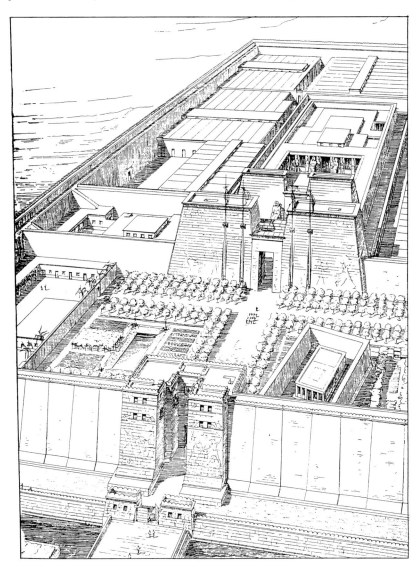

A reconstruction of the funerary temple of Ramesses III at Medinet Habu showing the trees and pool in the forecourt. XXth Dynasty. (Fig. 46)

court there is also a well. Hölscher called this the Palace Garden, but admitted that there was very little evidence for an actual garden. He had the

> Impression that it was a garden at the time of the Second Palace, and accessible from the harem court. Its main entrance was a monumental pylon in the centre of the north side; on its axis lay the well, source of all growing things. Along the south side stretched a terrace on which stood small buildings and a columned hall.[51]

The well in the 'palace garden' was a cylindrical shaft 5m. deep, which could have been emptied by means of buckets, for use in the garden and for filling the pool. No cultivation plots are recorded and no tree pits. The nature of the flooring is not mentioned. The 'garden' was about 30m. wide N-S.

4. In Roman times there was an avenue parallel with the outer wall on its east side.

At the entrance to the temple there was a large lake forming the top of the 'T'-shaped canal which led up to the temple. This was the main landing quay, over 10m. wide. 12m. deep and 7m. high.[52] Gardens were probably all round this pool, like the illustration of Karnak temple in the tomb of Neferhotep (Theban Tomb 49).

The wells inside the temple of Ramesses III, some of which are of later construction, probably had gardens around them.

Between the final sanctuaries and columned hall there are many scenes of offering bouquets which might indicate the presence of a garden in the vicinity. A special garden growing lettuces in honour of Amun-Min is illustrated on the pedestal upon which the sacred barque rested in the sanctuary. But where that garden was, or whether it even existed in reality, is not known.

Pools planted with flowers and trees are described by Ramesses, who says he: "Dug a canal (or pool) overflowing with Nun, green, and planted with all kinds of trees and colourful plants".[53] The mention of the god Nun suggests that either ground water, or the inundation, filled the pool. This description may refer to the pool in the forecourt of the temple, but the actual pool may have disappeared. Ramesses also says he dug a pool for libation water. He gave a gold and silver jug for libation water which was to come from this pool or canal which he had dug. But it is not clear where this pool was situated.

Ramesses III established many orchards and gardens all over the country to support his funerary temple at Medinet Habu. He speaks of the

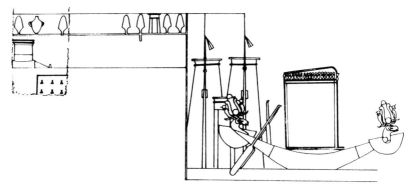

An avenue between two temples illustrated on blocks from the tomb of the Mayor Paser found at Medinet Habu. Reign of Ramesses III. XXth Dynasty. (Fig. 47)

far-flung 'strongholds' which had to produce offerings from their gardens for the festivals:

> I have collected for the herds of all small cattle, fields, domains of high land... gardens of... wild fowl descending into the pool in order to make festive thy oblations, with plenty...[54]

The original plan for Ramesses III's temple was for a pool outside the walls, with presumably trees and papyrus on the edges, and inside pools on the north side and near the palace. There were plantations in the front of, and on the north side, of the temple. In later times alterations were made and other water-sources were added.

A Funerary Temple depicted in the Tomb of Paser[55]

An avenue of trees lining the banks of a river or canal connecting two temples is illustrated on blocks from the mortuary chapel of the mayor Paser, which were found at Medinet Habu. A boat is travelling from one temple to another. The occasion may be the Festival of the Valley, and the temples, Karnak, and a funerary temple; Paser's own funerary chapel or, possibly the chapels of Hathor and Anubis at Deir el-Bahari. The temple visited has a garden in its first court, between the pylon and an altar. This garden is entered through a separate gate. Just beside the altar are 'T'-shapes, presumably offering-tables or pools. The approach to the temple is along a river, or canal bank, lined with trees.

A Garden at the Temple called Meniset

There was a garden at a temple which lies west of the funerary temple of Seti I, near the cultivation. Its plants are referred to on a stela, found among its ruins, which says:

Whoever is sprinkling water before this stela may Amen favour him.... May everyone love him if he is spreading water upon the leaves before my statue.[56]

This invocation suggests that there is a statue of the owner standing in a leafy place. The courtyard of the temple may have been a garden.

This temple and its garden may be illustrated in the tomb of Amenmose, First Prophet of the Temple of Amenhotep of the Court (Theban Tomb 19). A festival for the deified Ahmes Nefertari is in progress. Her boat is being towed on a 'T'-shaped lake towards a temple. On the banks of the lake are bowls of offerings between trees. There is a similar scene in the tomb of Userhet (Theban Tomb 51), in which the barque of Amun, containing the statue of a deified king (probably Tuthmosis I, since Userhet was priest of this king during the reign of Seti I), is being towed on a canal, past date and sycamore trees, beside which are booths with offerings, to a temple.

The Temple of Amenhotep of the Garden

A temple called the "Temple of Amenhotep of the Garden", was mentioned as a landmark by the scribes who inspected the royal tombs during the Twentieth Dynasty:

The (tomb) eternal horizon of Amenhotep (I) .. which is called... The High Ascent, north of the House of Amenhotep [Life, Prosperity, Health], of the Garden concerning which it had been reported that thieves had broken into it.[57]

The Amenhotep to whom the temple was dedicated was most probably Amenhotep I. The chapel on the terrace of Hatshepsut's temple at Deir el-Bahari contained a statue of Amenhotep of the Garden. This chapel was removed when Hatshepsut's temple was built, and it is not known whether this was the spot referred to by the inspectors, or whether it was the temple of Meniset, or somewhere else.

Summary

The earlier Theban royal funerary temples were landscaped in terraces against the western mountain. Groves of tamarisk and sycamore fig covered the slopes. *Mimusops laurifolia* were also planted. Under the trees were pools. These features were characteristic of the tomb of Osiris, which was stepped, surrounded by water, and sheltered by the kinds of trees which had special significance as the resting place for the god's soul. Later temples, like those of Ramesses II and Ramesses III, are less dramatically landscaped, but they contained gardens inside and out, and were built on sloping terrain. The gardens of funerary temples had to have trees outside and gardens inside. The main emphasis is on the garden within the pylon, in the first courtyard, where trees were usually planted.

Abydos

At Abydos, the early royal tombs may have had gardens. But it is not certain if the tombs are actual burial places, or memorials connected with the cult of Osiris at Abydos.

In the New Kingdom, the most spectacular representation of a tomb with its garden is the Osireion, surrounded by trees, which was never used as a burial place. There is also some written evidence for gardens at Abydos. One inscription, already mentioned, describes a now vanished temple built by Seti I and its lake and island. Another describes how Ramesses II (1279-1212 B.C.): "Founded (for the deceased king Seti I) offerings for his ka...wine, incense, all fruit. I cultivated trees growing for him".[58] Ramesses II also "planted many gardens, set with every (kind of) tree, all sweet and fragrant woods, the plants of Punt".[59] Gifts were made to the temple of Osiris, but it is a cult temple rather than a royal funerary temple.

VI   Gardens of Private Tombs

Planting for Eternity

> I went to the cemetery; I dug a pool one hundred cubits on each side
> (about 5m.) and round it planted sycomores.[1]

In this way, a rich man prepared for the afterlife, making a garden near his
tomb, as the Coffin Texts urged repeatedly: 'Build a domain in the west,
dig pools and plant sycomores.'[2] There the owner could: 'Walk as he
wished on the beautiful bank of his pool.....and draw water from the well
which he had installed for eternity and forever.'[3] The pool had a religious
meaning. It could be interpreted as the god, Nun, and as representing the
primordial 'Lotus lake' at Hermopolis, where life had begun, according to
the myths of that place. Both the 'T'-shaped pool and the rectangular pool
were places for making offerings.

*A garden painted in
the tomb of Ineni
(Theban tomb 81).
The owner is seated
in a kiosk in the
orchard and a ser-
vant brings him
offerings. Reigns of
Tuthmosis II-
Tuthmosis III.
Early XVIIIth
Dynasty. (Fig. 48)*

Ineni, who lived in the early part of the Eighteenth Dynasty, speaks of his garden of the West, "Which he had made while on earth." There he hoped to walk, "Cool under its sycomores," and "Admire its beautiful trees".[4] He listed the trees in this garden, which were all useful economically, being providers of fruit or wood.

A list of the produce of an orchard was written on a board held by a figure in a model granary which was found in the tomb of Ipiankhu at Saqqara. The list includes carobs and figs.

The progression from death to life is illustrated in the tomb of Amenemope (Theban Tomb 41). In the pillared courtyard of his tomb, with its pyramidal top, and surrounded by mourners, the deceased receives the 'Opening of the Mouth' rites which will restore his physical abilities.

The Goddess of the West greeting the deceased Amenemope (Theban Tomb 41). The mourners are shown beside his mummy. Reigns of Horemheb-Ramesses I. Late XVIIIth-early XIXth Dynasties. (Fig. 49)

He passes into the tomb, and is embraced by the goddess of the West. Then he arrives beside a 'T'-shaped pool under a sycomore-fig tree, where the tree-goddess pours life-giving water into his hands.

These 'gardens of the hereafter' are painted inside several New Kingdom and later tombs. The owners appear, both in the way they would have been in their lifetime, and as the recipient of life-giving, magical rites. For the deceased planned to come:

> Up to earth to see his house and the conduct of worship in the western sanctuary going back at his pleasure.[5]

On the occasion of the deceased's return to earth, the relatives brought him a 'Bouquet of Amun', a gift from the temple of Amun.

Continuation of Fig. 49. The Tree-goddess pours water for Amenemope and his soul, a human-headed bird with hands. The tree stands in a T-shaped pool. (Fig. 50)

The gardens illustrated in paintings have several features in common, although they are arranged differently, and not all are always included. There is the pool as a central focal point. It may be square, oblong or 'T'-shaped. In the pool are water-lilies, papyrus, ducks and fish. Sometimes the pool is covered by vines, or surrounded by a pergola covered with vines. On the edge of the pool, mandrakes, poppies and cornflowers are often growing. Beside the pool is either one sycomore-fig tree, or a row of them, or date and doum palms. Further away from the pool, a complete orchard of fruit trees is sometimes shown. The gardens in the paintings have religious significance, and so the ways in which groves and water were shown in the decoration of the tombs vary. All have meanings to do with resurrection and the afterlife, and invoke the mythology both of the sun god and of Osiris, as well as reflecting the real gardens and orchards visible in the countryside.

Gardens with the Goddess in the Sycomore-fig Tree

When the owner arrived in his 'Garden of the West', Nut, the sky goddess, appearing out of the sycomore-fig tree, or as part of the tree itself, told him how she would take care of him:

> I am Nut, I have come to thee bringing thee gifts. Thou sittest under me and coolest thyself under my branches. I allow thee to imbibe of my milk and to live and to have nourishment of my two breasts; for joy and health are in them... Thy mother provides thee with life. She

sets thee within her womb wherein she conceives.. ... I present to thee my bread, my beer, my milk, my meal, my figs...[6]

The scene of the tree goddess suckling the deceased, which first appeared in the tomb of Tuthmosis III, was once part of the decoration of royal tombs, and was taken over by the courtiers during the Eighteenth Dynasty. Occasionally the goddess in the sycomore tree is identified as Hathor or Isis, rather than Nut. The recipient is represented as the spirit of the deceased, a *ba*, either in the form of a bird with a human face, or as a human, with a bird on his or her head. In some tombs the tree goddess appears from the sycomore at the corner of a pool, holding out her gifts of fruit and drink. To drink water in the afterlife, and to be provided with gifts by the tree-goddess, are wishes expressed in one of the magical documents buried with the dead, called in modern times the Book of the Dead (Chapters 58-9).

Sometimes the scene is expanded so that a garden surrounds the pool from which the deceased, or the deceased and his wife drink, (e.g. Sebekhotep Theban Tomb 63) or beside which they kneel (e.g. Sennedjem Theban Tomb 1); and where they receive bread and water from the tree-goddess. It is both an offering place, as indicated by the 'T'-shaped pools, and place of nourishment. As one tomb-owner put it:

My heart rejoices on its earth to refresh itself under its sycomore, to walk among his own trees, to take the *ihi*-plants and the lotus, and gather the *hnw*-plants and lotus buds, the dates, the figs and the grapes. My sycomores wave in front of me, they give me bread which is in them, my basin offers water. My heart rests in its freshness.[7]

The garden painted in the tomb was expressly said by the owner of Theban Tomb 109, Min, to be his "Garden of the West", his future garden, where he and his wife would enjoy themselves, looking at everything that was growing. In this garden there is a pool filled with duck and fish and aquatic plants. The couple are seated, and their son presents a bouquet, with the words: "For your *ka*, the plants of your garden."[8] This scene is part of a general picture of the owner inspecting and counting produce from his estate. The garden was part of the estate and the agricultural year was depicted as unfolding before the owner, or the owner and his wife, who were seated, usually in an arbour or booth, watching the work being done on their estate. Similar scenes are in the tombs of Amenemhab (Theban Tomb 85) and Huy (Theban Tomb 14).

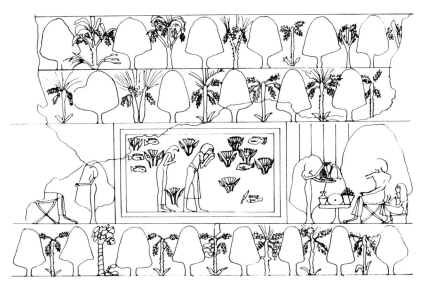

Sebekhotep and his wife drinking from a pool in the middle of their orchard. (Theban Tomb 63). Reign of Tuthmosis IV. XVIIIth Dynasty. (Fig. 51)

Home and Tomb-Chapel together in a Garden

In some paintings, the tomb-chapel and the home are shown close together, which suggests that the chapels were separate from the actual tomb. In some instances a tree-filled garden is attached to the tomb-chapel only; in others, both buildings have a garden. In the tomb of Ipuy (Theban Tomb 217) the tomb-chapel is shown in a garden, beside a lake or canal, while the tomb is in the mountain, some distance away.

In Theban Tomb 334 (the name of the owner is not known), the house and the tomb-chapel are shown, in plan, close together. There is a pool in front of the chapel, which is approached by steps up to a walled enclosure. A doorway leads into an open garden planted with four trees, in front of a building with three doors. The house beside it has four separate areas, each with its own door. This would be a modest dwelling for anyone who could afford a tomb at Thebes, and maybe this is only symbolic of his house or represents a garden-kiosk.

A painting in the tomb of Nebamun (TT 90), shows a house with a date tree growing in its courtyard, and a shrine in close proximity. The shrine is inscribed with the name of Amenophis III. In front of the shrine is a 'T'-shaped pool. Two figures bring offerings and pour a libation into a lotus cup in front of the shrine. Behind the figures is a vineyard. In both paintings (TT90 and 334), the deceased is sitting outside his house. This idealized architectural relationship between what is either his tomb-chapel, or a building with which he was intimately connected, near his house, indicates the ambiguous connection between this world and the next.

The 'Chief of Husbandmen', sitting outside his house beside his tomb-chapel with a pool in front of it and surrounded by trees. Theban Tomb 334. Reign of Amenophis III, XVIIIth Dynasty. (Fig. 52)

Ineni's house (Theban Tomb 81), and the orchard which he cultivated in his lifetime, become part of the afterlife, as we see him drinking from the pool in the orchard and receiving offerings in his garden-kiosk. A similar combination of this life, and the life to come, is illustrated in the papyrus of Nakhte (British Museum EA10471), where the deceased and his wife face Osiris across a pool covered with a vine and surrounded by trees. Their house with its windows and ventilators is behind them. This part of the picture is presumably of Nakhte's property, and he and his wife are about to cross over to Osiris who is there as an honoured guest.

Nakhte and his wife coming from their house with its sycomore fig and date palm towards Osiris. A vine makes a covered way from the pool to Osiris. XVIIIth Dynasty. (Fig. 53)

Gardens with a Pool on which the Statue or Shrine of the Deceased is towed

There are scenes in tombs in which a ritual of towing a boat towards the tomb-chapel is taking place. In the boat is the statue of the deceased or his sarcophagus. Sometimes a priest waits outside the chapel, which is not necessarily attached to the tomb itself. The ceremony with the statue, is either the burial, or a commemorative festival.

The Beautiful Festival of the Valley taking place in a Garden

The Beautiful Festival of the Valley, in which the family members brought the statue of the deceased out of the tomb, or joined it in a garden, where it was placed in a light booth during the ceremony, and then towed in a Neshmet boat round the pool in the centre of the garden, may be illustrated in the tomb of Rekhmire (Theban Tomb 100). The place is an orchard with rows of date palm, doum-palm and sycomore-fig trees, surrounding an oblong pool. But the location of the garden is ambiguous. For, an inscription on the tomb-ceiling speaks of Rekhmire, 'in his fair garden of the west',[9] which, 'affords him all manner of bread which is in it and all kinds of produce from his orchard'. He refers to the tomb chapel which was granted him by the king, who 'saw to it that it (the tomb chapel) should last me forever'.

The ritual in the tomb of Minnakht (Theban Tomb 87) appears to be the same celebration on water as that depicted in the tomb of Rekhmire, only the statue is either covered by a kiosk, or the object in the boat is a shrine containing his statue or mummy. An oblong pool or canal is surrounded by date palms and sycomore figs and a doum palm stands in the corner. A long flight of steps, shaded by vines, leads to the gate of a walled enclosure, in which there is a tomb-chapel containing four rooms. In the courtyard in front of this building are two trees. The ritual may also be the Festival of Osiris, when the statue was set up in a booth and presented with bouquets.

In the tomb of Ipuy (Theban Tomb 217), a similar scene is depicted. The prow of the boat is decorated with a ram's head, which indicates that the Festival of the Valley is taking place, since the boat must be the bark of Amun. The actual tomb can be seen in the mountain. The chapel in the painting may be the chapel built by Tuthmosis III, at the western end of the sacred lake at Karnak, rather than Ipuy's own tomb chapel. So there may be some conflation of ideas between the two ceremonies in honour of the deceased: one in Karnak and one on the west bank. The garden around this tomb-chapel has a variety of trees: there are willow, pomegranate, and sycomore-fig. The flowers are cornflower and poppy and the fruiting mandrake; the usual accompaniments to funerary scenes. Gardeners working hard to maintain the plants man a line of *shadufs*.

These scenes are reminders of the instructions which Hapzefa gave to his mortuary priests to take his statue at all the appropriate festivals to the nearby temple of Wepwawet in Asyut. The festivals in question are to do with the deceased being regarded as Osiris. At Abydos, the centre of worship of the god Osiris, the king, or his statue, was taken out and rowed on a lake in front of the temple in 'The great *neshemt*-barge' while the Followers of Horus cried out: 'Give unto him (the king) an eternity of Sed-festivals, (Jubilees) to double his years of life upon earth, accomplishing the reign of Atum'.[10] The lake was surrounded with trees, and in the centre were 'papyrus and reed and lilies abounding daily'.

Part of a similar scene may be illustrated in a painting from a Theban tomb, (TT 134) of the New Kingdom. A boat approaches a landing stage. Beyond, is a garden with sycamore trees between the pylon and a building. This building may well be a temple; but it could be a tomb, and thus be a good illustration of the forecourt planted with trees. What might be two stelae in the courtyard reinforce this conjecture. Priestesses, rattling the metal disks of their hoop-shaped sistra, welcome the boat; their presence indicates that this is either the day of the burial or a commemorative festival. However the owner was 'Prophet of Amenophis who navigates the Sea of Amun', and so the scene could be of a royal voyage rather than of his own funerary rites.

In some tombs there is a pool in front of the tomb-chapel, but no activities are taking place. The owner of tomb 334 has a pool in front of his tomb chapel and he is seated, facing away from them. Amenopet, the owner of Theban Tomb 215, sits beside a lake, under a palm tree, listening to music. The scene is very damaged, so it is difficult to see what else is there. A chapel in the tomb of Kenamun (Theban Tomb 93) is in front of a pool, again there is no activity on the pool, although in front of the chapel, there is a small figure with upraised hands, which is probably part of an inscription, rather than a priest waiting to receive the boat. The pool is surrounded by a pergola supporting a vine. Kenamun refers to the sycamores which he has planted. The rest of the scene consists of offering-bearers, the sycamore-tree goddess, and a spell for the preservation of the tomb.

A vine-covered pergola supported on wooden columns in the form of bundles of papyrus surrounding a pool. Tomb of Kenamun (Theban Tomb 93). Reign of Amenophis II, XVIIIth Dynasty. (Fig. 54)

The idea that the painted gardens are living places, where the cultivation of the plants is in progress, is demonstrated in the depiction of gardeners at work. Men working *shadufs* are incorporated in scenes in several tombs. In the tomb of Ipuy, there is even the detail of a dog sitting beside one of the workers. In the tomb of Rekhmire, men with buckets on yokes on their shoulders pour water into the channels around the trees. Gardeners are picking the grapes in the tomb of Minnakht. But these figures were not included because they were amusing; they were there to facilitate the life of the plants.

All the effort in gardening and agricultural work was for the purpose of, and culminated in, the meal which was to be enjoyed by the deceased in the afterlife, sometimes alone, and sometimes in company with his wife, children, family members and friends.

Feasting was one of the main activities the dead person looked forward to. He expected to be resurrected and to feast, according to the Book of the Dead chapter 110. In several tombs a great banquet is shown taking place with the deceased and his wife, their relatives and friends enjoying a vast meal to the accompaniment of music and dancing. Fruit and vegetables grown in the gardens were piled up in front of them including grapes, dates, figs, sycomore-figs, onions, leeks, cucumbers, melons and lettuces. The pool provided flowers to give to the guests. A servant at Rekhmire's funerary banquet says: "Take the scented flowers [of the pool] which I have brought thee from the pick [of the plants] which are in these [gardens]."[11] Flowers also decorated the tables and the food. Flowers and perfumes enhanced the enjoyment not only of diners, but also of lovers:

> Put incense and fine oil together to thy nostrils, and garlands of lotus and mandrake flowers upon thy breast, while thy sister whom thou lovest sits at thy side."[12]

The Garden as an Offering Place

A quite different 'garden' scene is represented in some of the tombs at Thebes and Memphis, often in the same tomb as the scene with the tree goddess, which indicates that the scenes are complementary in their messages. This scene shows a mythical place, containing religious symbols, trees and pools. The features in this space are, obelisks, a pool surrounded by palm trees, cultivation plots, sycomore-fig trees, offering-pools, a slaughtering area beside a pool, and offering-stands, of a type used both for libations and for burning incense. Shrines of gods surround the place.

The scene represents both eastern and western horizons of heaven, as described in the Pyramid and Coffin texts. The pool among the palm trees suggests the place on the eastern horizon where, according to the Pyramid Texts, the sun god purified himself before he went on his daily journey across the sky (Pyramid Text 519). The two sycomores were also on the eastern horizon (Pyramid Text 1433). To the western horizon, belong the two obelisks (Coffin Text Spell 1011), the offering stands and the slaughtering-area. The obelisks also signified Heliopolis, the sun city. There are an additional four offering-pools, in front of which are two women kneeling holding water (or milk) pots. Their ritual is either a libation to the desert, or, to the Goddess of the West.[13]

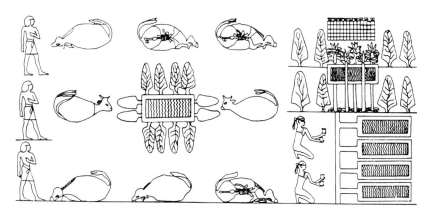

The garden of the 'Butic Burial'. A painting in the tomb of Rekhmire (Theban Tomb 100). Reigns of Tuthmosis III-Amenopohis II. XVIIIIth Dynasty. (Fig. 55)

The scene has been called by modern scholars the 'Holy Place' in the 'Butic Burial', because the pool and the palm trees are the characteristic features of the predynastic cities in the Delta, Pe, Dep and Djeba, which together constituted Buto, the main religious centre of Lower Egypt during the Predynastic period, where, according to the ancient myths, the world began.

The context for the scene is the burial ritual which is taking place in the adjacent scenes. This place represents the ideal of a garden where offerings were made to the gods, featuring a pool, palm trees, and cultivated plots. An actual garden imitating this idea may have existed at Tell Dabaa. Here outside a palace of the Thirteenth Dynasty (c. 1780-1750 B.C.) there was a row of six trees standing in front of six tombs. They were the burial places of Asiatics who had adopted Egyptian names and customs.

A Garden with an Island in a Lake

A garden setting, an island in a tree-lined lake, was illustrated in connection with other burial rituals; again, sometimes in the same tomb as

106

the 'Butic Burial' and the 'Tree-goddess' scenes. Trees and flowers grow on the banks of the lake, and flowers on the banks of the island. The trees are date palms, sycomore-fig, other fruit trees and tamarisks. The flowers, growing each in separate plots, are clumps of papyrus, poppies and cornflowers, alternating with mandrake fruits and mayweed.

Plants growing on the banks of the island where burial rituals are being performed. A boat containing the coffin approaches the island. At the lower left are steps up to the building on the island. A painting in the tomb of Hekmarenakhte Turo. Theban Tomb 222. Reigns of Ramesses III-IV. XXth Dynasty. (Fig. 56)

The symbolism of this setting combined the ideas of the Osirian Mound of Creation with those of the Field of Offerings in the 'Butic Burial' scenes. This island was illustrated on the walls of tombs at Saqqara and Thebes between the Eighteenth and Twentieth Dynasties.[15] The plant symbolism is evident in the trees chosen: date and doum palm had particular associations with resurrection. Date palms were sacred to Re, the sun god. and symbolized the triumph of life over death. The deceased was believed to become a date palm 'in order to drink water in the necropolis'.[16] The date-palm was a sacred tree in various religious centres, and was also the emblem of Upper Egypt. Date palms are illustrated together with sycomore figs and doum-palms on the banks of the lakes where burial rites were performed during the New Kingdom. They were planted in the forecourts of tomb chapels. Because of their long roots and ability to grow in dry places they survived in these inhospitable conditions. The date-palm was a sacred tree in the religious centers of Buto, Heliopolis and Akhmim, and was also the symbol of Upper Egypt. Hathor of Kom el-Hisn was Lady of the (male) Date Palms.

The doum-palm, like the date palm, was regarded as a source of water for the deceased. The doum-palm is shown growing beside water in the other world, and itself provided water for the deceased drinking beneath it.[17] Irinefer (Theban Tomb 290) asked to become a doum palm in order to drink water in the afterlife next to Min. The doum nut indeed contains fluid. The doum palm was sacred to the moon god, Thoth. The theme of the ape, the animal of Thoth, climbing the doum palm sixty cubits high, was illustrated on spoons and jars.

Papyrus had associations with Hathor, as goddess of the West and nourisher of the dead. Mandrake plants are not explained by the Egyptians. Collars of mandrake fruit were worn as a resurrection decoration in tomb-paintings and on statues. The ancient Egyptian written sources provide no explanations as to why poppy and cornflower were depicted in funerary scenes. They may simply be associated with the cornfields where the corn, representing Osiris, grew, and therefore they are his accompaniments and renew themselves annually. The Romans offered poppies to the dead, and regarded them as a moon-flower, dedicated to Venus. The cornflower was burned to drive away serpents.

In the Egyptian island scenes, the Field of Offerings is recreated with water, palm trees, animal offerings and four offering-pools. On the island, the 'Opening of the Mouth', to restore the physical powers of the deceased, and the purification rituals, are performed on the mummy of the deceased. An inscription accompanying one of these scenes states that the priests are:

> Performing the Opening of the Mouth for the Osiris, Neferhotep, justified. Your purity is the purity of Horus, ...of Seth... of Thoth... of Dunanui.[18]

In the island-scene in the tomb of Ipuia at Saqqara, the representation of the tomb occupies the same position relative to the island as does the tomb at the Osireion. (See Chapter 5). The deceased's statue is conveyed to an island in the centre of the lake, in a boat with lotus or papyrus prow and stern, called a *Neshmet* bark. Other boats, containing offerings and shrines, move towards the island. There is a gateway to the lakeside garden, and a landing-stage by the lake. On the banks are priests and mourners, stands, piled with offerings, and, a boy picking dates from a tall palm tree.

According to the Pyramid Texts, in the Field of Offerings there was an island: 'I have gone to the great island in the midst of the Field of Offerings on which the Swallow gods alight.' (Pyramid Text 1216)[19] The dead king also swam to an island, "Which is between the thighs of Nut" (Pyramid Text 1188). The journey of the statue on the lake may reflect these ancient memories, and also imitate the daily journey of the sun over the ocean of heaven. The waterlilies are reminders of the daily birth of the sun god, and offer the deceased hope of rebirth. The same connection with the sun is represented by the fishes, particularly the *Tilapia*, the red colour of which was likened to the sun.

The idea for this island was based in religious beliefs. It may have remained a mythical place, or been created on actual islands at Memphis and Thebes, for the performance of the ritual. By the late Eighteenth to Nineteenth Dynasties, there was an Island of Maat at Memphis to which a High Priest of Memphis expressed the wish to be taken: "Take me on the island of Maat, the cemetery of Memphis. I come in joy..."[20] Memphis itself was described as the 'divine island of ancient times'.[21] Plutarch says that the name of Memphis was interpreted as 'the tomb of Osiris'.[22] Whether real or imaginary, the lake in the garden was a place of rebirth and of refreshment in the afterlife.

The idea of island garden burial places and retreats continued in various forms up to modern times, including the island burial of Rousseau at Ermenonville.

Tombs painted with a Vine-Arbour

Some tombs have a vine painted across the ceiling of the burial chamber. In the tomb of Sennufer (TT 96), the vine rises beside a plan of his tomb, and covers the edges of the tomb ceiling. The rest of the ceiling is painted with a cloth, so that the tomb itself looks like a tent inside a vine-covered arbour. Picking the grapes in a vine arbour was something the dead person hoped to do in the afterlife, and it may have been a ritual symbolizing rebirth. A piece of ivory in Paris shows a small Amarna prince, perhaps Tutankhamun, picking grapes under a pergola of vines. In several tombs (e.g. Theban Tombs 158, 324), the deceased and his wife are fishing from a pool sheltered by a vine arbour, and men are picking grapes from their arbour. Fishing was a pleasure the deceased expected to enjoy in the next world: "I rise early in the morning (or I make love) and I fish".[23] Picking papyrus, marsh flowers, and waterlilies were other activities which occupied the dead, according to Spell 62 of the Coffin Texts.

Summary

The different types of gardens depicted were derived from different beliefs about the afterlife, which came into prominence at different times. They also show how the sun cult, and the cult of Osiris were used to assure the deceased that he would live forever. The garden with the tree-goddess was part of a scene in which the estate and its produce were the focus of attention. The tree goddess was part of the sky religion. The 'Butic' burial, and its pool amid the palm trees, and cultivation plots, was from an older tradition. The island in the midst of a lake had echoes, as a place of birth and renewal of life, of the island of Chemmis, where Isis gave birth to Horus, and so belonged to the Osirian cycle, but also incorporated elements from the Field of Offerings and the 'Butic Burial'. Herodotus, described a temple at Buto, on the Sebennytic arm of the Nile, where there was an island of Chemmis, which he said was floating, on which was a temple of Leto (Isis) surrounded by palm and fruit trees.

Physical and Documentary Evidence for Actual Tomb Gardens

While owners expected to live in the magical garden inside their tombs, and to enjoy all its produce, they also planted trees outside their tombs, and arranged for the gardens of their funerary chapels to be maintained.

The starting point for building a tomb was the beliefs about death and resurrection, which were the same for private, as for royal, tomb-owners. Everyone sought to imitate the Tomb of Osiris within the Mound, which appeared at the moment of Creation, and was protected by one, or several, trees. The deceased imitated Osiris, in the way the body was wrapped, and indeed with the title: 'The Osiris' followed by his or her name. The gods were involved in preparing a garden for the deceased. According to Spell 696, written on coffins of the Middle Kingdom, "Vegetation is planted in this garden by this Horus(?)." Often, the only plants, even highly placed officials could expect at the time of their funerals, were bouquets of papyrus decorated with flowers.

Private tombs had only some of the attributes of the tomb of Osiris. Most private tombs were built with a part above, and a part below, ground. The part above ground usually consisted of one or more open-air courts, which sometimes contained a garden. The part below ground was for the

The pool in Rekhmire's orchard. His statue is being towed across to a chapel. The trees round the edge are date and doum palm, and sycomore fig. The gardeners are watering the trees which are planted along a channel. (Pl. XIII)

Nebamun's house and the date palm in his garden. Above is the temple at which he probably officiated, with its two trees representing an avenue and a vineyard and pool. Theban Tomb 90. XVIIIth Dynasty. (Pl. XIV)

A model of a garden
found in the tomb of
Meket-re at Thebes.
XIth Dynasty. (Pl. XV)

Part of the garden painted in the tomb of Sennufer. Theban Tomb 96. (Pl. XVI)

A pool surrounded by trees and flowers in Nebamun's tomb. In the corner is the tree-goddess dispensing water and bread. (Pl. XVII)

The garden and chapel of Minnakht. Theban Tomb 87. (Pl. XVIII)

Gardeners at work. The tree on the left may be *Mimusops laurifolia*. Tomb of Ipuy. Theban Tomb 217. (Pl. XIX)

The temple of Queen Hatshepsut at Deir el-Bahari, Egypt. (Pl. XX)

burial, and the equipment left with the dead. In the Late Period there was a further development: a courtyard was built below ground level, but left open to the sky, so that plants could be grown in them.

Gardens around Private Tombs of the Old Kingdom

During the Old Kingdom, the kings were buried in pyramids, but the courtiers had a different type of tomb, called, in modern times, a mastaba, because it looked to early excavators like the bench, which the Egyptians call 'mastaba'. In early times, the outer face of the tomb was crenellated, like the wall of Zoser's burial complex.

A First Dynasty private tomb, which is remarkably like the ideal of the tomb of Osiris, was found at Helwan by Zaki Saad.[24] The tomb itself would have been covered with a mound of earth, and along each side was a row of trees.

At Saqqara, Ankh-ka, a high official of the First Dynasty, planted trees outside the enclosure wall of his tomb. Here, at a distance of about 1.25m. was a trench filled with earth, running parallel with the wall. It was 1.50m. wide and 0.70m. deep. At regular intervals of 1.60m. the excavators found the remains of small trees. Unfortunately the 'roots of the trees were too fragmentary for identification'.[25]

Outside tomb S 2185 also at Saqqara, dating from the reign of Djer, was an open area where there were holes, 'intended to hold lamp-stands or basins for offerings and the like'.[26] The excavator makes no mention of plant remains. But the holes could have been for trees.

Although the private tombs at Saqqara are very close together, there was an open space between two tombs where the excavators, Claus Bieger and Peter Munro, suggest there may have been a garden.[27] It is just outside the enclosure wall of Zoser's pyramid complex, and may date from his reign.

A priest at the pyramid of Teti (Sixth Dynasty), referring to his tomb at Saqqara, said "I have come from my town. I have gone down to my tomb. I acquired a piece of desert for my tomb."[28] He then states that he made a contract mentioning "every feast," which suggests that he appointed people to take care of his tomb. A similar statement is made by another owner who said he: "Made the desert plantation of my tomb".[29] This statement implies that he either made a garden outside his tomb, or that he arranged for an allotment nearby to provide offerings at his tomb.

Summary

In the crowded conditions at Saqqara and Giza there is little evidence for gardens around tombs during the Old Kingdom, apart from those which have been identified, although there were probably plantations nearby for providing the offerings at the tombs, and for supplying the people appointed to carry on the cult of the dead.

Gardens of Private Tombs from the End of the Old Kingdom to the End of the Middle Kingdom

The forecourt of a tomb-chapel is probably represented in two Eleventh Dynasty models from the tomb of Meket-Re at Thebes. The garden takes up about two thirds of the space, and consists of seven miniature sycomore-fig trees surrounding a pool. The excavator, Herbert Winlock, regarded these models as representing part of Meket-re's house. The pools may be intended as a place to put offerings, particularly a libation of water; though it is unlikely that any relatives could have come with the longed for water to such an inaccessible tomb, high above Deir el-Bahari.

At Asyut, the grand viceroy of Nubia in the time of Sesostris I, Hapzefa, contracted with priests to maintain the garden at his funerary chapel, where his statue would be kept. The contract was with the Overseer of the Cemetery-workmen and the Desert Guards. He agreed with them that they would accompany his statue:

> Which is in my garden, when it proceeds to the temple of Wepwawet on every festival of the beginning of a season which is celebrated in this temple.[30]

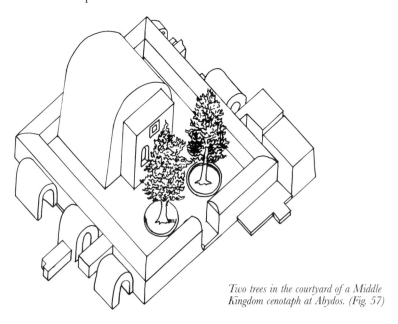

Two trees in the courtyard of a Middle Kingdom cenotaph at Abydos. (Fig. 57)

The statue represented Hapzefa, who, although he died in Nubia, and was buried at Kerma, had already arranged for his funerary rites to be carried on in Egypt, using the statue in the garden of his tomb-chapel.

At Abydos, some of the larger Middle Kingdom cenotaphs had trees, standing singly or in pairs, at the entrances.[31] These cenotaphs, which were like memorial chapels, rather than dummy tombs, faced onto a processional way which was used in the annual festival of Osiris.

A grove of four trees around a central tree was found by Eric Peet in front of a private tomb in the desert at Abydos.[32] Although the tomb dates from the Twelfth Dynasty, the planting of the trees is probably later, and to do with a re-use of the tomb.

Pottery Models of Gardens beside Buildings

Pottery models of open courtyards with a building or portico at the back, have pools and offerings of pieces of meat and bread laid out in them. These are cheap versions of the stone offering-tables found in tombs throughout Egyptian history. One of these pottery offering-trays has a palm tree in the courtyard.[33] Many of the others were found at Gizeh and Rifeh, but they do not have any garden features.

New Kingdom

The Setting of the Gardens of Private New Kingdom Tombs

The tombs of the courtiers and high officials at Thebes were on the slope of the western mountain. This mountain was believed to be inhabited by the goddesses, Hathor, Nut, and The Goddess of the West, who may all be aspects of the same benevolent being.

One of the most splendid private tombs, of which anything has survived, belonged to Amenophis III's architect, Amenhotep, son of Hapu. He was one of the few courtiers to be allowed a funerary temple alongside those of the kings. The arrangement of the forecourt of the temple is very like the models found in Meket-Re's tomb. The visitor to this temple would have entered through a pylon in the main enclosure wall, and arrived at a pool surrounded by trees. Twenty trees were growing in pits dug in the rock and filled with soil. The pits for the trees were 3m. to 4m. deep (double the height of an unusually tall man), and surrounded at the top with a square border of bricks. In them were pots filled with soil, in which the young plants had been raised. From this garden, three ramps, the central one of stone, and the two side ramps of brick, led to a portico in front of the second pylon before the temple proper. The excavators, Robichon and Varille, did not find any canal leading to this temple, although they looked for it. But the pool was deep enough to reach the ground water. The pool and garden took up about half the area devoted to the whole temple, and the site was terraced like the temples at Deir el-Bahari, and that of Tuthmosis IV.

Nineteenth Dynasty Tomb-Gardens at Thebes

In some Nineteenth Dynasty tombs in the cemetery at Deir el-Medineh, the village where the workmen who built the royal tombs in the Valley of the Kings lived, various instances of gardens have been found. Outside a few tombs (Theban Tombs 106, 216, 290) were the remains of a tree, or roots beside a basin for water. Outside another (Theban Tomb 1213) there were roots and plant-debris in large pots, on either side of the brick stairway leading into the sanctuary of the tomb chapel. But the excavator, Bernard Bruyère, was inclined to think that the vegetation was accidental. Other tombs at Deir el-Medineh have 'T'-shaped pools in their courtyards, which may indicate the presence of gardens. Basins, which were either receptacles for water, or planting-beds, have been found in the courtyards of several other tombs (e.g. Theban Tombs 3, 6, 10, 217, 218).

Trees growing in the garden of a tomb are shown in a painting in the Nineteenth Dynasty tomb of Huy at Thebes, beside his tomb with a pyramidal top (Theban Tomb 14). The mourners, and the 'Opening of the Mouth' scene indicate that the boat, visible at the side, is arriving at the tomb, but it is not clear if it is being carried, or is arriving by water, as the lower part of the picture has been destroyed.

The trees planted outside a tomb at Thebes, are illustrated on a stela showing a widow who has come, apparently alone, to perform rites for her deceased husband, Djedamunefankh. The tomb is in the desert. It has a

The mourning widow crouches outside the entrance to the tomb. Painted wooden stela of Djedamunefankh from Thebes. The Egyptian Museum, Cairo. XXIInd Dynasty. (Fig. 58)

gate in the form of a pylon, and steps up to the actual tomb building, which is crowned by a small pyramid. In front of it, apparently in the desert, and not within a courtyard, are two date palms and a sycomore-fig tree. Under the date trees is the offering table with a basin below it. There is a similar illustration of a tomb on the edge of the desert, which has a grove of palm trees and a sycomore in front of the tomb, and no enclosure visible. (Turin stela no.144)

Tomb Chapel Gardens at Amarna

Tomb-chapels, detached from the tomb, imitating the design of the royal funerary temples of Thebes, were built at Amarna. The reason for the separation of tomb and chapel may be that the rock in the cliff was too soft to make a tomb, or that the owners wished to have their tombs in a more concealed position. The tomb-chapels were built on the slopes of the broad open valley which runs down the promontory of low hills east of the main city.[34] The chapels consisted of two outer courts, steps up to a porch containing an offering table, and an enclosed room with niches round the wall. The outer courts were walled and had mud floors. In some, there were basins for water. The inner courts were up some steps, and had benches round, as if to provide seating for participants in rituals at the tomb. Some had gardens in the courtyard, and some had a 'T'-shaped pool, cut in the ground in front.[35] Cultivation plots, consisting of six rectangular compartments divided by low brick walls and a semicircular compartment, were found in the outer courtyard of tomb chapel 551. Some shafts were found a little higher up the slope behind the chapels.

Gardens in Private Tombs at Memphis

In the tomb of Paser at Saqqara, the cemetery for Memphis, pits, in which bushes or plants may have grown, were found in the courtyard. They were three shallow depressions scooped out of the chippings under the original floor in the north-east, south-east and south-west corners. There are possible traces of a fourth, containing small pottery fragments (for drainage?) in the north-west corner. No traces of roots were found.[36]

Gardens of Tombs of the Twentieth Dynasty to the Late Period

Memorial Chapels at Medinet Habu

At the back of Medinet Habu, the funerary temple of Ramesses III, outside the west gate, and aligned on it, were brick chapels (now no longer visible) built during the Twentieth Dynasty and reused in the Twenty-Second to Twenty-Fifth Dynasties for burials. In the Twentieth Dynasty, they were memorial chapels, and several had shrubs or flowers planted around a stela in front of them. Charred remains of wood were found in round holes filled with humus in their forecourts.[37]

Chapels in the forecourt at Medinet Habu, belonging to the Divine Wives of Amun, during the late period, had trees planted in their outer courts.[38] The Divine Wives held political as well as religious office, which developed from 'Divine Wife' being the title for the wife of the king, to their becoming the virtual ruler of Thebes.

Gardens on the Slopes of the Western Mountain

At Thebes, the western mountain continued in importance throughout the life of the city. Burials were made in this traditional place, and the idea of vegetation beside the tomb was still maintained. Coffins of the Twenty-First Dynasty are painted with scenes of tombs which are within the mountain and have trees standing outside.[39]

On the gently sloping ground between the temple of Hatshepsut and the river, the high officials of the Twenty-Sixth Dynasty and later, made their tombs. Some of these tombs have survived to a considerable height, and their courtyards are intact. In the open courtyards, the owners planted trees, and there is sometimes a cultivation plot for growing grain, which was part of the cult of Osiris.[40] Stones roughly put together and filled with Nile mud formed a bed for a tree in the forecourt of the tomb of Pabasa (Theban Tomb 279). Pabasa was Chief Steward of the God's Wife in the time of Psammetichos I (Twenty-Sixth Dynasty).

In a Thirtieth Dynasty tomb, that of Ankh-hor (Theban Tomb 414), trees were found outside and inside the entrance pylon. In the second of the courtyards, which is below ground level, and open to the sky, offerings were made by the living to the dead. In the centre of this court were offering tables and receptacles for plants, in which remains of a date palm tree and other plants were found. Other tombs of this period and before, have containers for growing plants in their courtyards.

The offering table and containers for water and plants still remaining in the open courtyard below ground in the tomb of Ankh-hor (Theban Tomb 414) at Thebes. XXXth Dynasty. (Fig. 59)

One owner, Ibi, begs visitors to water his plants:

> May the tree in the earth, dates on their stem as they grow, indeed the holy trees of the gods, be watered without lack in their place.[42]

Gardens buried with the Dead: The 'Corn Osiris'

The idea of Osiris as the restorer of plant life, and of the life of the deceased, was embodied in a so-called 'garden of Osiris', or 'corn Osiris'; which was a seed-bed in the form of the god Osiris, filled with grains, which was put in tombs. Germination of the seeds was thought to ensure that the deceased would flourish again, as the grain flourished. The dead person was regarded as: "This bush of life which went forth from Osiris to grow on the ribs of Osiris". (Coffin Texts, Spell 269) These Osiris figures have been found in several tombs, including that of Tutankhamun, who had a wooden frame filled with mud, in which the seeds had grown about three inches before they wilted. The mud figure was wrapped in linen, and the whole 'Osiris' was enclosed in a box. The ceremony of the 'Mysteries of Osiris in the month of Khoiak', in which the dead god was restored to life, is described in rooms on the roof of the temple of Hathor at Dendera.

Conclusion

The orchards and pools painted inside tombs were to encourage, by magical means, the perpetuation of life for the deceased into eternity. The

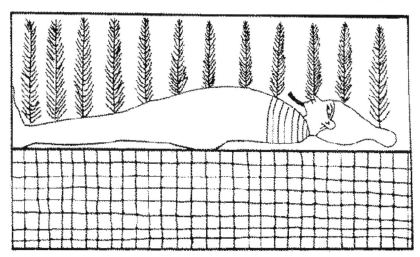

Corn growing from Osiris who is lying on a squared plot of ground. A painting on the coffin of Ankhrui found at Hawara. XXXth Dynasty. (Fig. 60)

tomb owners supervised the agricultural work at each season (the harvesting of different crops is shown to mark the seasons), and sat under their trees receiving the produce of their estates, and the magical gifts of food and drink from the goddess of the garden, and they drank from the pool, the water of which had a permanently life-giving quality. As Pentu says in his tomb at Amarna: "I drink water at the edge of my tank everyday without ceasing".[43] In these magical gardens, the main trees are the sycomore-fig, home of the sky goddess who provided food and drink, and the date palm, sacred to the sun god; the pool with waterlilies and fish were symbolic of perpetual drink and food being available. They are also emblems of rebirth. But the complete estate with its many agricultural activities, and the funerary banquet, were all part of the scene, and there is no division obvious between this life and the next.

The groves, imitating those round the tomb of Osiris, planted, in however minimal a way, at private tombs, show that the idea of imitating the burial of Osiris remained important, and was reinforced by the practice of placing germinating Osiris figures in the tombs. The essential features of the actual gardens outside the tombs, were date and sycomore trees and a basin of water. The tradition of planting gardens around one's tomb continued into the first century A.D. Strabo mentions the gardens and graves of the suburb called Necropolis, outside Alexandria, on the canal leading to Lake Mareotis, where there were many gardens and graves, and halting-places arranged for embalming the dead. The gardens at Alexandria were described by Hero (A.D. 100) who admired their devices for irrigation. The Roman Consul and *bon viveur*, Licinius Lucullus, may have derived inspiration from Alexandria, for his garden, which had aviaries, hare-warrens and fish-ponds.

VII   Gardens of Cult Temples

Introduction

The gardens of cult temples were for providing offerings. The kings repeatedly say that they have planted gardens in order to provide offerings for the gods, as Tuthmosis III records:

> My Majesty made for him a garden for the first time, planted with every pleasant tree in order to offer vegetables therefrom for divine offerings of every day.[1]

On special feast days, 'Live garden fragrance' was required in great quantity in the temples, and the gardens themselves were 'sweet in fragrance of all flowers'.[2]

The Egyptian temple represented heaven, the land of Egypt and the whole universe. Temples were earthly substitutes or representations of heaven. The keeper of the temple door was called the 'Door Opener of Heaven'.[3] On an obelisk, Hatshepsut described Karnak as 'The horizon on earth'. An inscription in the tomb of a priest asks his living colleagues to recite a blessing for him. He addresses them as : 'You who enter heaven (the temple) and behold those in it.'[4] Karnak was likened to: 'The heavens abiding on their four pillars'.[5] The different parts of the temple had heavenly counterparts. The pylon was the horizon. The shrine was as durable as 'the Pillars of Heaven'.[6] The lake was Nun, the primeval water.

The interior walls of temples are often decorated with relief carvings of a papyrus marsh. The symbolism of a growing organism pushing up out of the damp ground is continued in the columns, which are like the papyrus marsh, and like trees, with leaves and flowers in their capitals. The zone where men and gods interacted is depicted midway on the walls; above, is the sky, where the vulture and falcon deities fly amid the stars. The temple was also a replica of the world which the sun god passed over every day. The first court of the temple was the place where the whole land of Egypt, its produce and its gods, were celebrated.[7] Temples were also like offerings in stone to the gods. Columns were in the form of bouquets carefully constructed for presentation. Sometimes the stems are bound together with flowers inserted in the ties, as at the temple of Ptah, where the columns in front of the temple represent bouquets fixed in the ground. The plants most frequently mentioned as offerings are waterlily (lotus), and papyrus. The significance of the plants was both in their symbolism and in their perfume. The processional ways through the temple imitated routes through a lake flanked by tall papyrus clumps. The mode of transport of the statues of the gods was a boat, carried on the shoulders of priests. The papyrus columns in the central aisle led to the mound of creation at the heart of the temple. The papyrus marsh where Isis hid Horus is also evoked by this architecture. On either side were the shorter 'lotus bud' columns, which also supported the roofs of the lower chambers, deeper inside the temple.

But, the idea of the columns imitating a marsh of papyrus and waterlilies only occurred in the New Kingdom, and later. In earlier times the actual vegetation from which buildings were constructed was copied in stone: Zoser's pyramid complex is the most famous example. Later, columns were made in imitation of stems with a bud at the top, or were square or facetted, as in the chapel built by Hatshepsut and Tuthmosis III at Medinet Habu, or the funerary temples of Mentuhotep and Hatshepsut. In the Ptolemaic period and later, the symbolism of growing vegetation is more marked. The temple of Dendera has waterlily flowers carved round the outside which makes it look as if the temple was floating on Nun, the primeval ocean. In the Luxor temple, the courts built by Amenophis III all have 'lotus bud' columns. The processional way built by Tutankhamun has papyrus capitals, and these columns are taller than those in the court of Amenophis III, emphasizing the actual relationship between waterlilies and papyrus.

Temples were the dwelling places of the gods. The Egyptians referred to them as 'House of God', or a 'Monument for his (the god's) image'.[8] Every temple had an orchard, and a pool, in which the god could refresh himself. The early religious documents speak of the sun-god bathing in a pool, before he set off on his daily journey across the sky (Pyramid Text 253). Outside the temple, the 'sacred landscape' included a lake in which waterlily and papyrus grew, surrounded by palm trees. Gardens were part of the symbolism of growth, and the annual cycle from inundation to harvest. They were also living representations of creation, demonstrating how vegetation sprang from a mound of earth, beside the original pool of water. The gardens were also inhabited by the gods. Heaven itself was a garden with its entrance on the east flanked by two sycomore-trees of turquoise.

The layout of the gardens of cult temples was different from the form of the gardens of funerary temples. The landscape which was created was that of a royal house or estate. It did not represent a mythological place, such as the mound of creation, or the tomb of Osiris. The only special, religiously inspired, planting was that of lettuces for the cult of Amun-Min. Trees such as the palms and sycomores maintained the religious connotations. The separate areas of the gardens were avenues, vineyards, orchards, pools and plantations of vegetables.

Excavated Temple Gardens

Gardens were an integral part of temples. Since the temple was the house of the god, the arrangements were similar to those of a house. Gardens were laid out on the approaches and between the various temples, and inside the courts of individual buildings. Avenues led to the entrances of the temple. Inside the main gateway, there was an open space which often contained trees and flowers. Between the buildings were larger gardens, consisting of a vineyard and pools surrounded by papyrus, mandrake, poppy, cornflowers and crown daisies. In the pools grew waterlilies and papyrus, as well as various reeds and pondweeds. There were gardens inside courtyards, just as there were in the inner courtyards of palaces. Gardens were also created at points along the processional way between temples.

Often the only part of the garden to have been excavated is the avenue leading up to a temple. The practice of planting trees at the entrance to temples goes back to the most ancient sanctuaries, such as early Dynastic and Old Kingdom representations of the temple of Neith.

Gardens in Temples of the Middle Kingdom
At Medamud, a wall surrounded a sacred grove on a mound. The existence of the grove was indicated by the layer of ashes which was spread across the enclosure, and at intervals, a great tree trunk, which had burnt so fiercely that the roots had disappeared, because their remains had decomposed quickly in the damp ground. Under the two mounds were small shrines reached by twisting underground passages. In the corner of the temple there was a single tree, which illustrates the concept of a sacred tree in a particular place.

At Hermopolis, inside the first courtyard of the temple built by Amenemhat II, tree-pits were found. The holes were somewhat haphazardly arranged.

The Gardens of New Kingdom Temples
At Tell Dabaa, the post-holes for a pergola, and pits for the vines of a large vineyard have been excavated, outside the Eighteenth Dynasty

temple of Sutekh. The temple was surrounded by rows of trees inside the temenos wall, and outside it, for a distance of 65m. The size and depth of the pits suggests that the trees were palms. The arcading for vines was laid out in regular lines. In the Eighteenth Dynasty, gardens were created on the low islands in the river formerly used for houses. Tell Dabaa was the site of Avaris, near to Pi-Ramesse, where Ramesses III created gardens for the temple of Amun. An avenue leading up to the temple door, 'Brightened with the flowers of every land, *isi* plants, papyrus and mandrake flowers like sand'; and also date groves.[10] At the vineyard called Kanekame in the town of Ramesse, the vines were supported on olive trees.

At Soleb in Nubia, there was an avenue of trees which was later replaced by a meadow where sheep were kept. Then, the sheep were put into stalls, and finally they were replaced by ram-headed sphinxes of granite. Trees surrounded a pool in front of the temple:

> In front of the enclosure was a quay supporting a small building and giving on to a pool of water with curving banks, like the representations of the Buto lake. The quay and the pool were bordered with trees.[11]

The Gardens of Temples dating from the Late Period to Roman Times

At Tanis, in the Late Period, there was a sacred tree inside a brick enclosure, but not within a temple area.

Excavation at Hermopolis has revealed beside a well, a small grove of palm trees, where there was a mudbrick building near a ramp and stairway, which may have been where the sacred ibises were kept.

At the temple of Khnum at Elephantine, in the time of Nectanebo II, date trees were planted in pits inside the first court of the temple.

Taharqa (Twenty-Fifth Dynasty) said that he had given 'Numerous trees or shrubs' to the temple of Amun at Kawa near Dongola in Nubia, and listed the kinds: 'Incense trees, acacia, cedar, *shwab* (*Mimusops laurifolia*), and seeds of cypress.'[12] Pits for trees, some of which contained the roots of *Mimusops* and *Butyrospermum Parkii* (Shea butter tree), were found around the outside of the temple, as well as being "planted in a line with the south wall of the building" on the east side of Temple B.[13] There was also a sunken bed surrounded by a brick ledge with a stone drain in front of the pylon. The rest of the gardens had been roughly paved with sandstone chips, though traces of leaves and brushwood along the north and south edges may indicate that trees had been planted there.

The Use and Purpose of the Gardens

Cult temples were a dwelling for a god, or several deities, where the rites for their daily sustenance were carried out, and particular events in their myths were celebrated at regular intervals. In the gardens the offerings were grown for those services. The gardens were like Fields of Offerings situated in the temple enclosures. Ramesses III equipped the temple of Re, north of Heliopolis: 'With people and property in order to convey into thy house, gardens containing flowers for thy forecourt'.[14] He also described how temple gardens were used, 'for walking about'.

The plants which were cultivated in the temple gardens were needed both in the ceremonies in the temples, and for bouquets presented as ceremonial gifts to officials, and to the gods. The special lettuces needed as offerings to the god Amun were grown in the temple area. Incense trees were particularly important for providing the resin which was burnt during temple rituals. Many of the pharaohs boasted of bringing incense trees from afar as gifts to be grown in the temple gardens. Some trees are shown in Old Kingdom reliefs, and offerings lists speak of *anty* and *sentjer*. One of the most famous expeditions to bring living trees, as well as the dry resin, was made by Queen Hatshepsut, whose ships landed in Punt, and loaded up with trees, their roots protected by balls of earth cradled in baskets. Her successor, Tuthmosis III, also brought back incense trees from 'God's Land'. This expression was a way of referring to a foreign place which belonged, according to one interpretation of Egyptian beliefs, to the Egyptian god, Amun. Many Egyptian kings brought back incense trees from Punt, even into the Ptolemaic period, when such an expedition is recorded at the temple at Athribis near Sohag, which was excavated by Petrie. Olive trees provided the oil used to 'light the flame' in the god's house. Libations of wine, both from vines, and possibly pomegrantes, were poured out during the rituals. Sweet smelling flowers such as waterlily, *isi*, mandrake and myrrh were ordered by Ramesses III to be planted at Heliopolis.

The large temple staffs were fed and clothed from estates belonging to the temple, and probably not from the temple gardens themselves.

Ceremonies in Temple Gardens

Carvings on temple walls, and other written documents, record the ceremonies which took place in gardens. In cult temples, the god was presented with floral offerings, usually consisting of waterlilies, or papyrus, or both. The earliest known instance of this ceremony, is found in the reign of Mentuhotep (Eleventh Dynasty).[15] The kings presented bouquets to the gods, particularly at the great festivals. And also, every time a god's bark went out of its shrine, it had to be decorated with flowers. Bouquets were made in a special florists' workshop, one of which is illustrated on blocks from the temple of Akhenaten, now on display in the museum in Luxor.

The temple-priests were agents for the gods in giving presents of bouquets of flowers to the king and to courtiers. Neferhotep, who was Chief Scribe of Amun, showed himself in his tomb (Theban Tomb 49) receiving a bouquet in the porch at the entrance to the temple of Amun at Karnak, and bringing it out into the garden between the pylon of the temple and the river, to show, or give, to his wife, who was waiting there. The kings received bouquets from the gods, who, in return granted them long life and nourishment, power and victory over foreigners. Bouquets

Neferhotep receiving a 'Bouquet of Amun' from a priest in the porch of the temple of Amun at Karnak. Tomb of Neferhotep. Theban Tomb 49. Late XVIIIth Dynasty. (Fig. 61)

could be interpreted as a visual pun for the hierglyphic sign for life, *ankh*; in fact, 'life' *ankh*, is the word used for garlands. Other ceremonies consisted in picking fruits and flowers, in order to present them as offerings. At Abydos, a vase of wine was offered, in order that the gardens should prosper. The gardens in question were the vineyards.

Ceremonies on the Temple Lake

The lake was the central feature of a garden in the temple, and was surrounded by flowers and trees. These gardens became the place for certain ceremonies. One of which took place when the priests were about to enter the temple, and purified themselves, either in the temple lake, or in a shallow trough using water from the temple lake. Other ceremonies included rowing the deity on the temple lake, greeting the infant sun god, and hunting the hippopotamus.

Greeting the Infant Sun God

In two legends a divine infant was born: one was the sun god, who was born as a lotus (waterlily) flower, or, was daily reborn out of a waterlily as a child; the other was Horus, son of Isis and Osiris, who was born in the papyrus marsh of Chemmis in the Delta.

An aquatic ritual is illustrated on faience and metal bowls, and on chalices and decorative spoons.

The infant sun-god born out of a waterlily. A gold pendant in the Museum of Fine Arts, Boston. New Kingdom. (Fig. 62)

*A girl picking water-lilies. A
spoon for holding incense. The
bowl of the spoon is in the form
of the fruit of Mimusops laurifolia. XVIIIth Dynasty. Louvre,
Paris. (Fig. 63)*

In the scenes on the bowls and chalices, girls who swim, and men
(who do not), seize ducks and calves, and collect waterlilies and papyrus,
and carry them through the swamp, either in their arms or in canoes. The
presentation of the offerings is represented in decorated spoons, in which a
bouquet or animal is held out as an offering, or forms the spoon itself.
These spoons were for holding the incense before it was burnt in the
temple ceremonies. The deity appears on the bowls as a child on a lotus,
sometimes also with his mother, Hathor, as a cow or a woman. The child
was born out of the primeval water, Nun, represented inside these bowls as
a lake. These bowls and chalices were illustrated both as receptacles for
libations in temples, and as the receptacles of offerings in front of the dead,
as well as being the vessels from which the dead drank water in the afterlife.
One such vessel was the white lotus cup in the tomb of Tutankhamun (the
blue waterlily cup of alabaster was used as a light). Some of the spoons
were New Year gifts, as were the flasks with New Year inscriptions
decorated with scenes of a cow amid papyrus, and the head of the goddess

Girls swimming and catching ducks. A gold and silver bowl belonging to Undebaunded. Found at Tanis. XXIst Dynasty. The Egyptian Museum, Cairo. (Fig. 64)

Hathor. These scenes may also be to do with the rebirth of the deceased, and some of the bowls have inscriptions which indicate that they are funerary, like the bowl inscribed for the 'ka' of the deceased king, Sheshonq.[16]

Music was evidently part of this festival, since many of the girls on the spoon handles and painted on the inside of faience bowls, and on sculpted blocks, play musical instruments such as harp and lute. The festival which is represented, if it is not part of the New Year ceremonies, may be a version of the offerings to Horus depicted in the temple at Esna, or a festival of Hathor, since this goddess as woman and cow, is represented on many of the bowls.

Rowing the Deity on the Lake

At Karnak, the leonine goddess, Mut, was rowed on her horseshoe-shaped *isheru*-lake, at an annual festival aimed at appeasing her, because she was thought to have entered Egypt in an angry mood. The scene in the tomb of Tjauenany (Theban Tomb 134), the 'Prophet of Amenophis who navigates the Sea of Amun', could be of just such a 'navigation' which ends at a temple with trees in the forecourt (if it is not an illustration of a tomb - see Chapter VI).

At Dendera, the Festival of Rowing Hathor, who also had a leonine aspect, had the same purpose of pacifying the angry goddess after her adventures in the desert. The ritual included processions to the kiosk which was beside the temple lake.

Kings were also rowed on their lakes. The story of king Seneferu and the beautiful maiden, who lost her earring whilst rowing him on his lake, may be about a ceremonial aquatic outing. It is certainly connected with sun worship, and the fish-pendant that the girl is assumed to have lost, is a symbol of the sun-god. The passage of the king across the lake imitated the passage of the sun across the sky. Tuthmosis III arranged for a statue of himself to be made for rowing on the temple lake at Karnak, 'in procession...... for the water procession on the lake'.[17] At the Festival of Osiris in the Month of Khoiak, there was a procession around the lake at Karnak.

Hunting the Hippopotamus

Seth, the enemy of the sun, was sometimes portrayed as a hippopotamus, which Horus had to kill with a harpoon. The ritual was played out at Edfu temple, but it is not certain that it was on the temple lake.

Summary

Rituals were performed on the lakes of both funerary and cult temples. The best known of those performed on the lakes of cult temples, the temples of the 'living' as opposed to the 'dead' gods were: Rowing the Deity on the Lake, Rituals for the Birth of the deity, and Rituals for Hathor. These lakes would have been surrounded with trees and filled with papyrus and waterlilies.

The Birth of the Deity in the Mammisi of Temples

Both goddesses and mortals preferred to have their children in the quiet and shade of their gardens. Leafy bowers, made of papyrus entwined with convolvulus, which sheltered humans, were sketched on pieces of stone and faience. The birthing bower was called 'Beautiful Tent', and 'House of Protection'.[18] Goddesses had bowers made of stone beside their temples, with papyrus columns representing the papyrus marsh, where the infant Horus was born. These bowers have the modern name, mammisi. The birth of the god of a temple, or of the reigning king, was celebrated annually in the place, "Where appears the lord of the gods, the king of

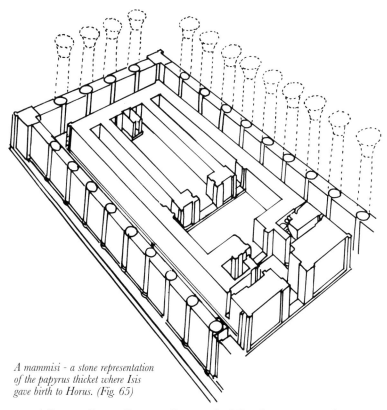

A mammisi - a stone representation
of the papyrus thicket where Isis
gave birth to Horus. (Fig. 65)

Upper and Lower Egypt," according to Seti I, who gave sandstone to
build: "The beautiful birth-house of the ennead," at the southern temple
at Wadi Halfa.[19]

The garden element is contained in the architecture, rather than in
any gardens discovered near birth houses. There may have been gardens
inside the mammisi. Evidence for gardens around birth houses in the Old
Kingdom, comes from documents which state that their forerunners, the
shrines of the goddess Meret, were in the garden of a temple (or a
palace).[20] Beside the temple of Hathor at Dendera, in the mammisi built
by Nectanebo there is a well in the forecourt, which could have provided
water for a garden. There was a lake, and presumably also a garden, beside
the mammisi at Armant, where the birth of Anthony's son, Caesarion, as
a winged scarab, is illustrated.

The architecture of the mammisi imitated the papyrus swamp where
Horus was born. An inscription on the outside of the mammisi at Edfu
states: 'This is the place where the infant has been born by his mother as
did Isis for her son in the hiding place'.[21] The idea of giving birth in a
garden also occurs in Greek mythology. Apollo was born to Leto in a
flowery place, while she held on to a palm tree.

Raising Animals for Offerings

Animals and birds were reared in the temple grounds, to provide offerings in the temples. During the Old Kingdom, birds were raised at the sun temple of Niuserre. Fowl-yards existed in the temple of Amun at Karnak during the reigns of Tuthmosis III, Akhenaten, and Seti II, who said they were, 'filled with geese, cranes, ducks, doves and [other kinds of fowl] to provide the divine offerings for his father Amun.'[22] A craftsman at the royal tombs dedicated representations of geese with the words: 'May the geese of Amun live forever'.[23] Pigs, to feed the temple staff - they were not used for divine offerings - were reared at Memphis in the time of Amenophis III.

In the Late Period, and in Ptolemaic and Roman times, at various cult temples, animals sacred to the deity of the temples were reared. These creatures would have occupied palm groves where they would have been sheltered from the sun, and would not have been able to do any damage to the trees.

Gardens growing Offerings at Karnak

The gardens of temples belonging to the living gods grew the offerings needed for the daily rituals. The temple of Amun at Karnak, enclosed many gardens, and was also surrounded by them. Avenues leading up to the temple have been excavated, and arrangements for planting and watering have been found.

Several gardens are illustrated on the walls of the tombs of the officials responsible for the temple gardens. In the time of Hatshepsut, Ineni (Theban Tomb 81) may have been been in charge of the garden inside the Karnak temple, since he had responsibility for the production of grain and offerings for the temple, but the garden illustrated in his tomb may also be his own garden. (Fig. 48) The Overseer of Fields and Gardens in Hatshepsut's reign was Senenmut, her chief architect, Amenophis II's chief gardener was Sennufer, who illustrated on the wall of his tomb (Theban Tomb 96), a garden which was probably on the north-western side of the temple. One of Sennufer's titles was "Overseer of the Gardens of Amun". His duties were to bring flowers and to present:

The 'scent of the marshes', flowers, and ... all kinds of plants from among the finest of the orchard which his Majesty has made anew for his Father Amun Re, ...on behalf of his Majesty.[24]

The painting on the wall of Sennufer's tomb, probably represents one of the gardens of the temple at the time of Amenophis II (1426-1400 B.C.), rather than his own garden. It was completely walled and hidden from view. The approach was by boat to a landing place in front of a gateway. Each part inside was walled, and had its own door. The vineyard was the heart of the garden. It was spread over a large area and surrounded by trees. The rows of vines made shady tunnels. This arrangement is the same as is shown in the garden of the queen's palace at Karnak, illustrated in the tomb of Neferhotep (Theban Tomb 49). Some of the villagers in Dakhlah oasis preserve this ancient pattern in their gardens. There were four fishponds, each in its own enclosure. Two had little kiosks at one end. All round were fruit trees: date palm and sycomore-figs, which shaded the water, and each other. Everything in this garden was for the offerings in the temple. The fruit was sweet and nourishing; the fish and ducks provided meat. Papyrus was pulled up and laid on the altars - as can be seen in the shrine of Amun at the end of the garden; it was also used for writing the religious texts needed to conduct the rituals. Wine was made from the grapes, which could also be eaten fresh or dried. Sennufer is shown in the scene next to the garden holding two geese as offerings, and the offering inscription belongs with this part of the scene. The building at one end of the orchard was a shrine for the god Amun, divided into three, containing statues of Amun, with offerings in front of him.

This garden is a forerunner in plan of the Persian *chahar bagh*, four orchards, with the four-fold division of the garden areas. But as far as can be seen from the copies of the painting, it was not a piece of ground divided by water channels, as was the case in later Near Eastern gardens. A canal, or the river, is shown flowing past the walls. The water may have been the waterway mentioned on doorposts found under the Second Pylon of the Karnak temple, the river, a canal, or even the temple lake. In the centre of one side there is a stone gateway inscribed with the name of Amenophis II. The doorposts, which may even be the doorposts for Sennufer's garden, or one nearby, state that the garden of which they were the entrance, grew marsh plants, waterlily flowers, fresh plants, waterlily plants, *hen*-plants and waterlily buds:

> The King of Upper and Lower Egypt (Amenophis II) has made as his monument for his father Amun-Re, the making for him of a cool and holy place (named) "Libation of Amun," of sandstone, the gateway of granite, the door leaves of copper. It is His Majesty who sanctifies this pool, adorned with reeds, and planted with sedges, lotuses, herbs, rushes, and lotus buds, that he might make all "given life" like Re forever.[25]

If Sennufer's garden was west of the Third Pylon at Karnak, beside the approach to the temple from the west, it is possible that a garden stood on the same spot for most of the New Kingdom, being illustrated again, although in a different way, in the tomb of Neferhotep (Theban Tomb 49) in the reign of the pharaoh, Ay, successor to Tutankhamun.

Trees in the temple garden at Karnak represented in the tomb of Neferhotep. Theban Tomb 49. A gardener is drawing water from a pool by means of a shaduf. The second tree from the right has a bag over a bunch of dates. Late XVIIIth Dynasty. (Fig. 66)

There was another garden on the western side of the temple of Karnak, opposite where Sennufer's garden may have been. It was around

The garden of the Queen's palace at Karnak where the wife of Neferhotep is receiving jewellery from the queen. An illustration in the tomb of Neferhotep. Theban Tomb 49. Reign of king Ay, late XVIIIth Dynasty. (Fig. 67)

the palace, where Neferhotep's wife received a reward in gold from Ay's queen. This palace and garden may have been on the same spot as Hatshepsut's palace, which probably stood north of the main entrance to the temple. It was near the quay in front of the temple as it existed in her time.

The queen's palace garden in the time of Neferhotep (Fig. 67) had a pylonic gateway, leading into an orchard of pomegranates, beyond which was a vine pergola shaded by sycomore-fig trees. The palace building was surrounded by trees.

Beside this 'harim' part of the palace, was the king's 'Window of Appearances', from which the king, Ay, dispensed gold to Neferhotep. The queen is shown beside him, which indicates that the two honourings were not simultaneous. There are two trees in the open courtyard where Neferhotep stands to receive the gold. The avenue which leads from the king's Window of Appearances, past the queen's Window of Appearances, apparently, ultimately led to Neferhotep's house. The relationship between the two royal palace gardens and the approach to the temple, is not clear. The scenes with the two presentations to Neferhotep and to his wife, and the ride home along an avenue, are shown together on one wall. The scene of presenting the bouquet, the forecourt of the temple and the quay, and the garden connected with the temple store-house, are illustrated together, in a different part of the tomb.

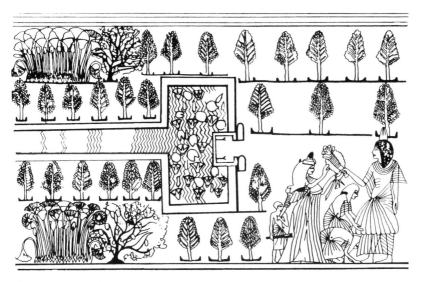

The avenue in front of the western entrance to the temple of Amun at Karnak. A pool filled with waterlilies surrounds the landing-quay. In the foreground, Neferhotep presents the 'Bouquet of Amun' he has just received (Fig. 61) to his wife. Tomb of Neferhotep. Theban tomb 49. Late XVIIIth Dynasty. (Fig. 68)

The avenue, illustrated in the tomb of Neferhotep, which led from the quay, at the head of the 'T'-shaped canal, to the western entrance to the temple, covered a distance of 800m. Beneath the trees, grew vines and papyrus. The name for the long avenue between the quay and the temple may have been the 'Way of Offerings'.[26] A succession of quays was built in front of the temple, as more buildings were added on the western side. If we take the painting in the tomb of Neferhotep literally, there was another orchard south of the 'T'-shaped pool, and west of the temple storehouse.

The orchard contained date palms and sycamore figs, which are being watered by gardeners using shadufs. A myrtle bush grows beside a pool from which a man is drawing water. There are two thorn-fenced enclosures. Men carry bulging sacks of produce on their shoulders to the temple store-house. The 'T'-shaped canal runs into two other canals, beside which men cut papyrus, ferry cattle, and fight.

An avenue leading to Karnak was described as: 'The glory of the cedar, beloved of Thebes, upon the way of the ram-headed sphinxes'.[27] It may have been the one on the west of the temple, leading from the Second Pylon to the quay, or it could have been on the southern side, between Karnak and the temple of Mut, before the human headed or lion-headed sphinxes were put in position. Or, indeed, it may have been the avenue in front of the temple of Khonsu. An avenue of sphinxes with flower beds in front of them, led to the temple of Khonsu in the time of Amenophis III,[28] and was remade in Ptolemaic and Roman times.

The ram-headed sphinxes, dating from the time of Ramesses II, with the present-day flower beds in front of them, on the western approach to the temple of Karnak. (Fig. 69)

At the western entrance to Karnak, in Ptolemaic times, a line of trees stood behind the line of sphinxes. Flowers were planted in front of the sphinxes in semi-circular basins, which were filled from a network of channels supplied by wells.

If Sennufer's painted garden was not on the west of the temple, on the approach between the temple and the river, it may have been on the south, where Amenophis II built a shrine.

At the southern entrance, an avenue led to the temple of Mut. This processional avenue was enclosed within a wall in the time of Nectanebo, and probably also earlier. Round brick basins for planting trees and channels to supply water were found where Nectanebo said he had, "Built a beautiful road for his father Amun, bordered by walls, planted with trees and decorated with flowers,"[29] between the Karnak and Luxor temples. This work was done on the occasion of the Feast of Opet. The route was flanked with lion-sphinxes. A quay, which was connected by a canal to the river, has been revealed on the processional way from Karnak to Luxor.[30]

Along the processional way between the two temples, in the time of Hatshepsut, were shrines or way-stations for the sacred barque. Three of them were surrounded by groves of trees. Lettuces sacred to Amun-Min grew in square plots beside, or in, these shrines.

These way-stations were illustrated on the walls of a shrine which itself stood in a garden, and whose inside walls were decorated with lettuce beds. Produce was said to come from a garden at Karnak which provided: 'All fresh and pure vegetables' for Amun. This garden is represented on Hatshepsut's shrine.[31]

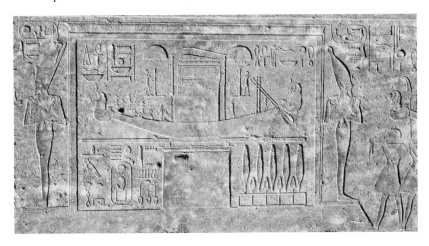

One of the way-stations on the route between the Karnak and Luxor temples, depicted on a block from a shrine set up by Queen Hatshepsut. The lettuces sacred to Amun-Min are shown in square plots on the right side. XVIIIth Dynasty. (Fig. 70)

More lettuces were grown in what looks like a field, since it is not walled. The Overseer of this garden was called Nakht (Theban Tomb 161).[32] He was also 'Carrier of the Bouquets of Offerings of Amun', and 'Gardener of the Offerings of Amun'. At one side of the field is a pool, filled with fish and waterlilies, and surrounded by clumps of papyrus growing in troughs. Beside the pool are latticed pergolas for vines, their bunches of grapes all ripe. It may be that the vine covered the pool. The three plots are divided into squares. In the first pair of plots, men with pots on yokes are watering. The identity of the crop is not indicated. Nakht is standing beside the fields, in a papyrus clump, watching the work proceeding.

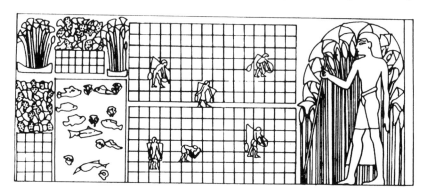

A garden, probably within the temple precinct at Karnak, in which the lettuces for the offering to Amun-Min were produced. The tomb-owner, Nakht, is standing watching the work, backed by a thicket of papyrus. A painting in the tomb of Nakht, Tomb 161. XVIIIth Dynasty. (Fig. 71)

Behind him are two men picking sycomore-figs from two trees. An orchard, or an avenue of sycomore-figs, may be indicated. Lettuces are growing in the upper of the central two plots. In the corner of this field there is a small house. This may be a gardener or guard's shelter, rather than Nakht's own house, but it does have an upper storey with windows. In the lower field, flax is growing; the blue flowers are indicated in Robert Hay's watercolour. The next pair of fields is flanked by two date palms, under which Nakht is seated, on one side, and standing on the other. In the top field, flax is growing, identified in Hay's painting by little red dots for the seed pods. In the lower field are lettuces. Another small house, this time with someone like a porter, sitting on a low stool, outside the door, who gives the impression that this is indeed Nakht's house, since he himself is sitting on a chair under the date tree, outside it. The funerary banquet is going on all round this scene, although the crops being cultivated are not provisions for the meal. These crops are clearly for supplying the temple with lettuces for Amun-Min and flax for the clothing for the statues and the priests and linseed oil.

Indoor Gardens inside Karnak

A garden was illustrated in the Sun Rooms in the Festival Temple of Tuthmosis III, in a very secret place. The entire suite of rooms could only be entered from a podium at the rear of the sanctuary of the Festival Hall, through an opening like a window. The 'garden' was an offering area, shaped like an offering table in the form of a 'T'. In the long part of the 'T' there was a stone shrine containing a statue of Amun. At the top of the 'T' there was a portico, supported by lotus-bud columns. Between the columns were sphinxes inscribed "Amun, Lord of Heaven, who resides in Akh-menu",[33] facing towards the sanctuary. Around the walls were niches which may have contained statues of deities. An enclosed corridor running from the portico to the north-west corner of the Festival Hall surrounded the 'T'-shaped area.

The walls of the 'T'-shaped area were decorated with the plants, animals and birds Tuthmosis III said he had brought back from his expeditions in Palestine and Syria: 'Plants which His Majesty found in the Land of Retenu. All plants that grow, all flowers that are in God's Land...' They were 'wonders' from a foreign land.

This part of the temple symbolizes the place of rebirth. Here life was given to the statues and to the king himself through the offering of a large bouquet.[34] The king had passed through the Sokar rooms, the part of the temple representing death, with scenes of the 'Voyage to Abydos', the Festival in the Valley and the Butic burial, into the realms of rejuvenation

Ruins of the shrine inside the Festival Hall of Tuthmosis III at Karnak, on the walls of which plants from Syria, the so-called 'Botanic Garden', are carved. The steps behind the lotus-bud columns lead into the central shrine of the Festival Hall. XVIIIth Dynasty. (Fig. 72)

and regeneration. This duality represented in temples, where the living Horus and the dead Horus are contrasted, emphasizes the perpetual cycle of death and regeneration. The purpose of the Festival Hall was to be a memorial to Amun-Re, described as the 'father' of Tuthmosis III, to perpetuate the names of his ancestors, and to ensure the service of offerings. In the room beside the 'Botanical Garden', the king was described as "Beloved of Amun who presides over his harems"; another reference to regeneration. The festivals celebrated in the Festival Hall were for the perpetual reconfirmation and regeneration of the king at his Jubilee, which took place at the New Year, at the beginning of the inundation. If the 'Botanical Garden' was open to the sky (although it seems to have been roofed), it is possible that some plants were grown in the space in front of the portico (in the long part of the 'T'). This garden, whether actual, or only in illustration, may be a forerunner of the sunken gardens at Amarna.

Not all the identifications of the plants and fruits on the walls of the 'T'-shaped room are certain, because the colour has disappeared, and it is not possible to tell what the sizes were in relation to each other; but those which can be recognized are: date and doum palm, sycomore-fig, common fig, pomegranate, vine, waterlily, iris, melon, and lettuce. There are also illustrations which may represent arum, crown daisy, teasel and bindweed. Others which may be illustrated, but of which only outlines remain, with no colour and no indication of relative size, are: myrtle, *Amygdalus* species, *Asphodelus* species, *Astragalus sanctus*, *Bellis sylvestris*, *Biarum angustatum*, *Capparis* species, *Balanites aegyptiaca*, *Cordia ovalis*, *Euphorbia abyssinica*, *Luffa aegyptiaca*, *Citrullus lanatus*, and *Mimusops laurifolia*.

Some of the plants carved on the wall of the 'Botanic Garden' within the Festival Hall of Tuthmosis III. The central plant may be teasel family (Dipsacus species), those on either side have not been identified. XVIIIth Dynasty. (Fig. 73)

138

The inscriptions say that the plants were from 'God's Land', which could mean all foreign regions, but in this case, Tuthmosis specifically identifies the land of Retenu, Syria, as the source, and states that they were for offerings to Amun. The first six fruits mentioned above (date, doum, etc.) were frequent, if not obligatory, offerings, and not un-Egyptian, although all (except doum) grew in Syrian regions also. There is no other ancient Egyptian illustration of an iris, unless the plants used for making perfume, which are usually described as lilies, are irises. Irises produce perfume which was an important element in offerings. They were found in a wreath from Hawara dating from the Ptolemaic to Roman periods. Plants which seem to be foreign, and not illustrated elsewhere in ancient Egypt, are the arum and calanchoe. The arum is a Mediterranean plant, but the calanchoe also grows in Yemen and Abyssinia. The plants could thus represent offerings from the North and the South. Some of the animals and plants seem to be 'monsters', anomalies of nature, and not either natural or heraldic. The 'monstrous' plants are said to be those which occur in threes. However fruits in threes are illustrated on the sycomore trees around the pool in the painting in the tomb of Nebamun (painting in the British Museum), and may simply represent abundance. The style also has echoes of the very much earlier Sumerian depiction of pomegranates and barley on a vase found at Uruk. Although plants, birds and animals are illustrated, each kind is kept more or less together with a few of the plants interspersed between the creatures.

Tuthmosis III had already expressed his enthusiasm for the gardens of Djahi (in Syria) after his fifth northern campaign. He wanted to show that these plants were special plants which grew in a remarkable way; "wonders" with many fruits and flowers on a stem. The Egyptians delighted in exotic produce, and proudly displayed animals, skins, tusks, and even human pygmies. Their enthusiasm was not simply collectors' mania, but a way of showing that Egypt's god and king had power over the world. If this is indeed a 'Botanical Garden', a collection of specimens of foreign and domestic plants, it would be the first known. Followers in this tradition were Aristotle, whose garden-curator was Theophrastus, several Renaissance scholar-princes, and even Montezuma.

The style of the presentation of the plants has also been regarded as unusual; being shown as 'specimens', on display, lined up side by side, as if laid out as offerings, and not as background for some activity. However other plants are illustrated in this manner at this period, for example, in the tomb of Amenemhab Mahu (Theban Tomb 85) where the owner is seen encountering a hyena. The lack of connection with the ground may be explained by the loss of the paint which would have finished off the composition. This was not the only garden Tuthmosis III made at Karnak.

My Majesty made for him (Amun) a garden anew, in order to present to him vegetables and all beautiful flowers.[35]

The whereabouts of this garden is not known. His biography carved on the walls of Karnak lists his gifts to Amun, and records that he made another garden for Amun, possibly for the festival of the "Going forth of Min":

For the first time, planted with every pleasant tree, in order to offer vegetables therefrom for divine offerings of every day which my Majesty ... as increase of that which was formerly... with maidens (beauties) of the whole land.[36]

On a statue, Tuthmosis III described himself as 'Menkheperre who offers fresh plants to Amun', and on a wall of a passage, as the one who is 'great in offerings'.[37] Tuthmosis III made arrangements for his commemorative rites, and instructed his priests to offer him "all fruit", and repeats that he has "consecrated a garden anew". Where these gardens were located is not known.

Garden-making continued under Amenophis II, as we know from the garden illustrated in the tomb of Sennufer, and the gate-posts bearing the king's name. The king said that he had made a 'garden anew' at Karnak for providing offerings, which may refer to one of these gardens.

In the time of Akhenaten, there may have been an estate in the temple grounds. It is illustrated on a block found near the Second Pylon. It was guarded by lions and consisted of four parts: a gate-house, a vineyard with a pool, an orchard and areas for animals.[38] There were also shrines surrounded by trees which are illustrated on other blocks found at the same place.[39]

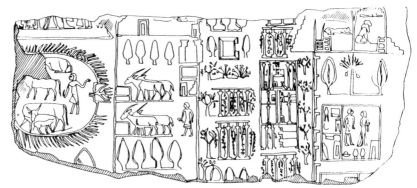

An estate probably belonging to the temple of Amun, depicted on a block of stone (a telatat) found at Karnak. Late XVIIIth Dynasty. (Fig. 74)

A temple of Ramesses II 'who hears prayers', which was on the east of the temple of Karnak, had 'a watered garden and a garden (or vineyard) planted with trees'.[40] The temple of Amenhotep of the Date Palm, with its single obelisk, represented as a small figure, is illustrated on the wall of the temple of Khonsu.[41] The 'Amenophis' may have been the deified Amenophis I, and both shrines may have been in the same place. In the time of Ramesses II, a grove within the temple area surrounded the House of Gold of Amun, where the temple treasures were manufactured. The workshop is illustrated in the tomb of Neferronpet (Theban Tomb 178). Other lakes in Karnak, in addition to the main temple lake, would have been surrounded by gardens. Several are mentioned in inscriptions. There was the northern lake, the portico of which faced north to catch the breeze from the north, and the 'northern sea of Amun' which may have been north of the Middle Kingdom temple. The whereabouts of the southern lake at Karnak is also unknown.

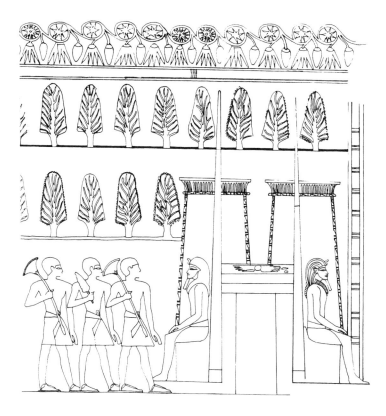

The avenue leading up to the eastern gate of the temple of Amun at Karnak flanked by colossal statues, illustrated in the tomb of Amenhotep-si-se. Theban Tomb 75. XVIIIth Dynasty. (Fig. 75)

Summary

The gardens at Karnak were numerous, diverse and changing over time. There were avenues at the western and southern entrances, gardens in between the buildings, and around the lakes and waterways. They were for the purpose of growing the offerings needed in the temple, and for providing the bouquets which decorated the statues and sacred barques and were presented as honorific gifts.

Literary and Pictorial References to Temple Gardens outside Karnak

Busiris

A shrine of Osiris at Busiris is illustrated on an unnamed tomb (Theban Tomb 147). A boat is about to land at the temple described as 'the beautiful temple which is in Busiris'. The name, 'The temple of Djedu', is inscribed above the door. There are trees either side of the doorway. Busiris was a town in the middle Delta (modern Abu Sir Bana), the old Djedu, the home of the god Osiris. It was a pilgrimage destination, like Osiris's other cult centre, Abydos.

Hermopolis

At the City of the Eight Gods, Khmunu, Hermopolis (modern Ashmunein) 180 miles south of Cairo, Merneptah planted orchards and flower gardens in the Temple of Amun and Thoth so that offerings could be made.[42] This temple was probably built originally by Ramesses II. Later, in the time of Persian domination (341-332 B.C.), a priest, Petosiris, restored it:

> I made an enclosure around the park,
> Lest it be trampled by the rabble.
> For it is the birthplace of every god,
> Who came into being in the beginning.[43]

He also complains that people had removed its shrubs and eaten the fruit from its trees.

> The fruit of its trees had been eaten,
> Its shrubs taken to intruders' homes;
> The whole land was in uproar about it
> And Egypt was distressed by it.

There were also orchards at the temple of Amun and Nehemet-Auay and Re in Hermopolis.

The Delta

Ramesses III's donations to temples in the Delta included plantations which would provide offerings for the temples. He planted olive groves and vineyards and dug lakes covered with waterlilies.

Heliopolis

At the new temple for Amun at Heliopolis, Ramesses III established gardens with fruit trees, vines, flowers and vegetables; and an orchard of two hundred persea (*Mimusops*) trees.[45] Ramesses III also created for the other temples at Heliopolis, lakes growing waterlilies and papyrus flowers, *isi*-flowers and flowers of every land, mandrake, myrrh and sweet and fragrant woods for the 'beautiful face' of the god. He gave date and olive groves, and the gardeners to work in them. In the sun temples at Heliopolis, gardens were planted so that flowers could be presented 'in the forecourt of the temple'. He also restored the sacred papyrus marsh at Heliopolis, which was a representation of the Delta marsh of Akh-Bit, where Isis had given birth to Horus.

Memphis

At Memphis, the ancient capital and city of Ptah the Creator, five groves and gardens were planted by Ramesses III with incense trees, brought from God's Land 'in order to satisfy the two Serpent Goddesses every morning.'[46]

Athribis

Benefits to Athribis by Amenophis III were recorded on a statue of Amenhotep, son of Hapu.[47]

At Athribis in the Thirtieth Dynasty (325 B.C.) a priest planted orchards at the Embalming House of the Falcon (Horus) in the necropolis in the north of the Athribite nome (Benha, Tell Atrib). "I had a garden made to the west of the Embalming house planted with every kind of sweet smelling tree".[48]

Bubastis

Herodotus described the temple of Bastet at Bubastis in his day. It was on an island in the middle of the city, on a lower level than the buildings. The waterways round the temple were thirty-three metres wide and overhung with trees. Inside the temple enclosure wall, was "a grove of very tall trees planted round the shrine, where the image of the goddess stands."

143

A paved route led through the market to the temple of Thoth, 'bordered by trees reaching up to heaven on either side.'[49]

Dendera

The names of the sacred gardens at the temple of Dendera are written up in the temple. There were gardens of the persea, palm, willow and fig trees.

Fayum

Offering-bringers, who are shown together with figures carrying trees, in the tomb of Puyemre (Theban Tomb 39), may represent places in the Fayum.

Trees appear to have flanked the entrance to the sanctuary of Sobek illustrated on a papyrus from the Fayum.

Summary

The literary evidence for cult temple gardens shows that the kings supported the endowments of the temples. The effect of this generosity was to maintain the links between the king and the powerful priesthoods. The types of gardens were: orchards, plantations for incense trees, lettuces and flax, and water-gardens where papyrus and waterlilies were grown.

VIII The Gardens at Amarna

The Pharaoh and the City

Splendid you rise, O living Aten, eternal lord!
You are radiant, beauteous, mighty,
Your love is great, immense,
Your rays light up all faces,
Your bright hue gives life to hearts,
When you fill the Two Lands with your love.
August God who fashioned himself.[1]

*The head of King
Amenophis IV,
Akhenaten. Luxor
Museum. (Fig. 76)*

Akhenaten was another of the great garden architects of Egypt. He moved his residence from Thebes to Middle Egypt, and built a city filled with parks and gardens. He chose a desolate sweep of desert on the opposite side of the river to Hermopolis (Ashmunein), the city of the Eight primeval gods in the Hare-nome, the ancient Wenu, and dedicated an area of about 15km. deep on both sides of the river for his new settlement. The area on the east was the main city, with temples and residences. On the west bank, were the fields which provisioned the city .

Why he moved from Thebes, and why he moved to this particular spot, have been the subject of speculation for many years. He seems to have wanted to devote himself to his new religion, unhampered by the existing priesthood of Amun, although he had built temples to his favoured deity, the Aten, within the precinct of Amun at Karnak.

Akhenaten created the sun-city *par excellence*, called the 'Light Land of Aten', or the 'Horizon of the Aten', Akhetaten. Symbols of the sun covered the buildings. The message of this city was of the royal family's devotion to, and dependence on, the sun, and, through the king and his family, the dependence of the entire populace upon the sun. Akhenaten did not identify himself with the sun, as did Louis XIV, but he proclaimed himself as the chosen instrument of the sun, and intermediary between this divine power and mankind.

> Your rays are on your son, your beloved,
> Your hands hold millions of jubilees
> For the king, Neferkheprure, Sole-one-of-Re,
> Your child who came from your rays.[2]

In the gardens created by Akhenaten at Amarna, the sun symbolism was everywhere: in painted relief sculptures of the king and queen worshipping the Aten, and making offerings of garden produce to the Aten, whose many hands reached down to touch the proffered gifts. The gardens were also decorated with paintings. Walls were painted on the inside and out with bright imitations of the plants which grew in them, including vines laden with grapes, and water plants, and with court and country life. In particularly significant buildings, coloured tiles and inlays were used instead of paint. This tradition of painting and tiling garden walls continued into Eighteenth Century Portugal, where painted tiles cover walls and summer houses of the Quinta de Sao Mateus Dafundo in Lisbon. In a northern climate, the painted palm trees and other exotic plants bloomed through the winter, just as in the desiccating summers of Middle Egypt, delicate flowers, which by May would have died, were still visible, delighting the king and the sun god. Another reason for the gardens at Amarna to have painted walls and pavements was that the city was a new creation, and few plants, and fewer trees would have grown up in the first years at all.

There were several garden pavilions in the great gardens built by Akhenaten to the south of his city, and a few in the private gardens of his most exalted courtiers. Such garden pavilions were another long-lived feature which continued throughout the Islamic period in the Near East.

Akhenaten's gardeners cannot have been pleased at the king's choice of site. It was an exposed stretch of desert, vulnerable to the blistering south winds in March and April, and to extreme swings of temperature, which could reach 48C in the summer, or freezing on a winter's night. Most of the plants would have to have been brought considerable distances from other royal gardens, presumably by boat. Since the soil was poor and dry, large numbers of pits had to be prepared to receive the trees, and gallons of water would have been needed to keep them alive. Date palms would have been difficult to transport because the 'heart', the growing point at the top of the tree, can easily break off if a tree is moved. But with care, large trees can be transplanted. Usually date palms are grown from suckers from a mature tree, so that the sex of the tree is known. Any grape vines which were brought in would have taken two to three years before they bore fruit. The wine-jar sealings in fact indicate that the wine which was consumed at Amarna came from already established vineyards in other parts of the country. Olives would have taken six years to mature. Even sycomore-figs and common figs take two to three years to grow from cuttings. On the other hand, annuals, such as are depicted in the paintings at Amarna, grow from seed; water plants, waterlilies, reeds and papyrus need not have been brought further than from the canal and river banks to the various pools in Akhenaten's gardens.

The plants which are painted on the walls and floors may express the desire of the king for a complete range of vegetation, from shady climbing plants, to lush riverbank reeds and flowers. Other water plants appear in abundance: papyrus, the gently waving reed *Phragmites australis*, *Cyperus alopecuroides*, the edible *Cyperus esculentus* and *rotundus* with convolvulus twined among them, as well as tall, feathery *Arundo donax*. Fruit trees which are illustrated are date palms, sycomore and common figs, and above all, grape vines and olives. Flowers of the fields which grew in these gardens were poppy, cornflower, *Chrysanthemum coronarium*, mandrake and various flowers of the hollyhock family.

The gardeners succeeded in making the trees grow during the fourteen years the city was occupied, at least in the workmens' gardens.[3] Vast amounts of food were needed to feed the population which came with the court. The grain, vegetables, oil, wine and other provisions were supplied by diverting the taxes which would have gone to Thebes, but some grains and meat were produced locally. The area of the city stretched from:

> Mountain to mountain, starting from the eastern horizon of the sky to the western horizon of the sky ...... consisting of its mountain(s) and desert lands, consisting of its marshes and new lands, consisting of its birds..... people.... herds..... everything which the Orb has brought into being and on which his rays shine.[4]

The Maru-Aten

The walled park, called *Maru*-Aten, was a sacred precinct with a lake, temples, offering pools and buildings, enclosed within a wall, which was supported by buttresses all the way round, and painted with vines and swags of petals. It lay about 5km. south of the main city. There were two enclosures. In the centre of the larger, northern, garden, was a lake oriented east-west, which occupied about a third of the space of the garden, and was surrounded by trees and flowers. Walled walkways linked the various buildings around the lake.

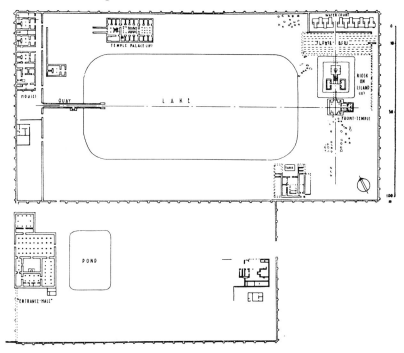

A plan of the Maru-Aten park at Amarna. (Fig. 77)

The Entrance to the Maru-Aten

The entrance to the two adjacent enclosures was in the southern one. The excavators believed that the northern one had been built later, thus bringing the larger enclosure nearer to the main city. A large building (Building viii) beside a pool formed the entrance. It led from the main road to a pool, through a palm-columned hall decorated with scenes of the king in procession, and receiving tribute, and the king and his family worshipping the Aten, whose hands stretched out to bless and to receive, by touching the proferred papyrus bouquets.

A throne or altar stood against the south wall of the open central court, on three sides of which were small, roofed columned halls. Across from the entrance, approached through a garden planted with trees and shrubs, was another building (Building vii) on the eastern side of the southern garden.

The Northern Enclosure

The Lake

Having come into the southern enclosure through a columned entrance and passing an ornamental pool, the visitor would enter the northern enclosure through a small gateway in the wall. There, spreading almost the entire length of the enclosure lay a large, cartouche-shaped lake, 120m. long and 60m. wide. and a metre deep. A quay jutted out into the centre, for about a third of its length, with, at its eastern end, a stone gateway, decorated with reliefs of the king worshipping the Aten. There were also captives, soldiers running, and offering-bringers holding bundles of papyrus, bowing before the entrance to a temple, which might have been the one opposite the gateway, across the lake. The gateway also had columns with palm-leaf (papyrus ?) capitals, and a cavetto cornice with a palmette frieze and cobra heads. Steps led down from the gateway into the water, evidently the point at which a boat could arrive and leave. On the land side, half way along the quay were steps down to cultivation plots. Arriving and leaving the quay would thus be through a flowery ground.

The Temple at the Eastern End of the Lake, the Small Temple (Building ii)

Directly in line with the end of the quay, on the eastern shore, was a small temple, also oriented east-west. It was only 16m. long and 10m. wide. Its pylonic gateway, set in the centre of its side wall, provided entrance to this temple, and to the island shrine beyond. Inside an inner pylon, was a roofed court, the decoration of which suggests offerings of ducks and plants. The reeded columns were painted green, and decorated with waterlily flowers and leaves, inlaid with blue and green paste, and modelled

149

bunches of grapes and 'laurel' leaves.[5] Below the name of the king, painted in bright yellow, ducks hung head downwards. The lintels over the door were of alabaster, and the walls were covered with reliefs and swags of ducks. In the inner shrine, was an altar, or throne, at the east end. The decoration of the temple walls consisted of faience inlays, which must have included a large composition of the king and queen, although only their heads have survived.

The Island at the Eastern End of the Lake

Beside this temple was an artificial island surrounded by a shallow moat.

A reconstruction of the island in the Maru-Aten at Amarna. Small bridges indicate the crossing over the narrow moat to the island. On the island is the temple with flags, and, in front of it, one of the porticoes. On the left is the small temple which stood at the end of the lake. (Fig. 78)

On this island stood two confronted porticos before steps leading up to a shrine on a slightly raised platform. This shrine was similar in plan to the shrines in private gardens in the central part of the city. All the buildings on the island were made of stone and precious materials.

The shrine on the island was open to the sky; on the inner face of the walls were scenes of the king worshipping the Aten. Painted on the outside were palm and acacia trees, part of a lakeside with papyrus and reeds growing on the bank, and waterlilies in the water. There was also a lion lying under a vine, and a calf lying down, a bird flying towards a bunch of dates, and offerings in the form of ducks hanging on a pole. Inside, there was a black granite stela showing the royal family worshipping the Aten. Shallow flights of steps, walled on either side, led to a raised platform on which stood an altar or throne. The columns were decorated in an unusual way with waterlily flowers in high relief, some upright and some bending, as if part of a growing clump. The capitals were carved like palm leaves, and papyrus, and painted green. A frieze of crimson-eyed snakes' heads, inlaid with black granite, guarded the top of the shrine. Similar royal reptiles guarded the inside of the two one-roomed porticos on the south side of the shrine, where long-stalked waterlily flowers, similar to those in the shrine, decorated the shafts of the pilasters, and clumps of papyrus carved in relief, formed the capitals. A palm leaf pattern was inlaid around the cornice. The floors were of alabaster, and the walls were covered with tiles, decorated with flowering plants. Inscriptions were carved on the thin screen walls across the front. Trees surrounded the island, on the east side of which were traces of an inner enclosure wall.

The Cultivation Plots beside the Island

To the north of the island, was an area, about 13m. wide, of cultivation plots, in front of a mudbrick building which contained eleven 'T'-shaped offering-pools.

The Eleven Offering Pools in the North-Eastern Corner of the Enclosure (Building i)

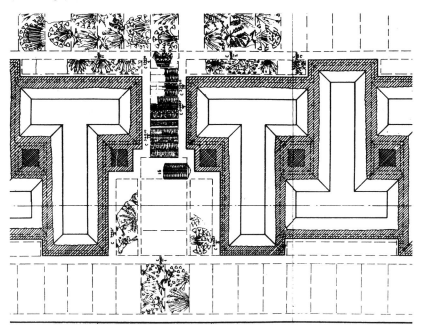

A plan of the 'T'-shaped pools in a building in the Maru-Aten at Amarna. (Fig. 79)

A brick building covered eleven 'T'-shaped pools dug into the ground. In them 'masses of broken wine-jars' and their mud-sealings were found. The entire inside of the building was painted with growing plants. On the floors around the pools were imitation flower beds each containing clumps of papyrus, poppy and cornflowers, and on the parapet surrounding them, vines and pomegranates were painted on a yellow background. The basins were large: 6m. long, 4m. wide, and 1m. deep.

Inside they were painted with white and yellow stripes, topped with a narrow black line. The entrance to the building was slightly off-centre, lining up with the shrine on the island. The pools themselves were arranged in two uneven groups, of four on the west side, and seven on the east side, of the pathway leading from the island. How the pools were used is a matter of conjecture. The birthday of the Aten, the sun's globe, may have been celebrated every month by throwing whole jars of wine into the pool designated for a particular month.[6] Rituals for the twelfth month may have been celebrated on the island, or at the lake. Or, each basin may have represented one hour of the night, with the twelfth hour being celebrated at the island. Since the Aten had created time: 'Thou creator of months and maker of days, and reckoner of hours',[7] an indicator of time dedicated to him is in keeping with the ideas about him; for he was believed to renew himself daily.

Paintings on the floor round the 'T'-shaped pools in the Maru-Aten at Amarna. Duck flying over papyrus, willow-herb (?) or pond-weed and reeds. (Fig. 80)

A Garden Kiosk (Building iv)

Another small garden-building stood on the northern side of the lake. It was approached by a walled pathway. In the central room was an atrium. When they found it, the excavators were reminded of houses at Pompeii. The central area of this peristyle garden, was surrounded by a brick wall 0.20 m. high, inside which were cultivation plots, each compartment being surrounded by a low partition, and filled with mud. Around the courtyard were small rooms. Beside the open area were six columns, making a portico. In each corner, on the west side, were steps to an upper story. The walls of the courtyard were painted white to a height of 0.40 m. where there was a black line. Above this line, was a yellow zone, and above that, a zone imitating stone: painted blue, black and red, and above that decoration, grapes and pomegranates and rectilinear panels. A room on the south side of the court contained a recess with a bench.

Beyond the peristyle, on the east side, was a columned hall decorated on the walls or ceiling, with bunches of black grapes and green leaves, with red stems and tendrils, on the all pervasive yellow background, which usually indicated gold and the colour of the sun. Around the ceiling was a garland of blue and white waterlily petals; the flutings of the columns were painted alternately blue and red. Storage for wine jars occupied the surrounding small rooms .

The room on the western side of the peristyle court contained a throne or altar at the top of a flight of steps, with a brightly painted balustrade, red, green and blue on a white ground, with a red top. Six columns may have supported a roof over it. The walls were painted in broad bands of white, black, yellow, red and blue. The door frames were white picked out in blue. This building could have been used as a rest-house for a small group of people: possibly for the king and his immediate entourage. It could have been a place to have meals: a small banqueting house; while the columned halls at the entrance could have served as a banqueting house for the larger retinue. Or, it may have been purely ceremonial. It may be comparable with the 'palace' on the north-west side of Karnak, and have had a similar function.

The Building beside the Lake and surrounding its own Pool (Building iii)

At the south-eastern side of the lake, an avenue joined the 'Small Temple' at the eastern end, with another building, which had its own pool enclosed on three sides by loggias and cellars. It occupied an area of 13m. x 10m. Impressions of the waterlilies which had grown in the pool in Akhenaten's time were still visible when it was excavated. This building may also have been a resthouse for the king, where he could sit and enjoy the breezes from the north blowing across the main lake and the pool in front of him.

Houses

Both sacred areas, at Amarna and Karnak, included houses among their buildings. The excavators suggested that those at Amarna, at the western end of the lake, were for gardeners, but they were more likely for priests, as were the houses at Karnak.[8]

The Meaning of the Gardens

These two enclosed gardens, with their lavishly decorated buildings, processional routes, and abundance of vegetation and water, were religious in inspiration and purpose. The northern garden, or a part of it, is described in an inscription as the *maru* of the Aten. A *maru* was a sacred enclosure, a courtyard or a temenos, containing a resting place for the god's boat, a lake and flower-beds. It was where the divine king's power was displayed to his own people, and to foreign emissaries. Ceremonies for the New Year and other seasons, such as Inundation, may have been celebrated on the island. A lake is an essential part of a *maru*, and represented the god Nun, primeval water. In the Amarna religion, the king replaced Nun.

Amarna was the place where the Aten came into being: his 'Seat of the First Occasion, which he had made for himself that he might rest in it'.[9] The island may represent the stepped mound of creation on which the Aten, like the sun's boat, rested, as illustrated in Chapter 110 of the Book of the Dead, and be the place where rituals of recreation for the Aten would have been celebrated. At Karnak, a shrine at the western end of the temple lake was for the jubilees of the king, Tuthmosis III; this arrangement would translate at Amarna to a ceremony in honour of the Aten, rising at the eastern end of the lake; or a ceremony for the king and the Aten together. Beside the island-mound were the eleven offering pools, and the garden growing offerings. This arrangement is similar to that at Karnak temple, where the Field of Offerings is beside the central shrine.

The word *maru* has to do with seeing,[10] and thus the *maru* of the Aten is the Viewing Place of the Aten, where the deity was 'seen' by the priests or the king. One of the priests at Amarna, Meryre, was called 'Great Seer of the Aten'.[11] It has been called 'the observatory of the Aten'. But this seeing went both ways, from god to humans, as well as from humans to gods, since the Amarna god created by seeing, as a poem to the Aten puts it:

> By the sight of your rays
> All flowers exist
> What lives and sprouts from the soils grows when you shine
> Drinking deep of your sight all flocks frisk.[12]

The word which means seeing has a further meaning of visit,[13] which gives the idea of 'seeing' a reinforced power of presence, making the shrine the 'god's gazebo'.[14]

The 'Shade' of the Sun God

A temple in the '*maru*-Aten' was called a 'Shade' of the sun-god . A 'shade' of the sun god Re was the place where the king, or a member of his family, was celebrated as the living incarnation of the sun god. It was where the shade or shadow of the sun fell upon the royal person imbuing him or her with divine power.[15] The 'Shade of Re' in the '*maru*-Aten' belonged at first to a queen called Kiya, and then to the king's daughter, Meritaten. It is surprising to find any queen except Nefertiti associated with Akhenaten, but Kiya was an important woman at court, with similar ranking to the Queen Mother, Tiye. It is not known where this building was situated.

The Symbolism of the Maru-Aten

The *Maru*-Aten seems to have represented both the beginning point of life on earth, and the Field of Offerings on the horizon of heaven. It was a garden in which the Aten was to flourish, or enjoy himself. It may even have been for the king and the Aten to enjoy together, just as other estate owners say they delighted in their gardens, and listened to the lapping water, and contemplated the scenery.

The lake was certainly large enough for processions of boats and even aquatic spectacles, being roughly comparable in size to the pool in front of the Palm House at the Royal Botanic Gardens at Kew. Hatshepsut had created a garden for Amun to walk in, at her temple at Deir el-Bahari. Vegetation and offerings were represented in painting, sculpture and reality.

Paradise for the Egyptians was where life began and continued forever, the Fields of Reeds, and of Offerings, where there was bread and fresh air. It was the goal of an afterlife journey, where the route of the 'Two Ways', described on coffins, ended. It was also connected with the idea of Ro-setau, the tomb entrance, opening to the world beyond. But at Amarna the emphasis was on the present: the afterlife was unclear, but could be spent in a garden. The garden of the *Maru*-Aten is a theatre, but we can only guess at the play.

Akhenaten's worship of the sunlight is expressed in hymns to the Aten, which his courtiers recorded in their tombs at Amarna. He describes all living creatures and plants as drawing life from the sun. Although Akhenaten's descriptions of nature are subsidiary to his praise of the Aten, they contain delightful observations which echo the paintings in expressing the exhuberance, and the harmony of nature:

> When the chick in the egg speaks in the shell
> You give him breath to sustain him.

And

> All beasts browse on their herbs
> Trees, herbs are sprouting,

Birds fly from their nests
Their wings greeting your *ka*,
All flocks frisk on their feet
The fish in the river dart before you...[16]

This enthusiasm for the open air was regarded as an aberration by the Assyrian ambassadors who were 'kept standing in the sun', according to a letter to Akhenaten from their, king Ashuruballit I, who complained:

(The ambassaors) will die in the open sun. If it does the king good to stand in the open sun, then let the king stand there, and die, in the open sun.[17]

The '*Maru*-Aten' would have been shaded from the sun once its trees had grown up. When they visited the park, the king and queen rode in chariots, which they either drove independently, or together in one curricle. Sometimes one of the princesses rode with them and was allowed to encourage the horses with her own little whip. Soldiers, carrying their standards, spears and shields ran beside, and in front of, the royal couple, while the younger princesses followed, driven in their individual chariots. Once inside the '*Maru*-Aten' the king, may have continued in a chariot, or been carried in his magnificent throne guarded by lionesses and female sphinxes, with fan bearers walking backwards in front of him, creating some shade over his face and the back of his neck. Nefertiti had a similar throne, and the two were carried side by side on the shoulders of barefooted young soldiers. The king may also have had a boat in which he would have been rowed across the lake.

The 'Northern Maru'

At the northern end of Amarna, about 3km. from the central part of the city, there was a smaller, and in some ways similar, garden, to the '*maru*-Aten', which may have been called the 'Northern *Maru*'. It measured 115m. by 144m. E-W. Its layout followed the same general design of the *Maru*-Aten, in that it had a central pool, which, in this case was surrounded by buildings, all much closer together, within a built setting, rather than in the more open park. The 'Northern *Maru*' was only 120m. wide and 290m. long. It had the same open-air altars, and enclosed, garden as the other *Maru*. The central pool was surrounded by a terrace planted with trees or shrubs, and a portico providing a shaded walkway. In the enclosed garden, which was also sunken, steps led down to small rectangular flower-beds, watered from the central pool by a channel which passed under the

View across the 'Northern Maru', as it is today. (Fig. 81)

floor of the intervening room, and round the edge of the flower beds. A balcony overlooked this garden. The walls were painted with pictures of plants and processions. The sunken garden was surrounded by narrow, open cells, the walls of which were each decorated with a bird, geese and storks, or animals within a border, like a framed picture. One of the rooms on the north side of the garden had a 'window', looking out on the flowers, and the walls, which were decorated with birds flying among the foliage of a papyrus marsh; small niches cut in the walls may have been for bird-cages. The ceiling of the rooms and passage round the garden was covered with a painted trellis of vine, and moulded bunches of grapes at the top. This idea must have been copied by the Romans, who passed it on to the Renaissance popes and cardinals.

Beside the sunken garden area, was a dias for a throne on the central axis of the pool on the east side. It was approached through two columned halls, but had a view out to the pool. This room was about 5m. square. The name of Meritaten, daughter of Akhenaten and Nefertiti, was carved on the doorposts, indicating that the enclosure had a special connection with her. At the opposite, western, end was a court with the remains of a throne or kiosk, flanked by altars.

Tethering rings, and mangers, decorated with carvings of ibex, gazelle and antelope, indicate that animals were kept in a building beside the pool. They may have been syolic of the power of the Creator. Animals in an enclosure are illustrated on a block dating from the time of Akhenaten, found at Karnak, but in addition, lions in their cages guard the gateway. A menagerie is very much part of a royal garden. That other Sun

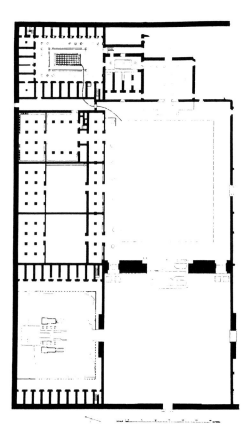

A plan of the 'Northern Maru'.
(Fig. 82)

King, Louis XIV, had one at Versailles. A surprising survivor is in the modern Jardin des Plantes in Paris, which was formerly a royal garden. Here a bear and lion still remain, amongst the botanical specimens, reminders of the king's beasts of medieval times.

An idea of what a *Maru* looked like is illustrated in the tomb of the High Priest of the Aten, Meryre.[18] What this illustration represents, whether a temple, or the palace, or Meryre's own garden, is not known. The main elements of a *Maru* are represented in this garden: pools, altars, shrines and trees. There a large expanse of ground divided into walled areas, each with their own pylonic entrances, in which several buildings are set among trees.

Various individual elements are similar to parts of the '*Maru*-Aten' and the 'Northern *Maru*', but the whole illustration is not identifiable with any area excavated hitherto. It does however give an idea of how the '*Maru*-Aten' may have looked, with its buildings surrounded by trees in their mud-walled pots, particularly the entrance building with its pool in front, and the open air courts, filled with altars and offering-tables. Echoes

158

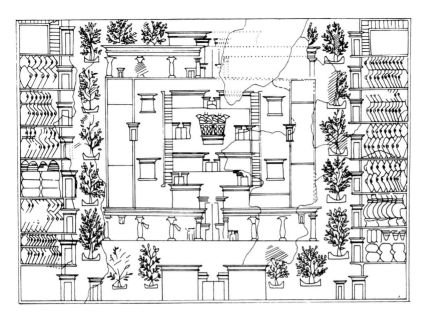

The trees in the gardens around buildings depicted in the tomb of Meryre, High Priest of the Aten, at Amarna. (Fig. 83)

of the 'Northern *Maru*' are found in the altar courts, and in a stable, in which horses are feeding, which parallels the tethering rings found in the stable of the 'Northern *Maru*', and the illustrations of wild game, gazelle and antelope, carved on the mangers. In the tomb-relief, the majority of the trees are either olive or sycomore-fig, but in a walled orchard around a pool, from which a gardener is collecting water in the pots on his yoke, there are pomegranate, date-palm, doum-palm, castor oil bushes (?), sycomore-figs and vines. There seems to be a berm, a canal or a moat outside the garden, which may be a protective device for safe-guarding the orchard. (Fig. 84)

The *Maru*-Aten was no mere landscape of allusion, like the gardens of classical Rome or Eighteenth Century England, for it recreated a true microcosm of the universe, with the primaeval water, the mound of creation, and abundant vegetation; its landscape reflected Egyptian myths about the life-giving power of the sun. The garden was in defiant contrast to the surrounding desert, and those brooding hills, in which the king made his tomb. Nature was divine, and only the divine Akhenaten could operate in this setting.

Kom el-Nana

There were more gardens in the area known as Kom el-Nana, south of the main city. It was an enclosed area, rather similar in some respects to

159

An orchard on the estate illustrated in the tomb of Meryre at Amarna. It appears to be surrounded by a moat or berm. (Fig. 84)

the '*Maru*-Aten'. It measured 230 x 250m. and was, 'surrounded by a brick wall braced by square buttresses and cut by entrances flanked by pylons.'[19] Inside the enclosure were ceremonial buildings. One of these was a pavilion (the south pavilion) inside which were apparently 'Windows of Appearances', which is the name given to balconies, where the king appeared on ceremonial occasions, and small sunken gardens, on the eastern and western sides. Its principal entrance lay exactly opposite the south pylon, and it provided exits to the great court on the west, and to a group of houses. Pieces of painted pavement were found in the western garden. Another garden was found inside the walls north of the east pylon entrance.

Marus in Other Places

It is just possible that the 'Northern *Maru*', usually assumed to be at Amarna was, in fact at Karnak, where the block mentioning it was found, although the text refers to 'the Horizon of Aten'.[20] Amenophis III had made a *maru* for Amun at Thebes, with a pool, flowers and vineyards, as a 'Place of flourishing' or 'enjoyment', for the god; in its midst was a temple. The location of this *maru* is not known. It was probably not in the lotus-columned courtyard built by Amenophis III at the Luxor temple, because the ground, which has recently been excavated was solid with stone.[21] But it could have been where the court built by Ramesses II now stands, or further outside. Another location which has been suggested is at Amenophis's funerary temple on the west bank, or even, in the temple of Mut at Karnak.[22]

There was a *maru* at Edfu, where the ceremony of choosing the new sacred falcon was carried out. In Ptolemaic times it may have been a building within an open court. This ceremony took place at the beginning of the sowing season, at the end of the inundation. There may have been a *maru* here as early as the Thirteenth Dynasty, as there was at Dendera.

The Central Ceremonial Area at Amarna

The landscaping of the temple gardens at Amarna is illustrated on the walls of some of the courtiers' tombs (those of Tutu, Parennefer and Pentu) and excavation has confirmed that the avenues of trees shown as leading up to the great temple, in the centre of the city, did indeed exist. Remains of two trees were found in front of the 'House of Rejoicing', a shrine within the main temple enclosure.

The Sunken Atrium Gardens of the Central 'Palace'

A little to the south of the temples was a ceremonial area which included two enclosed, sunken gardens which were part of the central ceremonial building. These garden areas were decorated with paintings and inlaid walls. They were called by the excavators: the northern and southern 'harems of the palace'.[23]

The Northern Sunken Garden

This garden was beside a large open court surrounded with statues of the king. The only entrance was through courts which connected with the road. The plan of the northern garden is similar to that of the sunken garden at the 'Northern *Maru*'. It has a central flower bed and surrounding colonnade, off which open small rooms (about 2 x 3m.). Inside the rooms were brick blocks. Petrie, who excavated the area, suggested they were to support benches for sleeping, but more likely, they were for storage-shelving. Along the west side, within the colonnade, were bins made of painted bricks. The sunken area was terraced, and trees were planted in oblong pits on the terraces. These trees shaded the flower beds which were watered by a channel leading from a water tank and a well. The garden area was 20m. long and 10m. wide. The colonnade of light wooden posts could have supported a roof, which would have shaded the plants from the fierceness of the sun. Nefertiti's name was carved on the coping of the well-head, over which was a kiosk. The well was 4.60 m. deep. This area was one of the most elaborately decorated of all the buildings at Amarna. The columns around the pool were inlaid with faience in imitation of bundles of papyrus, and the capitals were inlaid with tiles imitating papyrus umbels. These clumps of artificial papyrus stood round the pool, imitating an actual papyrus thicket. The columns, which supported the kiosk over the well, were decorated with figures of the royal family making offerings. On the east wall, were paintings of waterlilies, men tending cattle, a canal and boats. The small rooms round the sunken area were decorated with red pottery offering dishes piled with grapes. Painted wine jars and vases, resting in bowls, decorated the other rooms.

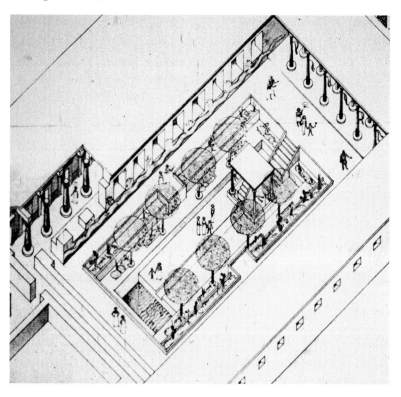

A reconstruction of the northern sunken garden in the central 'palace' area at Amarna. (Fig. 85)

The decoration and provision for storage suggests that wine offerings were made here, possibly in the pool; and wine-jars were apparently stored in the narrow rooms round the pool. The symbolism of this garden is that this is the place where the king and his family make offerings into a pool in the midst of a papyrus thicket.

Southern Sunken Garden

The southern peristyle garden (M and N on the plans) lay north of the 'bridge', beside the courtyard inside the main entrance from the road.[24] It was 26m. long, with a central bay containing a pool (making a width of 30m. at its widest), and was flanked by porticos on the east and west. The excavators' description of the garden is as follows:

> In the centre is a long garden court running north and south, giving directly on to the bridge. The garden itself is sunk and stone steps lead down to it from the south. It was filled with Nile mud and was apparently watered by means of a trench which runs from the entrance above mentioned into its north-west corner. Round it runs a path. Rather to the north of the centre, a court (M) opens to the east, a layer of plaster with the markings of blocks probably indicating the position of a stone threshold. This open court is paved with bricks. Not quite in the centre is an oblong tank lined with plaster which shows the marks of stone round the edge. In the middle of this was found a great oblong slab slightly askew. It may have been an ornamental pond with some central structure.

The water tank was 30cm. long and 10cm. wide. The excavators wondered whether there had been a fountain here. The portico, facing the pool across the garden, had a painted pavement. It would have been a vantage point, facing east. The entrance to the series of rooms around the garden was from an open courtyard between the two sunken gardens.

Painted Pavements representing Gardens in the Central Building

Between the two actual gardens were columned halls, on the floors of which were painted pools, with beside them, foreign captives lying bound. Anyone approaching the northern garden, would walk along a pathway, between the painted pools, treading on the bodies of Asiatic and Nubian prisoners who lay beside the pools.[25] These figures were life-sized, and the pools in the room called by the excavators the 'Main Hall', were about 3m. long and 1m. wide. The sides of the pools were painted to represent steps, just like in the real garden in the adjacent part of the building, only with limestone and granite paths between the water-channels on each level.

Waterlilies grew in the painted pools with fish swimming amongst them. On the second and third levels up from the pool were tall reeds and papyrus, with duck flying above, and nesting, and butterflies and dragonflies settling on the reeds. Calves leapt among the poppies, cornflowers and convolvulus. Offerings of bouquets and incense cones (or piles of fruit, possibly grapes, in bowls) were arranged at intervals around the edge. Some of the piles are coloured blue, others green, which may indicate a difference in content, or simply be the fading of the pigment. The four

Plants and animals on the edge of a pool. Part of a painted pavement in the central 'palace' at Amarna. (Fig. 86)

columns either side of each pool probably represented the trees shading the water. The bound Asiatic and Nubian prisoners with their weapons, three bows, between each, symbolized the subjugation of foreign lands. This pavement is similar to one found in Amenophis III's palace at Thebes (Malqata).

In the cross-hall nearest to the northern garden (Room E), there was a pool either side of the pathway of captives. The column bases were on the banks of the pools, flanking the processional way. In this hall there was an outer path on which stands piled with unguent cones or piles of incense and bouquets were painted. A pathway led into another columned hall on the east side of the main hall (Room F). In this room were two pools. Here the outer border of bouquets and stands is better preserved than in the Main Hall, and two kinds of bouquet are discernable: one is made of papyrus only, and the other has poppies stuck in among the papyrus. There were thus eight painted pools beside a processional way, leading to a real pool, in the northern, sunken garden. This series of pools is a reminder of the series of eleven pools in the '*Maru*-Aten', and it is tempting to think that there may have been ceremonies connected with a cycle of eight days, followed by a special day. On one side of a hall, between rooms E and F with the scene of pools, was a painted flower-bed of growing plants: cornflower, poppy, hollyhock or mallow and giant reed (*Arundo donax*), *Cyperus rotundus* and *Cyperus papyrus*. These paintings were substitutes in secco for the real plants growing in the gardens.

The actual designs of the plants and animals around the pools in the central building or 'palace', and in the '*Maru*-Aten', are very similar. Both feature calves and bulls leaping among the clumps of papyrus, as well as birds and fish; but a lion attacking a bull is only depicted on the 'palace' pavements. The plants in the 'palace' are not shown in separate plots, but overlapping each other, as if growing wild.

The combination of bouquets, incense and prisoners, comprised the offerings made to the gods and illustrate the abundance of nature and plants, birds, fish and animals, ready for offerings.

Illustrations of Atrium-gardens inside the 'Palace'

Illustrations in the tombs of courtiers at Amarna show rooms in the palace which appear to have a garden, or a painted pavement decorated with plants. These rooms are the royal bedroom and dining-rooms. The bedroom in the palace at Malqata had trees outside it; the pits for which still remain.[26] A porticoed building which may be part of one of the palaces at Amarna is shown in a tomb of one of the courtiers, May. It fronts on to the river, or a canal, and has a 'garden' in front of it filled with papyrus and other plants.

Parts of gardens are illustrated on blocks from buildings at Amarna, which were later taken as building material to Hermopolis.[27] One shows a squared patch of cultivation and a gardener coming up out of a lake or the river, with pots on a yoke. Part of another block shows another part of a garden beside water. The main feature in the illustration is the royal barge; the garden is in the background, fenced, with square plots growing a single plant in each plot. A block now in the Louvre (E.14325), illustrates trees outside a palace, and courtyards and altars. The bushes outside might be vine or castor oil, and sesbania or acacia. Lakes are illustrated on several blocks and there are many decorated with a variety of plants. The plants shown growing and being collected are mainly papyrus.

The Vineyard

In the 'Palace', to the south of the sunken gardens was a pillared area which may have been a vineyard.[28] The pillars were of brick and beside them were pits for trees, or more likely, vines. The area was surrounded by a thick wall. It was called the 'Great Pillared Hall', and the 'Coronation Hall', by the excavators. The Egyptians called it, 'The Domain of Smenkhkare in the House of Rejoicing of the Aten'. The whole length of the west side was covered with green glazed tiles decorated with daisy-like flowers, cornflowers and a blue bud with yellow sepals or calyx. It may have been completely open to the sky, or the central aisle may have been roofed and painted with vines on a yellow background. This elaboration of decoration would indicate that it was a pleasure garden, shaded from the sun and protected from wind. Decorative plaques were also found on the outside of the building, but they may have got there in the general destruction. The wine jars found at one end of this enclosure once contained wine from the Delta, which suggests that this vineyard was for the production of grapes only.

Exactly the same system of brick pillars supporting vines is used today by the Luxor farmers in the fields beside the road to the airport.

The Garden of the 'King's House'

Across the central highway from the 'Palace', outside the building called the 'King's House' by the excavators, was another garden. This garden, roughly 60m. square, may have been terraced, with trees forming an avenue up to the 'King's House'. Outside the pylon at the entrance were more trees and flower beds. It is possible that this avenue was a ceremonial approach to the throne-room.[29] Irrigation channels led to the trees, and a well provided water. On the lowest terrace, there was a kiosk, approached by steps, and its roof supported on square brick piers. Pieces of a half life-size statue of the king, and a statuette, were found in the garden, but they need not necessarily have been part of the statuary of the garden. They may just have been discarded there.

This garden, approached by an avenue from the outside, and rising in terraces up to the royal apartments, is clearly a setting for ceremonies intended to impress the court and foreigners with the power of the king. It parallels the palace gardens at Karnak, illustrated in Neferhotep's tomb (Theban Tomb 49), where Neferhotep and his wife received rewards from the king and queen at 'Windows of Appearances'. But the Amarna setting is more impressive because it is larger and terraced, and visible on the ground.

Private Gardens with Shrines

Some of the gardens of officials at Amarna contained a sacred building in the form of a kiosk,[30] inside which was a mural, and sometimes a stela, showing the king, Akhenaten, often with his wife, Nefertiti, and their children, worshipping the Aten. Trees formed an avenue to the shrine, or stood sentinel, one on either side of a mud path, or surrounded the shrine.[31] The pits in which the trees had been planted were filled with Nile mud, and some were linked by irrigation channels. Sometimes there was a papyrus clump beside the ramp up to the shrine. A few of the

166

gardens had a pool in front of the shrine, reminiscent of the arrangements at a Theban funerary temple, and of the kiosk and pool in the painted gardens of some Theban officials. A terraced pool was found in the garden of House Q 46.1 on the excavators' plan.[32] This very extensive property belonged to the Overseer of the Cattle of the Sun God in the Temple of the Aten. These shrines, and their gardens, were separated from the rest of the estate by walls. An illustration of a garden enclosing a shrine at the entrance to Meryre's house appears in a relief in his tomb.[33] The excavated shrines varied in size from about 2m. square, to 25m. square.[34] The gardens around them, including the shrines, were from about 70m. long, and 35m. wide, to about 12m. square. Usually the gardens were longer than they were broad. The orientation of the shrines was roughly east-west, with the steps both on the east and the west, which indicates that the position of the officiant was more important than the orientation of the building. Nearly all the shrines were built of mud brick. The houses with large gardens were laid out along a street, which the excavators called the 'High Priests' Street', since so many of the most important people in the city had their large houses and grounds there. Many of these houses had pools and wells in their grounds, even if no shrines have survived. Among the owners whose names are known are Pawah, The Great Seer of the Sun's disc in the temple of the Sun god, Re, the General Ramose, and the sculptor, Tuthmosis, who made the famous head of Nefertiti now in Berlin.

A model representing the houses at Amarna with shrines in their gardens. Egyptian Museum, Cairo. (Fig. 87)

Illustrations of Private Gardens at Amarna and Thebes

Meryre, the Superintendent of Nefertiti's household at Amarna, illustrated a shrine in the garden of his house. Indeed he is shown arriving there after being honoured by Akhenaten. There is a 'T'-shaped pool in the entrance courtyard, and trees line the route up to the shrine.[35] Pentu had an atrium garden in his house, or a pavement painted with plants.[36]

A few of the officials at Thebes have left impressions of their houses and gardens. Some of the houses are surrounded by trees in containers, like those of Thay and Mosi (Theban Tombs 23 and 254) and there is sometimes an avenue leading up to them as at the houses of Amenemope and Neferhotep (Theban Tombs 41 and 49). Nebamun (Theban Tomb 90) had date trees in the courtyard of his house, and Nakhte (papyrus in the British Museum, Fig. 53) had sycomore and date trees outside his. A much larger pool than is shown at Meryre's Amarna shrine, one on which a boat

Date palms and sycomore fig-trees flanking Thay's house or gatehouse. He returns from an honouring ceremony with a bouquet which he is showing his wife. The main gate into his estate is behind him. Theban Tomb 23. XIXth Dynasty. (Fig. 88)

168

could sail, is illustrated beside the house of Djhutyhetep (Theban Tomb 80). Pools were a feature of house gardens about which their owners boasted: 'I am one who owns a beautiful garden and pool and tall sycomores'.[37] Another said he had 'Made a garden with a pool... eighty-eight and a half cubits wide in which three hundred sycomores are planted.'[38]

What this building, which is referred to as a house, really is, is not clear. Most of these buildings are small for the residence of a high official. It may be just the gate-house into the property, comparable with the building illustrated at the entrance to the estate on a block found at Karnak.[39] (Fig. 74) The building illustrated in the tomb of Thay (Theban Tomb 23) inside the entrance pylon, and sited in a tree-lined courtyard could be just such a gatehouse.

Another interpretation would be that an estate contained many buildings, and the particular one illustrated was one of many pavilions used for various purposes, the arrangement of which would be comparable with Topkapi in Istanbul.

Sycomore fig-trees protected by brick containers, and date-palms growing in the ground, beside the house of Mosi. He is showing the bouquet he has just received to his wife on the steps outside the house. Theban tomb 254. XVIIIth Dynasty. (Fig. 89)

The atmosphere in the gardens at Amarna might have been like that in the garden at el-Saff in summer, although this garden was much further north, being only seventy miles from Cairo:

The tenseness of throbbing life in the fastening rhythm of rising temperatures... the gradual approach of the hush and lull of midday with some coolness lingering in the dark shady recesses, still filled with the dampness of the morning. Insects and birds then rest dreamily while the sun blaze is so intense that colours fade for a few hours, only to brighten up again in the peace of the early afternoon. Turtle doves start to coo once more in soft cheering tenderness, hoopoes call out with subdued intensity their three-fold note and ever invisible wild doves raise their pleasant elusive voices in a suspended rhythm. Although spring is over, tiny unseen warblers still twitter jubilantly and a few 'bulbuls' persist in singing their gay little phrase of soft liquid notes. Sunset is the time for the grey herons to wake up and start for their fishing places. For a moment the air resounds with their brief rallying cries.[40]

The gardens at Amarna were magnificent theatres for the enactment of ceremonies, celebrating Akhenaten and his deity. In these open spaces, the power and splendour of the king were made manifest for all the world to see. They were also sacred landscapes, with special characteristics appropriate to the worship of the sun god, and the places where the enormous quantity of offerings needed for the service of the Aten were grown.

Offerings piled up in honour of the Aten, while Akhenaten, Nefertiti, and Tiye, the Queen Mother, and princess Meritaten, enjoy a meal together. Relief carving in the tomb at Amarna of Huya, Superintendent of the house of the Great Royal Wife, Tiye. (Fig. 90)

Postscript

Ancient Egyptian gardens stand at the beginning of garden-making as an art. The designers were concerned with creating particular landscapes which reflected the mental images they had of how the world was created and sustained. They were also economic units providing the raw materials necessary to perform the rituals intended to sustain the natural order and rhythms of the world, and to maintain the communities who performed this activity.

The gardens around tombs were theme-parks mirroring the religious ideas of their time; theatres for the performance of life-giving rituals. Those who owned the gardens, about which most evidence has survived, were the highest and wealthiest in the land, the king and his courtiers. Many of the designs for gardens which were adopted throughout the Near East, and passed on to Rome and Europe, as well as to India, derived from Egypt: symmetrical arrangement of elements, focus on water, terraces, and avenues. Inscriptions were an integral part of Egyptian gardens and do much to explain their design and symbolism. Brightly coloured garden pavilions served a variety of purposes, as shrines, dining-rooms and viewing points. Bright colours for garden buildings were even used in 18th century Kew by William Chambers.

More and more evidence is becoming available about the ordinary cultivators who grew crops for their own use, and about the range of plants which were growing in the area. The quantity of plants which did not have religious significance, or whose religious significance is as yet unclear, are being revealed by the use of new scientific techniques, and as more information becomes available it will be possible to build up a more detailed picture of the whole ecosystem in which the ancient Egyptians lived. For, if we know what plants were present, we can work out what animals could live on those plants, and build up a picture of the whole landscape.

Effort in the future should be devoted to finding out more about the layout of gardens, by the kind of careful excavation which is now being practised, and to the analysis of soils and material remains in order to find out what plants were growing in the neighbourhood of an excavated site. Modern techniques make it possible to extract much more information from an archaeological site than was possible at the time many of the sites described in this book were excavated. Another strand of research is into the living examples of ancient plants: their habit and conservation. Many of these plants are endangered, and every effort should be made to collect seed where available, and to try to propagate new plants which will keep the strains alive. There are plans to have a collection of 'ancient Egyptian' plants at the Agricultural Museum in Cairo; I hope this idea succeeds. Some of the plants, like the doum palm are already there, but others need to be added. The Botanical Island at Aswan is another place where some of the ancient plants are grown, but others, which survive only further south in Africa, and in Arabia, need to be preserved, and, if growing conditions allow, re-introduced to Egypt.

Abbreviations

ASAE	Annales du Service des Antiquités de l'Egypte
BIE	Bulletin de l'Institut de l'Egypte
BIFAO	Bulletin de l'Institut français d'archéologie orientale
BMMA	Bulletin of the Metropolitan Museum of Art
CdE	Chronique d'Egypte
CG	Catalogue général des antiquités égyptiennes du Musée du Caire
EEF	Egypt Exploration Fund
GM	Göttinger Miszellen
IFAO	Institut français d'archéologie orientale
JARCE	Journal of the American Research Center in Egypt
JEA	Journal of Egyptian Archaeology
JNES	Journal of Near Eastern Studies
LÄ	Lexikon der Ägyptologie
MDAIK	Mitteilungen der Deutschen Archäologischen Instituts, Abteilung Kairo
MDOG	Mitteilungen der Deutschen Orientgesellschaft
Pyr.	Pyramid Text
SAK	Studien zur Altägyptischen Kultur
TT	Theban Tomb
Urk.	Kurt Sethe, Wolfgang Helck, Urkunden der 18. Dynastie, (in translation), Berlin 1955-61.
ZÄS	Zeitschrift für Ägyptische Sprache und Altertumskunde

Notes

Introduction

1. James L. Wescoat, Jr. 'Early Mughal Gardens' , in John Dixon Hunt, ed. *Garden History: Issues, Approaches, Methods*, Dumbarton Oaks, 1992, 333. Wescoat's view of history is based upon Hyden White's 'Formalist and Contextualist Strategies in Historical Explanation', a paper presented at the University of Chicago, 7 April, 1989 and *Metahistory: The Historical Imagination in 19th century Europe*, Baltimore, 1972; *Tropics of Discourse: Essays in Cultural Criticism*, Baltimore, 1978.

2. Seti I inscription, Speos Artemidos, H. W. Fairman, Bernard Grdseloff, 'Hatshepsut and Seti I inside Speos Artemidos', *JEA* 33 (1947), 23; Sinuhe B 305-6 uses the same phrase.

Chapter *I*

1. Norman de Garis Davies, *The Rock Tombs of El-Amarna*, i, London, 1903, pl. xxxii, Meryre reliefs and in houses.

2. Giulio Farina, *La Pittura egiziana*, Milan, 1929, pl.clxii; André L'Hote and Hassia, *Les chefs d'oeuvres de la peinture égyptienne*, Paris, 1954, pl. 109.

3. Jean-Claude Hugonot, *Le Jardin dans l'Egypte ancienne*, Frankfort-am-Main, 1989, 9-20

4. Pierre Anus, 'Un domaine thébaine d'époque amarnienne', *BIFAO* 69 (1970), 70-71.

5. Ramesses III Kanekame, James H. Breasted, *Ancient Records of Egypt* iv, Chicago, 1906-1908, 216. Papyrus Harris.

6. Günther Düriegl, Irmgard Hein, eds. *Pharaonen und Fremde Dynastien im Dunkel*, Exhibition Catalogue, Vienna, 1994, 93.

7. Manfred Bietak, 'Eine Palastanlage aus der Zeit des späten Mittleren Reiches und andere Foschungsergebnisse aus dem Östlichen Nildelta (Tell Dabaa 1979-1984), *Anzeiger Österreiches Akademie der Wissenschaften* 121 (1985), 312-349.

8. Abdel Ghaffar Shedid, *Stil der Grabmalerei in der Zeit Amenophis' II. Untersucht an den Thebanischen Gräbern Nr.104 und Nr. 80*, 1988, pls. 49, 54, 65.

9. e.g., Theban Tomb 19, Georges Foucart, *Tombes thébaines: Le Tombeau d'Amonmos*, Cairo. 1932-5, pl. xi; Theban Tomb 277, J. Vandier d'Abbadie, *Deux tombes thébains à Gournet Mourrai*, Cairo, 1954, pl. xxiii.

10. Patrick F. Houlihan, *The Birds of Ancient Egypt*, Warminster, 1986, nos. 53, 54, 55, 59, 28.

11. Werner Kaiser, et al. 'Stadt und Tempel von Elephantine', *MDAIK* 38 (1982), 310-314, fig. 18-19:

12. Ricardo Caminos, *Late Egyptian Miscellanies*, Providence, 1954, 143.

13. Manfred Bietak, 'Ein altägyptischer Weingarten in einem Tempelbezirk', *Anzeiger der Phili-. hist. Klasse der Österreichischen Akademie der Wissenschaft* (1985), 267-278; Günther Düriegl, Irmgard Hein, eds. *Pharaonen und Fremde Dynastien im Dunkel*, Exhibition Catalogue, Vienna, 1994, 93. *Proceedings of the British Academy*, 1979, 269; Arne Eggebrecht, Und nochmals: Khatana-Qantir Importance... Zum Auftakt der Hildesheimer Grabungen in Qantir', *MDAIK* 37 (1981), 139-142.

14. Sir Geoffrey Jellicoe, Susan Jelllicoe, P. Goode, and M. Lancaster, eds. *Oxford Companion to Gardens*, Oxford, 1986, 63-64.

15. William T. Stearn, *Flower Artists of Kew*, London, 1990, 7.

16. Stearn, *Flower Artists of Kew*, 10.

17. Label in Victoria and Albert Museum for Temporary Exhibition, 1995, cf. Gill Saunders, *Picturing Plants. An analytical History of Plant Illustration*, London, 1994.

18. Kent Weeks, *Egyptology and Social Sciences*, Cairo, 1979, 69.

19. Heinrich Schäfer, Trans. John Baines, *Principles of Egyptian Art*, Oxford, 1974 ed., 43.

20. William Stevenson Smith, *A History of Sculpture and Painting in the Old Kingdom*, Oxford, 1946, p. xiii.

21. "Laws" 656 translated by John Tait in Schäfer, *Principles of Egyptian Art*, 1986 ed., 349.

22. N. de Garis Davies, 'Mural Paintings in the city of Akhetaten', *JEA* 7 (1921), 4.

23. Alexander Badawy, "Compositions murales à système modulaire dans les tombes égyptiennes de l'ancien empire, " *Gazette des Beaux Arts* (Feb. 1981), 49-52.

24. John Baines, 'Color Terminology and Color Classification: Ancient Egyptian Color Terminology and Polychromy', *American Anthropologist*, 87 (1985), 282-297.

25. Henri Frankfort, ed. *Mural Painting at el-'Amarneh*, London,1929, 4; cf. Cyril Aldred, *Akhenaten*, London, 1968, 7.

26. James H. Breasted, *Ancient Records of Egypt*, ii, 975, Chicago, 1906, inscription cut on the rocks at Aswan.

27. William Stevenson Smith, A *History of Sculpture and Painting in the Old Kingdom*, Boston, 1964, 351-8; see also review of Stevenson Smith by John A. Wilson, *JNES* 6 (1947), 231-248; D. A. Lowle, 'A remarkable family of draughtsmen painters from Early Nineteenth Dynasty Thebes,' *Oriens Antiquus* 15 (1976), 91-106.

28. Sir Alan Gardiner, *Egyptian Grammar*, Oxford, 1927, Sign List, M. 11.

29. Carter nos. 540, and 551: Howard Carter, *The Tomb of Tutankhamun*, iii, London, 1933, frontispiece.

30. E. V. Pischikova, 'Representations of ritual and symbolic objects in Late XXVth and Saite Private Tombs,' *JARCE* 31 (1994), 69-70, who maintains that the lily, *Lilium candidum*, was only introduced in the Late Period.

Chapter II

1. Sir Alan H. Gardiner, 'The Dakhleh Stela', JEA, 19 (1933), 22, 22nd Dynasty.

2. Josef Dorner, Manfred Bietak, *Österreichisches Archäologisches Institut Grabungen 1984;* Manfred Bietak, 'Ein Altägyptischer Weingarten in einem Tempelbezirk. Tell el Dabaa 1 Marz bis 10 Juni 1985', Anzeiger der Österreichischen Akademie der Wissenschaften, Wien 121 (1985), 273-278.

3. LÄ i, 77 Bewässerung ; Francis Ll. Griffith, 'Excavations at el-'Amarnah, 1923-1924,' *JEA* 10 (1924), pl. xxxiv house garden; Amarna house N.49.9, Ludwig Borchardt, Herbert Ricke, *Die Wohnhäuser in Tell el-Amarna*, Berlin, 1980, plan 73; Barry J. Kemp, *Amarna Reports*, iv, London, 1987, 51-52, fig. 4.5, fig. 4.6

4. Jean Vercoutter, 'Mirgissa III', *Kush* 15 (1973), 275-276.

5. Michela Schiff Giorgini, 'Soleb campaigns 1961-1963', *Kush* 12 (1964), 87-95.

6. Charles Bonnet, *Kerma, royaume de Nubie*, Geneva, 1990, 37. It is not clear what the date of the plots at Kerma is, or whether they were connected with the buildings around.

7. Peter L. Shinnie, 'Preliminary report on the Excavatons at `Amarah West, 1948-1949 and 1949-1950', JEA 37 (1951), 9.

8. Jean Vercoutter, 'Fouilles de Mirgissa', *Bull. Soc. Fr. d'Égyptologie* 43 (1965), abb. 3.

9. Barry J. Kemp, *Amarna Reports*, iv, London, 1987, 124-125 fig. 9.6. Well area: Q 48.4 and Kemp, *Amarna Reports* v, 1-14.

10. James H. Breasted, *Ancient Records of Egypt*, Chicago, 1906, iii. 45ff. ll.32-35 note (d); Jean-Marie Kruchten, *Le décret d'Horemheb*, Brussels, 1989,125; a tax on gardens was current in Ptolemaic times, W. L. Westerman, 'Orchard and vineyard taxes in the Zenon papyri', *JEA* 12 (1926), 38-51.

11. J. E. Quibell, *Excavations at Saqqara* 1906,1907, 8. pl. xiii. Tomb of Karenen. Painted wood and stucco 60 x 50 cms. floor eaten by ants. Early Middle Kingdom. But compare roof of weavers' shop, James H. Breasted, *Servant Statues*, New York, 1949, 52, pl. 47.

12. Plan *LÄ* vi. 1169-1182; Dieter Eigner, 'Gartenkunst im alten Ägypten', *Die Gartenkunst* 7/1 (1995), 104-108.

13. C. Desroches-Noblecourt, 'La cueillette du raisin à la fin de l'époque Amarnienne: Toutankhamon fut-il portraituré sous l'aspect d'un petit prince?', *JEA* 54 (1968), 82-87.

14. Miriam Lichtheim, *Ancient Egyptian Literature*, iii, Berkeley, 1980, 173.

15. Günther Roeder, 'Bericht über die Ausgrabungen der Deutschen Hermopolis Expedition 1935', *MDAIK* 7 (1937), pl. 4b.

16. Henri Frankfort, *The Cenotaph of Seti I at Abydos*, London, 1933.

17. L. P. Kirwan, 'Preliminary Report of the Oxford University Excavations at Kawa, 1935-1936', *JEA* 22 (1936), 199.

18. In the *Maru*-Aten actual containers were found, T. Eric Peet and C. Leonard Woolley, *The City of Akhenaten*, i, London, 1923, 115. pls. xxxi, Fig. 2.

19. T. Eric Peet, C. Leonard Woolley, *City of Akhenaten*, i. London, 1923, 48; L. Borchardt, 'Ausgrabungen in Tell el Amarna 1912-1913', *MDOG* 52 (1913), 12; Ludwig Borchardt, Herbert Ricke, *Die Wohnhäuser in Tell el-Amarna*, Berlin, 1980, 26; Francis G. Newton, 'Excavations at el-'Amarnah 1923-1924', JEA 10 (1924), 295; C. Robichon, A. Varille, *Le temple du scribe royal Amenhotep fils de Hapou*, Cairo, 1936, 35, pl.xxviii; Günther Roeder, *Amarna-reliefs aus Hermopolis*, Hildesheim, 1969, pls. 8a, 41, 88.

20. Pierre Montet, 'Les travaux de la mission Montet: Tanis et Behbeit el Hagar en 1948 à 1949', *ASAE* 50 (1950), 40-42, fig. 5.

21. Robert Mond, Oliver H. Myers, *The Bucheum* i, London, 1934, 180-1, iii, pl.v, cii.

22. Werner Kaiser, et. al. 'Stadt und Tempel von Elephantine', *MDAIK* 38 (1982),310-314, fig. 18-19.

23. LÄ v. 809 Seelenhaus, fig. 3, Warsaw no. 139 502, A. Niwinski, 'Plateaux d'offrandes et 'maisons d'âmes', genèse, évolution et fonction dans la culte des morts au temps de la xie dynastie', *Études et Travaux* 8 (1975) 73-112A; LÄ v, 806; Charles Kuentz, 'Bassins et tables d'offrandes', BIFAO 81 (1981), 248-253, fig. 9- 10.

24. Richard A. Parker, 'A late demotic gardening agreement , Medinet Habu Ostracon 4038', *JEA* 26 (1941), 88, C (26)-(35).

25. Houses Q 44.1 and Q 46.1 Ludwig Borchardt, Herbert Ricke, *Die Wohnhäuser in Tell el-Amarna*, Berlin, 1980.

26. British Museum Label for Exhibition of shabtis. Chapter 6 of the Book of the Dead.

27. Miriam Lichtheim, *Literature of the Ancient Egyptians*, Berkeley, 1973, i, 187.

28. Richard A. Parker, 'A late demotic gardening agreement', *JEA* 26 (1940), 85-113.

29. T.G.H.James, *The Hekhanakhte Papers and other early Middle Kingdom documents*, New York, 1962, 32.

30. James H. Breasted, *Ancient Records of Egypt*, Chicago, 1906, iv. 682, Stela found at Abydos.

31. Miriam Lichtheim, *Literature of the Ancient Egyptians*, iii, Berkeley, 35.

32. F. Laming Macadam, *The Temples of Kawa*, ii, Oxford, 59.

33. Wilhelm Spiegelberg, 'Neue Beiträge zum dem altägyptische Titelsammlungen', *RT* 19 (1897), 92ff; Alan H. Gardiner, *Ancient Egyptian Onomasticon*, London, 1947, i, 66.

34. Edouard Naville, *The XIth Dynasty Temple at Deir el Bahari*. EEF Memoir. 28. London, 1907. pl.xxiv, p. 58, 69.

35. James H. Breasted, *Ancient Records of Egypt*, Chicago, 1906, iv, 600. Katha = *Carthamus tinctorius*, Gérard Charpéntier, *Recueil de matériaux épigraphiques relatif à la botanique de l'Égypte antique*, Paris, 1981, 1276.

36. Miriam Lichtheim, 'The Songs of the Harpers, *JNES* 4 (1945), 184.

37. Miriam Lichtheim, *Ancient Egyptian Literature*, Berkeley, 1973, ii, 99.

38. TT 241. Alan W. Shorter, 'The Tomb of Aahmose, Supervisor of the Mysteries of the House of the Morning', *JEA* 16 (1930), 55; and Paheri, el Kab , Christiane Desroches Noblecourt, 'Les trois saisons du dieu et le débarcadère du ressuscité', *MDAIK* 47 (1991), 67-80.

39. Francis Ll. Griffith, 'The Abydos Decree of Seti I at Nauri,' *JEA* 13 (1927), 199.

40. Jean Yoyotte, 'Le Bassin de Djaroukha', *Kêmi* 15 (1959), 29.

41. Christopher J. Eyre, 'The water regime for orchards and plantations in pharaonic Egypt', *JEA* 80 (1994), 75.

Chapter III

1. M. Nabil el Hadidi, *The predynastic of Hierakonpolis*, Taeckholmia, a. vol. 1, Cairo, 1981; *BIFAO* supplement (1981), 468.

2. Jane Renfrew in Barry J. Kemp, *Amarna Reports*, ii, London, 1985: analysis of more than 26 items.

3. See references in Dieter Eigner, 'Gartenkunst im alten Ägypten, Grabungsergebnisse der Zweigstelle Kairo des Österreichischen Archäologischen Instituts', *Die Gartenkunst* 7/1 (1995), 98-109.

4. Robert J. Wenke et al. 'Kom el-Hisn: Excavation of an Old Kingdom Settlement in the Egyptian Delta,' *JARCE* 25 (1988), 19-23; Marie-Francine Moens, and Wilma Wetterstrom, 'The agricultural economy of an Old Kingdom Town in Egypt's West Delta: insights from the plant remains,' *JNES* 47 (1988), 159-173.

5. Nigel Hepper in Geoffrey Martin, *The Sacred Animal Necropolis at North Saqqarah*, London, 1981, 146-151.

6. e.g., in the body of Ramesses II which was found with the royal mummies at Deir el-Bahari, ed. Lionel Balout and C. Roubet, *La Momie de Ramsès II*, Paris, 1985, 160.

7. See Ludwig Keimer, *Die Gartenpflanzen im alten Ägypten*, i, Hamburg-Berlin, 1924, ii, ed. Renate Germer, Mainz, 1984; Renate Germer, *Flora des pharaonischen Ägypten*, Mainz, 1985; Renate Germer, 'Plant remains in the Manchester Museum,' *JEA* 73 (1987), 245-246; Renate Germer, *Katalog der altägyptischen Pflanzenreste der Berliner Museen*, Wiesbaden, 1988; Renate Germer, *Die Pflanzenmaterialen aus dem Grab des Tutanchamun*, Hildesheim, 1989; Nathalie Baum, *Arbres et Arbustes de l'Egypte ancienne. La liste de la tomb thébaine d'Ineni (no. 81)*, Louvain, 1988; F. Nigel Hepper, *Pharaoh's Flowers: The Botanical Treasures of Tutankhamun*, London, 1990; F. Nigel Hepper, *Planting a Bible Garden*, London, 1987; F. Nigel Hepper, *Illustrated Encyclopedia of Bible Plants*, Leicester, 1992; Colette Roubet, 'La parure florale de Ramsès II: documents conservés dans l'herbier du Musée de Paris et au Musée de l'Agriculture au Caire', *Prospection et Sauvegarde des antiquités de l'Egypte. Actes de la table ronde organisée à l'occasion du centenaire de l'IFAO* ed. Nicolas-Christophe Grimal, Cairo, 1981, 151-161; Lise Manniche, *An Ancient Egyptian Herbal*, London, 1989.

8. James Henry Breasted, *Ancient Records of Egypt*, Chicago, 1906-8, iv. 380.

9. *Mimusops laurifolia = Mimusops schimperi*, Gérard Charpentier, *Recueil de matériaux épigraphiques relatifs à la botanique de l'Egypte antique*, Paris, 1981, 1078; Ib Friis, 'The taxonomy and distribution of *Mimusops laurifolia* (Sapotaceae)', *Kew Bulletin* 35 (1981), 785-792; I. Friis, F. Nigel Hepper, Peter Gasson, 'The botanical identity of the *Mimusops* in ancient Egyptian tombs', *JEA* 72 (1986), 201-4. Possible illustration in

tomb of Ipuy TT 217, Norman de Garis Davies, *Two Ramesside Tombs*, New York, MMA, pl. XVIII, last tree left of shrine.

10. Agricultural Museum, Cairo, no. 4055.

11. Agricultural Museum, Cairo, no. 1405.

12. Renfrew in Kemp, *Amarna Reports*, ii, 184. Also an example without provenance in the Louvre: M-A. Beauverie, 'Description illustrée des végétaux antiques du Musée Egyptian du Louvre', *BIFAO* 35 (1935), 133, pl. v, no. 1417.

13. Personal communication from Mme. Reem Samir who is preparing a study on *Mimusops schimperi* in the Dept. of Botany at Cairo University.

14. Sheila Collenette, *An Illustrated Guide to the Flowers of Saudi Arabia*, London, 1985, 440 growing at 2800 ft in untended groves along a river bank.

15. Hepper, *Pharaoh's Flowers*, 15.

16. BM 41147, 43180, 44923-4, from Deir el-Bahari, Edouard Naville, *The XIth Dynasty Temple at Deir el-Bahari*, iii, London, 1913, pl. xxv.2, p. 17, described by Geraldine Pinch, *Votive Offerings to Hathor*, Oxford, 1993, 282, as persea. Also Agricultural Museum, Cairo, no. 4462.

17. Louis Keimer, 'Interprétation de quelques passages d'Horapollon', *Supplément aux Annales du Service des Antiquités de l'Egypte* 5 (1947), 39, fig. 35; Germer, *Tutanchamun*, 53, Carter no. 585 = JE 61871, exhibition no. 708.

18. Keimer, *Gartenpflanzen* i, 37, but see Charpentier, *Botanique*, Paris, 1981, 198.

19. Ph. Derchain, "Le lotus, la mandragore et le persea', *CdE* 50/99 (1975), 85 quoting D. Bonneau, *La crue du Nil*, 49-50.

20. Anthony G. Miller, Miranda Morris, *Plants of Dhofar*, Oman, 1988, 242.

21. First Dynasty, Ludwig Keimer, 'Note sur le nom égyptien du jujubier d'Egypte (*Zizyphus spina Christi* Willd)', *ASAE* 42 (1943), 280; Agricultural Museum, Cairo nos. 3371-2, Pharaonic period.

22. Agricultural Museum, Cairo no. 379.

23. Dieter Arnold, *Der Tempel der König Mentuhotep von Deir el Bahari*, Mainz, 1981, 81.

24. In the tomb of Amenophis II, no. 2783 in the Egyptian Museum, Cairo.

25. Walter Draper, *Gardening in Egypt. A Handbook of Gardening for Lower Egypt*. London, 1895, 98.

26. UCL 35653. Abydos, Umm el Qaab surface. Janine Bourriau, *JEA* 76 (1990), 157. Compare Cairo JE 71297 from the tomb of Hemaka.

27. Pyr. Utt, 440. Raymond O. Faulkner, *Ancient Egyptian Pyramid Texts*, Oxford, 1969.

28. A. Lucas, *Ancient Egyptian Materials and Industries*, 4th ed. 1962, 437.

29. Ricardo Caminos, *Late Egyptian Miscellanies*, Providence, 1954, 74.

30. Breasted, *Ancient Records*, iv. 301.

31. Collenette, *Flowers of Saudi Arabia*, 500.

32. K. C. Sahni, *Important Trees of the Northern Sudan*, Khartoum, 1968, 84.

33. Abdel Ghaffar Shedid, *Die Felsgräber von Beni Hasan in Mittelägypten*, Mainz, 1994, abb.140 in colour.

34. Täckholm, *LÄ*, ii, 268.

35. B. Verdcourt, 'A synopsis of the Moringaceae', *Kew Bulletin* 40, 5 (1985), 1ff.

36. *Egypt Exploration Society Report*, 1989-90, 6.

37. *Grewia asiatica* grows on the Aswan Botanic Island acccording to the catalogue of the plants there, Esmail Ali Moussa, *Aswan Botanic Island*, Cairo, 1970s (?)

38. Miller, Morris, *Dhofar*, 284.

39. Thomas. J. Abercrombie and Lynn Abercrombie, 'Arabia's Frankincense Trail', *National Geographic Magazine* 168/4 (Oct. 1985), 475-513.

40. Wolfgang Helck, *Materialen zur Wirtschaftsgeschichte des Neuen Reiches*, Wiesbaden,1961-70, 13.

41. F. Nigel Hepper, 'Arabian and African Frankincense Trees', *JEA* 55 (1969), 69, figs. 1, 2.

42. Edourd Naville, *The Temple of Deir el Bahari*, London, 1895-1908, iii, pls. lxix-lxxix;F. Nigel Hepper, 'An ancient expedition to transplant live trees', *Journal of the Royal Horticultural Society* 92 (1967), 435-438.

43. Hepper, *Illustrated Encyclopedia*, 136.

44. Nigel Groom, *Frankincense and Myrrh, A study of the Arabian Incense Trade*, London, New York, 1981, 25 thinks that *antyw* is myrrh because it is turned into an ointment which cannot be done with frankincense; also myrrh trees grow in Africa which is where the expedition went. Cf. Théodore Monod, 'Arbres à Encens', *Bulletin du Musée National d'Histoire Naturelle*, Paris, 1979, 4th series.no. 1, Section B. no. 3., 131-169, for a study and illustrations of how the tree grows. Also Jean Dupéron, 'Contributions à l'étude de *Boswellia Sacra*: anatomie de la plantule et de la tige âgée' in the same volume.

45. Collenette, *Flowers of Saudi Arabia*, 91.

46. Gérard Charpentier, *Botanique*, 252 and 970; Adolf Erman, Hermann Grapow, *Wörterbuch der ägyptischen Sprache*, 7 vols. Leipzig, Berlin, 1926-1963, list many words for myrrh of which *antyw* is the most common in dynastic times, apart from words which appear in medical texts and which have been equated with myrrh. The rest of the words were introduced in Ptolemaic times. Charpentier, *Botanique*, 252 says that *antyw* is incense-oliban in dynastic times, and resin or perfume in general, in Ptolemaic times. *Sentjer* 970 is 'resin de térébinth' in Dynastic times, and resin in general in Greek times. The word *sentjer* is written on a label of a jar in the tomb of Tutankhamun, Jaroslav Cerny, *Hieratic inscriptions from the Tomb of Tutankhamun*, Oxford, 1965, no. 57, Carter 494. Balls of incense were found separately in the tomb, Germer, *Tutankhamun*, 79. Carter no. 32t. 2.2 cm. diam., Carter notes that they were: "suggestive of frankincense" after a sample had been burnt. Hepper, *Pharaoh's Flowers*, 20, 23.

47. Renate Germer, *Untersuchung über Arzneimittelpflanzen im Alten Ägypten*, Hamburg, 1979, 63-69, 69-82.

48. *LÄ* vi. 1116-1117, Weihrauch.

49. Norman de Garis Davies, *The Tomb of Ken-Amun at Thebes*, pl. ix, Miriam Lichtheim, 'The Harpers' Songs', *JNES* 4 (1945), 182, Amenhotep-sise TT 75 Norman de

Garis Davies, *The Tomb of Two Officials of Tuthmosis iv*, London, 1923, pls. v, xvii, p. 5 *antyw* which Davies translates as frankincense.

50. Charpentier, *Botanique*, 970 adopts the translation of terebinth for *sentjer*; Abdel-Aziz Saleh, 'Some problems relating to the Pwenet reliefs at Deir el-Bahari', *JEA* 58 (1972), 140-158, who thinks that *sntr* is incense, the sweet smelling resin, and *antyw* is resin and shrubs.

51. Millar, Morris, *Dhofar*, 178.

52. Charpentier, *Botanique*, 234.

Chapter IV

1. Miriam Lichtheim, *Ancient Egyptian Literature*, ii, Berkeley, 1976, 192. Love poem in Papyrus Harris 500.

2. Sylvia Schoske, Barbara Kreissl, Renate Germer, *"Anch" Blumen für das Leben. Pflanzen im alten Ägypten*, Munich, 1992, abb. 45.

3. For the plants mentioned see Ch. III, note 7: Renate Germer, *Untersuchungen über Artzneimittelpflanzen im alten Ägypten*, Hamburg, 1979; Georg Schweinfurth, 'Ueber Pflanzenreste aus alt-aegyptischen Gräbern', *Berichte der deutschen botanischen Gesellschaft*, Berlin, 2 (1884);Vivi Täckholm, *Student's Flora*, Beirut, 1974; Johanna Dittmar, *Blumen und Blumensträusse als Opfergabe im alten Ägypten*, Munich-Berlin, 1986; Sheila Collenette, *An illustrated Guide to the Flowers of Saudi Arabia*, London, 1985; and for the names of the plants, Gérard Charpentier, *Recueil de matériaux épigraphiques relatifs à la botanique de l'Egypte antique*, Paris, 1981.

4. K. Bosse-Griffiths, 'Fruit of the Mandrake' *Fontes atque Pontes*, (Festschrift Brunner), Wiesbaden, 1983, 67 suggests all fruits represented are mandrake and none are *mimusops*.

5. Herbert E. Winlock, *Material used for the embalming of Tutankhamun*. MMA. Papers. no. 10. New York, 1941, 17. See Renate Germer's reconsideration of this material in 'Die Blütenhalskragen aus RT 54' in *Miscellanea Aegyptologica. Wolfgang Helck zum 75 Geburtstag*, ed. Hartwig Altenmüller and Renate Germer, Hamburg, 1989.

6. Johanna Dittmar, *Blumen und Blumensträusse als Opfergabe im alten Ägypten*, Munich-Berlin, 1986, 29.

7. Mrs. M. Grieve, *A Modern Herbal*, London, 1974 reprint, 651.

8. Mark David Merlin, *On the trail of the ancient opium poppy*, Rutherford, 1984, could find no proof of opium poppies in Egypt.

9. Dr. Ragab being one of those who has restored the papyrus to Egypt, Hassan Ragab, *Le papyrus*, Cairo, 1980, 66-79.

10. F. Nigel Hepper, T. Reynolds, 'Papyrus and the adhesive properties of its cell sap in relation to paper-making', *JEA* 53 (1967), 156.

11. Moh. M. Saghir, *The Papyrus and Lotus in Ancient Egyptian Civilization*, Cairo, 1985; Stephan Weidner, *Lotos im alten Ägypten. Verarbeiten zu einer Kulturgeschichte von Nymphaea lotus, nymphaea coerulea und Nelumbo nucifera in der Dynastischen Zeit*,

Pfaffenweiler Centaurus Verlagsgesellschaft, 1985; W. D. Spanton, 'The waterlilies of ancient Egypt', *Ancient Egypt* 4 (1917), 1-24.

12.   TT 90. Norman de Garis Davies, *Two Tombs of Two Officials of Tuthmosis the Fourth*, London, 1923, 31, pl. xxxiii.

13.   The difference between the blue and white lotuses is shown on a faience bowl where the two kinds alternate. The upper row is the blue lotus, *Nymphaea caerulae sav* and the lower row *Nymphaea lotus* L., L. Keimer, 'The decoration of a New Kingdom vase', *JNES* 8 (1949), 1-5, pl. vii.

14.   Wilma Wetterstrom, 'Paleoethnobotanical studies at predynastic sites in the Nagada-Khattara region' in F. Hassan, *Predynastic Studies in the Nagada-Khattara region*, reported by Marie-Francine Moens and Wilma Wetterstrom, 'The agricultural economy of an Old Kingdom town in Egypt's West Delta: insights from the plant remains', *JNES* 47 (1988), 163.

15.   Lionel Balout and C. Roubet, *La Momie de Ramsès II*, Paris, 1985, 163.

16.   Vivi Täckholm, *Flora of Egypt*, iii, 1954, 347-348.

17.   Ludwig Keimer, *Die Gartenpflanzen im alten Ägypten*, ii, ed. Renate Germer, Mainz, 1984, under '*Sesbania sesban*'.

18.   Ed. Lionel Balout and C. Roubet, *La Momie de Ramsès II*, Paris, 1985, 165.

19.   Hildegard von Deines, Hermann Grapow, *Wörterbuch der ägyptischen Drogennamen*, *Grundriss der Medizin der alten Ägypter*, iv, Berlin, 1959; Renate Germer, *Untersuchung über Arzneimittelpflanzen im Alten Ägypten*, Hamburg, 1979.

20.   Miriam Lichtheim, *Ancient Egyptian Literature*, i, 69, Old Kingdom.

21.   Alfred Lucas, *Ancient Egyptian Materials and Industries*, ed. John R. Harris, London, 1962, 85-90; *LÄ*, iv. 910.

22.   Nadine Cherpion, 'Le "Cone d'onguent"', *BIFAO* 94 (1994), 79-106..

23.   Old Kingdom: Richard Lepsius, *Denkmäler aus Aegypten und Aethiopien*, ii, Berlin, 1849-59, 96; Frédéric Caillaud, *Recherches sur les arts et métiers, les usages de la vie civile et domestiques des anciens peuples de l'Egypte*, Paris, 1831, pl. 15A.

24.   TT175 Lise Manniche, *The Wall Decoration in Three Theban Tombs*, Copenhagen, 1988, fig. 30.

25.   E.g., Louvre, E. 11377, Georges Bénédite, 'Un thème nouveau de la décoration murale des tombes néomemphites. La cueillette du lis et le "lirinion" à propos d'un bas relief et d'un fragment de bas-relief au Musée du Louvre', *Fondation Eugène Piot. Monuments et Mémoires publiés par l'Académie des Inscriptions et Belles-Lettres*, vol. 25, Paris, 1921-22, 1-28; Louvre 11162, Christiane Ziegler, *Le Louvre. Les antiquités égyptiennes*, Paris, 1990; Turin 1673, Ippolito Rosellini, *I Monumenti dell'Egitto e della Nubia. Monumenti Civile*, ii, Pisa, 1934, 66; Henry Fischer, 'The early publication of a relief in Turin', GM 101 (1988), 31-32; Lisa Montagno Leahy, 'The puzzling history of Turin 1673', *GM* 105 (1988), 55-56; Täckholm, *Flora*, iii, 279; *LÄ* iii, 1205-6.

26.   M-A. Beauverie, 'Description illustrée des végétaux antiques du Musée égyptien du Louvre', *BIFAO* 35 (1935), 125, pl. iii.

27.   Lucas, *Materials and Industries*, 87.

28. Ethelbert Blatter, *Records of the Botanical Survey of India*, vol. vii. Calcutta, 1914-1916, 201.

29. James H. Breasted, *Ancient Records of Egypt*, Chicago, 1906-8, 4, 308.

30. Dieter Arnold, *The Pyramid of Senwosret I, i, The South Cemeteries of Lisht*, New York, 1988, pl. 51.

31. Täckholm, *Flora*, iii, 104, ff.

32. Collenette, *Flowers of Saudi Arabia*, 159 .

33. Nabil el-Hadidi, 'Notes on Egyptian weeds of Antiquity' in *The Followers of Horus. Studies in honour of Michael Hoffmann*, ed. Renée Friedman, Barbara Adams, Oxford, 1992, 323-325, fig. 2a.

34. Marie-Francine Moens, Wilma Wetterstrom, 'The agricultural economy of an Old Kingdom Town in Egypt's West Delta: insights from the plant remains', *JNES* 47 (1988), 159-173.

35. Agricultural Museum, Cairo, no. 1219.

36. James P. Mandaville, *Flora of Eastern Saudi Arabia*, London, 1990, 387.

37. Mandaville, *Flora of Eastern Saudi Arabia*, 329.

38. Ludwig Keimer, 'La *Potamogeton lucens* L. dans l'Egypte ancienne. Un exemple de tradition dans les réprésentations figurées égyptienne', *Revue de l'Egypte Ancienne*, i, 3-4 (1927), 182-197. *Potamogeton schweinfurthii, P. crispus*. Potamogeton appearing to stand up in certain OK reliefs. *Potamogeton* covering the statuettes of hippopotami. Probably grew in Upper as well as Lower Egypt; crocodiles could hide under the *Potamogeton*, L. Keimer, 'La vache et le cobra dans les marecages de papyrus de Thèbes', *BIE* 37/1 (1956), 216.

39. See Täckholm, *Flora*, i, 288 for list; more recent excavations at Amarna, Memphis and Kom el-Hisn, Marie-Francine Moens and Wilma Wetterstrom, 'The agricultural economy of an Old Kingdom Town in Egypt's West Delta: insights from the plant remains', *JNES* 47 (1988), 159-173.

40. Germer, *Flora*, 23 says *Cannabis sativa* was not known in Egypt.

41. *The New Encyclopedia of Textiles*, Englewood Cliffs, NJ, 1980, 140.

42. U. S. Dept of Agriculture. *A report on the flax culture for fiber in the US*, Washington, 1892.

Chapter V

1. Miriam Lichtheim, *Ancient Egyptian Literature*, i, Berkeley, 1973, 160.

2. Jacques Vandier, *Manuel d'archéologie égyptienne*, Paris, 1952- 62, ii, 2 fig. 319.

3. Francis Ll. Griffith, 'The Decree of Seti I at Nauri', *JEA* 13 (1927), 198.

4. Walter Bryan Emery, *Hor-Aha Excavations at Saqqara 1937-1938*, Cairo, 1939, 8 (S 3357) and Emery, *Great Tombs of the First Dynasty*, Cairo, 1949, iii, 2-3.

5. James E. Quibell, *Archaic Mastabas*, Cairo,1923, pl.vii, no. 1.

6. Ernesto Schiaparelli, *Relazione sui lavori, la tomba del dignitario "Cha" nella necropole di Tebe*, Turin, 1927, ii, 19, fig. 16; Herbert Ricke, *Bemerkungen zur Ägyptischen Baukunst*

des Alten Reiches, Cairo, 1950, *Beiträge zur ägyptischen Bauforschung und Altertumskunde*, Heft v, 21, fig. 4.

7. Cairo CG 1570A.Henry Fischer, 'An invocatory Offering Basin of the Old Kingdom', *MDAIK* 47 (1991), 130.

8. *Urk*, iv, 1632, 2. Trans. Barbara Cumming, *Egyptian Historical Records of the Later Eighteenth Dynasty*, Fasc. iii, Warminster, 1984.

9. Rainer Stadelmann, 'Pyramiden und Nekropole des Snofre in Dahschur, Dritter Vorbericht über die Grabungen des Deutschen Archäologischen Instituts in Dahschur', *MDAIK* 49 (1993), 261.

10. Dieter Arnold, *Der Tempel des Königs Mentuhotep von Deir el-Bahari, i, Architektur und Deutung*, Mainz, 1974; D. Arnold, *The Temple of Mentuhotep at Deir el-Bahari. From the Notes of H. Winlock*, New York, 1979.

11. Arnold, *Winlock Notes*, 21-22. pl. 17d.

12. = *T. articulata*, M. Nabil el-Hadidi, Loutify Boulos, *Street trees in Egypt*, Cairo, 1968, pl. 45; I. L. Smith, *Landscaping Plant Book*, Riyadh, 1986.

13. Claude Vandersleyden, 'Le jardin de Montouhotep', *Bull. Soc. Ég. de Genève 13* (1989), 161ff.

14. Arnold, *Winlock Notes*, 22.

15. Arnold, *Winlock Notes*, 22-23, pl. 15a, 19a, 49, 50.

16. Raymond O. Faulkner, *Ancient Egyptian Coffin Texts*, ii, Warminster, 1973, 247, Spell 682.

17. W. M. Flinders Petrie, G. Burton, Margaret A. Murray, *Lahun, ii, The Pyramid of Senusret II*, 5.11, pl. iv, viii.

18. Suzanne Ratié, *La reine Hatchepsout, sources et problèmes*, Leiden, 1979, 73.

19. Ludwig Keimer, Die *Gartenpflanzen im Alten Ägypten*,i, Berlin, 1924.

20. Edourd Naville, *The Temple of Deir el-Bahari*, London, 1895-1908, vi,1, pl.clxxii; Arnold, *Winlock Notes*, pl. 44; *LÄ* i, 1019.

21. Herbert Winlock, 'The Egyptian Expedition 1923-1924. The Museum's Excavations at Thebes', *BMMA* (1924), pt. 2 p. 18.

22. Herbert E. Winlock, *Excavations at Deir el-Bahari 1911-1931*, New York, 1942, 90.

23. Faulkner, *Coffin Texts*, spell 62.

24. Naville, *Deir el-Bahari*, v. pl.cxlii.

25. Note: in this translation by James Breasted the word for incense is translated as myrrh but for clarity 'incense' has been substituted, James H. Breasted, *Ancient Records of Egypt*, Chicago, 1906, ii, 293.

26. TT 143, Norman de Garis Davies, 'The Egyptian Expedition 1934-1935. Work of the Graphic Branch', *BMMA* 30 (1935) Nov. Sect. ii, 48.

27. A. Lucas, ed. John Harris, *Ancient Egyptian Materials and Industries*, 92, Lucas suggested the 'bare' trees might be frankincense.

28. F. Nigel Hepper, 'Arabian and African Frankincense Trees', *JEA* 55 (1969), 70.

29. F. Nigel Hepper, 'An ancient expedition to transplant live trees', *Journal of the Royal Horticultural Society* 92 (1967), 435-438 who says they were *Boswellia* which yield

frankincense, and not *Commiphora* which yield myrrh; Naville, *Deir el-Bahari*, iii, 15; The piles of gum shown with the trees are more like the gum of myrrh, Lucas, 'Cosmetics, perfumes and incense in ancient Egypt,' *JEA* 16 (1930), 50; Abdel Aziz Saleh, 'The Pwenet reliefs at Deir el-Bahari', *JEA* 58 (1972), 142-147.

30. *Boswellia sacra*, F. Nigel Hepper, *Planting a Bible Garden*, London, 1987, 80; Gus van Beek, 'Frankincense and myrrh', *Biblical Archaeologist* 23 (1960), 70-95; Frank N. Howes, *Vegetable Gums and Resins*, Waltham, Mass., 1949, 149-152.

31. Nigel Groom, *Frankincense and Myrrh. A study of the Arabian Incense Trade*, London, New York, 1981, 106 quoting Birdwood.

32. Groom, *Frankincense and Myrrh*, 119 quoting R. E. Drake-Brockman, *British Somaliland*, London, 1912, 242-5, 302-5.

33. Nigel Groom, *Perfume Handbook*, 154, 166 and personal communication; Howes, *Vegetable Gums and Resins*, 153.

34. Sheila Collenette, *An Illustrated Guide to the Flowers of Saudi Arabia*, London, 1985, 88.

35. Edward Brovarski 'Senenu, High Priest of Amun at Deir el-Bahari', *JEA* 62 (1976), 59-62.

36. Winlock, *Excavations at Deir el-Bahri*, 6, fig. 1, pl. 68; Jadwiga Lipinska, *Deir el-Bahari*, ii, *The Temple of Tuthmosis III*, Warsaw 1977, 60, fig. 63; Pierre Gilbert, 'Le Temple de Thoutmosis III', *CdE* 52 (1977), 252-259; Manfred Bietak, 'Theben-West: Vorbericht über die ersten vier Grabungskampagnen (1969-1971)', *Österreiches Akademie der Wissenschaften, Sitzungsberichte der phil.-hist. Klasse*, 278 Band, 4 (1972), Abhandlung, 17.

37. Dieter Arnold, J. Settgast, 'Vorbericht über die vom Deutschen Archäologischen Institut Kairo im Asasif unternommenen Arbeiten', *MDAIK*, 20 (1965), 56-57.

38. Dieter Eigner, 'Gartenkunst im alten Ägypten', *Gartenkunst* 7/1 (1995), 103.

39. Georges Legrain, 'Notes d'inspection. Sur le temple Manakhpirri-henq-ankh', *ASAE* 7 (1906), 183-7.

40. Herbert Ricke, *Der Totentempel Thutmoses' III, Beiträge zur ägyptischen Bauforschung und Altertumskunde*, Cairo, 1939,19-20. pl. v.

41. Gerhard Haeny, *Untersuchungen im Totentempel Amenophis III. Beiträge zur Ägyptische Bauforschung und Altertumskunde*, Wiesbaden, 1981.

42. Breasted, *Ancient Records*, ii, 883.

43. Marcelle Baud, *Dessins ébauchés de la necropole thébaine*, Cairo, 1935, 248-9. fig. 116.; Wilkinson Mss.v 148 [1-5]. 271 [2-4]; Norman de Garis Davies, *The Tomb of Neferhotep*, New York, 1933, i, fig. 9; Monique Nelson, 'Les fonctionnaires connus du temple de Ramsès II. Enquête à partir des tombes thébaines', *Memnonia. Bulletin édité par l'association pour la sauvegarde du Ramesseum*, 1 (1990-1991), 127-133.

44. Paraphrase of Wolfgang Helck, 'Ramessidische Inschriften aus Karnak', *ZÄS* 82 (1957), 120-121.

45. Breasted, *Ancient Records*, iv, 17.

46. Breasted, *Ancient Records*, iv.189.

47. Breasted, *Ancient Records*, iv, 194.

48. Breasted, *Ancient Records*, iv. 189.

49. Uvo Hölscher, *The Excavation of Medinet Habu*, iv, The Mortuary Temple of Ramses III, pt. ii, Chicago, 1951, 19, and vol. i (1934), pls, 3, 4.

50. Uvo Hölscher, *Excavations of Medinet Habu, i. General plans and views*, Chicago, 1934, pl. 2; Uvo Hölscher, *Medinet Habu*, ii, pl. 2. fig. 1, 2.

51. Hölscher, *The Excavation of Medinet Habu, iii, The Mortuary Temple of Rameses* III, pt. i, 67-78.

52. Hölscher, *Medinet Habu*, iv, 11-13, folio vol. i, pl. 25; Uvo Hölscher, *Das Hohe Tor von Medinet Habu. Eine Baugeschichtliche Untersuchungen*, Leipzig, 1910, pl. ii.

53. Harold Nelson, *Medinet Habu*, ii, pl.107, 20-21; W. F. Edgerton and J. A. Wilson, *Historical Records of Rameses iii*, vols. i and ii, Chicago, 1936, 132.

54. Breasted, *Ancient Records*, iv.141. 23-4.

55. Identified by Siegfried Schott, *Wall scenes from the mortuary chapel of the Mayor Paser at Medinet Habu*, Chicago,1957,14 pl. iii.

56. Marquis of Northampton, Wilhelm Spiegelberg, Percy Newberry, *Report on some excavations in the Theban Necropolis during the winter of 1898-99*, London, 1908, 8; Wilhelm Spiegelberg, 'Eine Inschrift aus dem Tempel der Ahmes-Nefret-ere', *ZÄS* 45 (1908), 87-88;Charles C. Van Siclen, III, 'The Temple of Meniset at Thebes', *Serapis*, 6 (1980),191.

57. Breasted, *Ancient Records*, iv, 513.

58. Breasted, *Ancient Records*, iii, 268.

59. Breasted, *Ancient Records*, iii, 527.

Chapter VI

1. Jacques Vandier, 'Une tombe inédite de la VIe dynastie', *ASAE* 36 (1936), 36.

2. Raymond O. Faulkner, *Ancient Egyptian Coffin Texts*, Warminster, 1973, CT ii, 134, 144; vi, 171, 173.

3. TT 82 Kurt Sethe, *Urkunden der 18. Dynastie*, Leipzig, 1906, iv 1064, 6-10, Wolfgang Helck, *Übersetzung zu den Heften 17-22 Urkunden der 18. Dynastie*, Berlin, 1961; Amenemhat, Nathalie Baum, *Arbres et arbustes de l'Egypte ancienne. La liste de la tombe d'Ineni (no. 81)*, Louvain, 1988, 31.

4. Ineni TT 81, *Urk.* iv. 73, Baum, *Arbres*, 28-32.

5. Norman de Garis Davies, *The Tomb of Kenamun at Thebes*, New York, 1930, 53.

6. Davies, *Kenamun*, 46.

7. Jean-Claude Hugonot, *Le Jardin dans l'Égypte ancienne*, Frankfurt-am-Main, 1989,130-131.

8. Phillippe Virey, *Sept tombeaux thébains*, Mémoires publiés par les membres de la Mission archéologique française au Caire, Paris, 1889, v. 2. (Khem), fig. 3. Burton Mss. British Library Add. Ms. 25638, 73, the ducks, fish and waterlilies are sketched by Burton.

9. Norman de Garis Davies, *The Tomb of Rekhmire at Thebes*, New York, 1943, 12-13, pl. xlvi 2D.

10. F. Ll. Griffith, 'The Abydos Decree of Seti I', *JEA* 13 (1927), 198.

11. Davies, *Rekhmire*, 78, pl.cxii. Scenes of collecting flowers in tombs of Djau, Deir el Gebrawi and Neferbauptah, Giza, Jacques Vandier, *Manuel d'archéologie égyptienne*, Paris, 1952-62, v, 1, figs. 198-199.

12. Miriam Lichtheim, 'The Harpers' Song', *JNES* 4 (1945), 195.

13. Jürgen Settgast, *Untersuchungen zu altägyptischen Bestattungsdarstellungen*, Glückstadt, 1963, 64-65.

14. Manfred Bietak, 'Zu den heiligen Bezirken mit Palmen in Buto und Sais - ein archäologischer Befund aus dem Mittleren Reich', *Zwischen den beiden Ewigkeiten, Festschrift für Gertrud Thausing*, Wien, 1994, 1-17; Günther Düriegl, Irmgard Hein, eds. *Pharaonen und Fremde Dynastien im Dunkel*, Vienna, 1994, 39, fig. 24.

15. Listed and illustrated by Beatrix Gessler-Löhr in Jan Assman, *Das Grab des Amenemope*, Mainz, 1991, 166-182. Add TT 31, Khons, Norman de Garis Davies, Alan H. Gardiner, *Seven Private Tombs at Kurneh*, London, 1948, pl. xii, for the corner of one such scene, and TT C4, Lise Manniche, *Lost Tombs*, London, 1988, 115, pls. 34, 42; Boyo Ockinga, *Bulletin of the Australian Centre for Egyptology* 2 (1991), 81 ff, tomb of Sennedjem at Awlad Azzaz at Sohag; Daniel Polz, *Das Grab nr. 54*, Diss. Heidelberg, 1988;see also Caris-Beatrix Arnst, 'Die Inselheiligtum im Gartenteich', *Altorientalische Forschung* 16 (1989), 203-215.

16. Ramses Moftah, 'Le défunt et le palmier-doum', *GM* 127 (1992), 63-65.

17. TT 218 Amennakht. Ingrid Wallert 'Bild des Alltags oder mehr?' in Helmut Brunner, *Wort und Bild*, 1979, 177.

18. Gessler-Löhr, in Jan Assman, *Das Grab des Amenemope*, Mainz, 1991, 172 says that the inscription indicates that the Opening of the Mouth and the purification are part of the same ceremony.

19. Pyr. 1216. 'The swallows are the Imperishable stars'. Raymond O. Faulkner, *Ancient Egyptian Pyramid Texts*, Oxford, 1969.

20. Adolf Erman, 'Aus dem Grabe eines Hohenpriesters von Memphis', *ZÄS* 33 (1895), 22, Berlin, 12410, name unknown.

21. Kurt Sethe, *Amun und die Acht Urgötter von Hermopolis*, Berlin, 1929, §250.

22. Plutarch, *de Iside et Osiride*, 20. Ed. and Trans. J. Gwyn Griffiths, Cardiff, 1970.

23. Coffin Text 467: Leonard H. Lesko, 'The field of *hetep* in the Coffin Texts', JARCE 9 (1971-72), 96.

24. Tomb I H3, Zaki Y. Saad, *Royal Excavations at Saqqara and Helwan* (1941-1945), Supplément aux ASAE cahier, no. 3 1952, 164.

25. Walter B. Emery, *Great Tombs of the First Dynasty*, Cairo, 1949, i, 73, tomb 3036.

26. Cecil Firth, James E. Quibell, *Excavatons at Saqqara (1912-1914)*, Cairo, 1923, pl. vii.

27. Claus Bieger and Peter Munro, 'Das Doppelgrab der Königinen Nbt und Hnwt in Saqqara', *SAK* 1 (1974), 36; Peter Munro, 'Das Unas Friedhof Nord-West', *GM* 59

(1982), 77-102; Hugonot, *Jardin*, 179; Uvo Hölscher, Peter Munro, 'Das Unas-Friedhof in Saqqara', SAK 3 (1975), 126.

28.   Cecil Firth, Battiscombe Gunn, *Teti Pyramid Cemeteries*, Cairo, 1926, pl. 85 (7), 289.

29.   Florence stela 1774 (Middle Kingdom) Ernesto Schiaparelli, *Museo archeologico di Firenze*, Rome, 1887, 489-490. The owner, Samentuser, built his house in the town and his tomb in the necropolis, Baum, *Arbres*, 30.

30.   George Reisner, 'The Tomb of Hepzefa Nomarch of Siut', *JEA* 5 (1918), 88; also known as Djefaihapi, LÄ, i, 1105.

31.   David O'Connor, The 'Cenotaphs' of the Middle Kingdom at Abydos, *Mélanges Gamal Eddin Mokhtar*, vol. ii. ed. Paule Posener-Kriéger, 1985,171-3, figs. 5-6. pl.i.

32.   T. Eric Peet, *The Cemeteries of Abydos*, ii, London 1914, 74-5, figs. 37-8, pl. xi. C. 81.

33.   Andrzej Niwinski, 'Plateaux d'offrandes et "maisons d'âmes", genèse, évolution et fonction dans la culte des morts au temps de la xiie dynastie', *Études et Travaux*, (1975), 105, figs. 20-21 not funerary, from Edfu.

34.   T. Eric Peet, C. Leonard Woolley, *City of Akhenaten*, i, London, 1923, 92.

35.   Ann Bomann, *The Private Chapel in Ancient Egypt*, London, 1991, passim; chapel 450, Barry J. Kemp, 'Preliminary Report on the el-Amarna expedition 1979', JEA 66 (1980), 14, fig. 5.

36   Geoffrey T. Martin, *The tomb of Paser and Ra`ia*, 1985, London, 4.

37.   Uvo Hölscher, *Excavations at Medinet Habu*, iv, pt. ii, Chicago, 1951, 22-25, pl. 42

38.   Uvo Hölscher, *Excavations at Medinet Habu, General Plans and Views*, i, Chicago, 1934, pls. 9, 10.

39.   Ludwig Keimer, 'La vache et le cobra', *BIE* 37/1 (1954-5), 226, figs. 9, 10.

40.   Klaus-Peter Kuhlmann, W. Schenkel, *Das Grab des Aba*, Theben n.36, Mainz, 1983, 131 roots found, pp. 113-113, pl.111b, see vol. 2.

41.   Dieter Eigner, *Die monumentale Grabbauten der Spätzeit in der thebanischen Nekropole*, Vienna, 1984, 170-172.

42.   TT 36. Ibi. Klaus-Peter Kuhlmann, 'Eine Beschreibung der Grabdekoration mit Aufforderung zu kopieren und zum Hinterlassen von Besucherinschriften aus Saitischer Zeit', *MDAIK* 29, 2 (1973), 209.

43.   Norman de Garis Davies, *The Rock Tombs of el-Amarna*, iv, 1, 20-30, pl. iv.

Chapter VII

1.   James H. Breasted, *Ancient Records of Egypt*, Chicago, 1906, ii, 567.

2.   Breasted, *Ancient Records*, ii, 903.

3.   Nebneteru. Priest of Amun, Miriam Lichtheim, *Ancient Egyptian Literature*, iii. Berkeley, 1980 .

4.   Lichtheim, *Literature*, iii.43. Stela of Somtutefnekht. c.340 B.C.

5.   Breasted, *Ancient Records*, ii. 601.

6.   Breasted, *Ancient Records*, ii, 376.

7. Paul Barguet, 'La cour du temple d'Edfou et le cosmos', *Livre du Centenaire, 1880-1980*, ed. Jean Vercoutter, IFAO, Cairo, 1980, 14.

8. Breasted, *Ancient Records*, ii,894.

9. Manfred Bietak et al., *Ägypten und Levante* 4 (1994), 18; Manfred Beitak, 'Ein altägyptischer Weingarten in einem Tempelbezirk', *Anzeiger der phil.-hist. Klasse der Österreichischen Akademie der Wissenschaften* 122 (1985), 275.

10. Breasted, *Ancient Records*, i, 215.; Mahmud abd er-Razik, 'Die altägyptische Weingarten (*k3nw/k3mw*) bis zum Ende des Neuen Reiches', *MDAIK* 35 (1979), 230-231.

11. Michela Schiff Giorgini, 'Soleb, Campagnes 1961-1963', *Kush* 12 (1964), 92-93.

12. Macadam's translations should be evaluated in the light of the more recent work of Gérard Charpentier, *Recueil de matériaux épigraphiques relatifs à la botanique de l'Egypte antique*, Paris, 1981.

13. L. P. Kirwan, Oxford University Excavations at Kawa, 1935-1936, in Macadam, *The Temples of Kawa* II, 208, *Mimusops*, fig. 4, site iii.

14. Breasted, *Ancient Records*, iv, 274.

15. Johanna Dittmar, *Blumen und Blumensträusse als Opfergabe im alten Ägypten*, Munich-Berlin 1986, 79; Hathor chapel at Dendera, Labib Habachi, 'King Nebhepetre Mentuhotep: his monuments, place in history, etc.', *MDAIK* 19 (1963), 24-25.

16. Pierre Montet, 'Vases sacres et profanes du tombeau de Psousennes', *Monuments et memoires, Fondation E. Piot*, vol. 43, 1949, 26; also illustrated by Keimer, *ASAE* 52 (1952), fig. 2.

17. Kurt Sethe, *Urkunden der 18. Dynastie, Dynastie*, Leipzig, 1906, Wolfgang Helck, *Übersetzung zu den Heften 17-22. Urkunden der 18. Dynastie*, Berlin, 1961, iv. 1257. Translation by Barbara Cumming, *Egyptian Historical Records of the Later Eighteenth Dynasty*, Warminster, 1982.

18. *LÄ*. vi, 1282; Hellmut Brunner, *Die Geburt des Gottkönigs. Studien zur überlieferung eines altägyptischen Mythos*, Wiesbaden, 1964, 61ff.

19. Breasted, *Ancient Records*, iii,161.

20. *LÄ* ii, 378.

21. Alexander Badawy, 'Architectural symbolism of the mammisi-chapels', *CdE* 38 no.75 (1963), 81.

22. Herbert Ricke, 'Der Geflügelhof des Amon in Karnak', *ZÄS* 73 (1937), 124 ff. ; David Berg, 'The 29th Dynasty Storehouse at Karnak', *JARCE* 24 (1987), 48, store-house not fowl-yard.

23. Hans Kayser, 'Die Ganse des Amon', *MDAIK* 16 (1958), pl. xiv, 193.

24. Sethe, *Urkunden der 18. Dynastie*, iv. 1418. Translated into English by Barbara Cumming, *Egyptian Historical Records of the Later Eighteenth Dynasty*, Warminster, 1984.

25. Charles Van Siclen, *Two Theban monuments from the reign of Amenhotep II*, San Antonio, 1986,16.

26. Michel Gitton, 'Le palais de Karnak', *BIFAO* 74 (1974), 63-64.

27. Charles Nims, 'Places about Thebes', *JNES* 14 (1955), 112.

28. Jean-Claude Hugonot, *Le Jardin dans l'Egypte ancienne*, Frankfort-am-Main, 1989, 30, fig. 14.

29. M. Abd el Raziq, 'Study on Nectanebo Ist in Luxor and Karnak', *MDAIK* 23 (1968), 156-159, according to an inscripton on one of the sphinxes (no. 2 W), Hassan S. Bakry, 'The sphinx avenue of the Luxor temple' in *Actes du Premier Congrès ICE*, ed. Reineke, 1979, 84.

30. El-Sayed Hegazy, 'The Great Processional Way of Thebes', *Journal of the Ancient Chronology Forum* 3 (1989-90), 82-85.

31. Pierre Lacau, Henri Chevrier, *Une Chapelle d'Hatshepsout à Karnak*, Cairo, 1977, 75.

32. *La Tombe de Nakht. Notice Sommaire.* Marcelle Werbrouck, B. Van de Walle, Fondation égyptologique Reine Elisabeth. Brussels, 1929. Illustrated by Hay, British Library, Add. Mss. 29822, 93 and 96, Lise Manniche, *Ancient Egyptian Herbal*, London, 1989, 16-17.

33. Jean Lauffray, 'Le secteur nord-est du temple jubilaire de Thoutmosis III à Karnak: état des lieux et commentaire architectural', *Kemi* 19 (1969), 198-199.

34. Paul Barguet, *Le Temple d'Amon-Re à Karnak essai d'exégèse*, Recherches d'Archéologie, de Philologie et d'Histoire, Cairo, 1962, 287; Translation of inscription in 'Botanical Garden', Barguet, *Temple*, 199, and Nathalie Beaux, *Cabinet de curiosités de Thoutmosis III: plantes et animax du 'Jardin botanique' de Karnak*, Louvain, 1990, 300.

35. Breasted, *Ancient Records*, ii,161.

36. Breasted, *Ancient Records*, ii, 566-7.

37. Eberhard Otto, *Topographie des Thebanischen Gaues*, Berlin, 1952, 27.

38. Pierre Anus, 'Un domaine thebaine d'époque amarnienne', *BIFAO* 69 (1970), 73-79. figs. 3, 5.

39. Donald Redford, 'Studies on Akhenaten at Thebes', *JARCE* 10 (1973), 91.

40. Maria Plantikow-Münster, 'Die Inscrift des B3k-n-hnsw in München', *ZÄS* 95 (1969), 117-131.

41. Charles F. Nims, 'The Eastern Temple at Karnak', in *Beiträge zur Ägyptischen Bauforschung und Altertumskunde Heft 12 Zum 70 Geburtstag von Herbert Ricke*, ed. Gerhard Haeny, Wiesbaden, 1971.107-111; *Temple of Khonsu*, OIP, 100, (1970), 15, n.(a), pl. 29,8.

42. Beatrix Gessler-Löhr, *Die Heiligen Seen Ägyptischer Tempeln*, Hildesheim, 1983, 241.

43. Miriam Lichtheim, *Ancient Egyptian Literature*, iii. Berkeley, 1980, 47.

44. G. Roeder, 'Zwei hieroglyphische Inschriften aus Hermopolis', *ASAE* 52 (1952), 345, 394.

45. G. A. Gaballa, 'Three documents from the reign of Ramesses III', *JEA* 59 (1973), 113.

46. Breasted, *Ancient Records*, iv, 333; Mahmud abd er-Razik, *MDAIK* 35 (1979), 231.

47. Breasted, *Ancient Records*, ii, 919.

48. Elizabeth J. Sherman, 'Djedhor the Saviour', *JEA* 67 (1981), 90.

49. Herodotus, *History*, ii, 138, Trans. Harry Carter, London, 1962.

Chapter VIII

1.   Miriam Lichtheim, *Ancient Egyptian Literature*, ii, Berkeley, 1974, 91.

2.   Lichtheim, *Literature*, ii, 93.

3.   Barry J. Kemp, *Amarna Reports*, ii, London, 1985,176.

4.   William J. Murnane, Charles C. Van Siclen, *The Boundary Stelae of Akhenaten*, London, 1993, 104.

5.   T. Eric Peet, C. Leonard Woolley, *The City of Akhenaten*, London, 1923 i, 120-121.

6.   C. Desroches Noblecourt, 'Les trois saisons du dieu et la débarcadère du ressucité' *MDAIK* 47 (1991), 72-80.

7.   Donald Redford, 'The sun disc in Akhenaten's program. Its worship and antecedents, ii', *JARCE* 17 (1980), 24.

8.   Pierre Anus, Ramadan Saad, 'Habitations de Prêtres dans le temple d'Amon à Karnak', *Kemi* 21 (1972), fig. 17.

9.   Donald B. Redford, *Akhenaten, the heretic king*, Princeton, 1984, 139.

10. Jean Winand, 'Champ semantique et structure en égyptien. Les verbes exprimant la vision', *SAK* 13 (1986), 308-314.

11. Alexander Badawy, 'Le symbolisme de l'architecture à Amarna', in *L'Egyptologie en 1979: axes prioritaires de recherches*, ii, Paris, 1982, 188.

12. Lichtheim, *Literature*, ii, 92.

13. Waltraud Guglielmi, 'Humor in Wort und Bild auf altägyptischen Grabdarstellungen', in Hellmut Brunner *et al. Wort und Bild*, Munich, 1979, 194.

14. Redford, *Akhenaten*, 149.

15. Lanny Bell, 'Aspects of the cult of Tutankhamun', in *Mélanges Gamal Eddin Mokhtar*, 35; Rainer Stadelmann, 'swt-Rw als Kultstätte des Sonnengottes im Neuen Reich', *MDAIK* 25,2 (1969), 159-160.

16. Lichtheim, *Literature*, ii, 97. Tomb of Ay.

17. Redford, *Akhenaten*, 235.

18. Norman de Garis Davies, *The Rock Tombs of el-Amarna*, London 1903, i. Meryre ii, 34, pl.xxxii.

19. Barry Kemp, 'Discovery and renewal at Amarna', *Egyptian Archaeology* 1 (1991), 19-22.

20. Sayed Tawfik, 'Amarna Kalkstein, Telatat aus Karnak,' *GM* 26 (1977), 55-62; Donald B. Redford, 'Studies on Akhenaten at Thebes. A report on the work of the Akhenaten temple project of the University Museum. University of Pennsylvania', *JARCE* 10 (1973), 81, pl. iii, 5, 7.

21. Personal communication from Dr. Raymond Johnson to whom I am most grateful for passing on his observation.

22. Alexander Badawy, 'Maru-Aten: pleasure resort or temple?' *JEA* 42 (1956), 60; Rainer Stadelmann, 'Tempel und Tempelnamen in Theben-Ost und-West', *MDAIK* 34 (1978), 179; Lanny Bell, 'Luxor Temple and the cult of the royal ka', *JNES* 44

(1985), 275; Lise Manniche, 'The *maru* built by Amenophis III: its significance and possible location', in *L'Égyptologie en 1979*, ii, 271-273.

23. John D. S. Pendlebury, *The City of Akhenaten*, iii, London, 1951, 38; Petrie, *Amarna*, 7, 9 believed the gardens were part of the harem of the palace, but later writers consider that none of these buildings were domestic, Jan Assmann, 'Palast oder Tempel?', *JNES* 31 (1972), 144.

24. "Southern Harem", Pendlebury, *City*, iii, 44-45, pls. xiii-xiv, xxiv; Petrie, *Amarna*, 14; Pendlebury, ' Summary report on the excavations at Tell el`Amarnah, 1935-1936', *JEA* 22 (1936), pl.xvii; Elfriede Reiser, *Der Königliche Harim im alten Ägypten und seine Verwaltung*, Vienna, 1972, 35-41.

25. Fran Weatherhead, 'Painted pavements in the Great Palace', *JEA* 78 (1992), 95-114, figs. 1-2.

26. I am most grateful to Dr. Raymond Johnson for drawing my attention to this feature. See plan in William Stevenson Smith, *The Art and Architecture of Ancient Egypt*, London, 1958, fig. 55 .

27. Günther Roeder, *Amarna Reliefs aus Hermopolis*, Hildesheim, 1969, 325-329.

28. Claude Traunecke, 'Sur la salle dite "du couronnement" à Tell el-Amarna', *Bulletin de la Société d'Egyptologie de Genève*, 9-10 (1984-5), 288.

29. Barry J. Kemp, 'The Window of Appearance at el-Amarna and the basic structure of this city', *JEA* 62 (1976), 82 fig. 1.2; Fran Weatherhead, 'Wall paintings from the King's House at Amarna', *JEA* 81 (1995), 95-114.

30. Salima Ikram, 'Domestic shrines and the cult of the Royal Family', *JEA* 75 (1989), 89-101.

31. Henri Frankfort, *The City of Akhenaten*, ii, London, 1933, 63-4, pl. xv, xxii.6, xxiii.3.

32. Ludwig Borchardt, Herbert Ricke, *Die Wohnhäuser in Tell Amarna*, Berlin, 1980, 26, plan 2.

33. Davies, *Rock Tombs of Amarna*, ii, pl.xxxiii,xxxvi, Jean-Claude Hugonot, *Le Jardin dans l'Egypte ancienne*, Frankfort-am-Main, 1989,144, figs. 118-120 comparing it with Amarna houses U.25.7 and U 25.11, ibid, figs. 127-128.

34. Barry J. Kemp, *World Archaeology* 9 (1977), fig. 4.

35. Davies, *Rock Tombs*, ii, pl. xxxiii; Hugonot, *Jardin*, fig. 120 .

36. Davies, *Rock Tombs*, iv, pl. viii.

37. Stela Florence 6365, 3-5, Elmar Edel, 'Untersuchungen zur Phraseologie der Ägyptische Inschriften des Alten Reiches', *MDAIK* 13,1 (1944), 49.

38. Cairo 45600, Edel, *MDAIK* 13,1 (1944), 49.

39. Pierre Anus, 'Un domaine thebain d'epoque "Amarnienne"', *BIFAO* 69 (1970), 73-79.

40. Warda M. Bircher, *Gardens of the Hesperides*, Cairo, 1960, 62. I am most grateful to Mrs. Bleser-Bircher for allowing me to quote this passage.

Short Bibliography

Nathalie Baum, *Arbres et arbustes de l'Egypte ancienne. La liste de la tombe d'Ineni (no.81)*. Orientalia Lovaniensia Analecta 31. Departement Orientalistik, Leuven, 1988.

Gérard Charpentier, *Recueil de matériaux. épigraphiques relatifs à la botanique de l'Egypte antique*, Paris, 1981.

Sheila Collenette, *An Illustrated Guide to the Flowers of Saudi Arabia*, London, 1985.

Dieter Eigner, 'Gartenkunst im alten Ägypten', *Gartenkunst* 7/1 (1995).

Johanna Dittmar, *Blumen und Blumensträusse als Opfergabe im alten Ägypten*, Munich-Berlin, 1986.

Renate Germer, *Flora des pharaonischen Ägypten*, Mainz, 1985.

Renate Germer, *Untersuchung über Arzneimittelpflanzen im alten Ägypten*, Hamburg, 1979.

Nigel Groom, *Frankincense and Myrrh. A study of the Arabian Incense Trade*, London, New York, 1981.

Wolfgang Helck, Eberhard Otto, Wolfhart Westendorf, eds. *Lexikon der Ägyptologie*, Wiesbaden, 1972-

F. Nigel Hepper, *Pharaoh's Flowers. The Botanical Treasures of Tutankhamun*, London, 1990.

Jean-Claude Hugonot, *Le jardin dans l'égypte ancienne*. Hildesheim, 1989.

Sir Geoffrey Jellicoe, Susan Jelllicoe, P. Goode, and M. Lancaster, eds. *Oxford Companion to Gardens*, Oxford, 1986.

Heinrich Schäfer, Trans. John Baines, *Principles of Egyptian Art*, Oxford, 1986.

Ludwig Keimer, *Die Gartenpflanzen im alten Ägypten*, 2 vols. Berlin 1924 and vol. ii, Mainz am Rhein, 1984, ed. Renate Germer.

Vivi Laurent-Täckholm, *Faraos Blomster*, Copenhagen, 1952.

Lise Manniche, *An Ancient Egyptian Herbal*, London, 1989.

Vivi Täckholm, *Students' Flora of Egypt*, Cairo University, Cairo, 1974.

Index